COMING OF AGE IN UTOPIA

ALSO BY PAUL M. GASTON

The New South Creed: A Study in Southern Mythmaking

Women of Fair Hope

Man and Mission

COMING OF AGE IN UTOPIA

The Odyssey of an Idea

~

PAUL M. GASTON

NewSouth Books
Montgomery | Louisville

NewSouth Books
105 South Court Street
Montgomery, AL 36104

Library of Congress Cataloging-in-Publication Data

Gaston, Paul M., 1928–
Coming of age in utopia : the Odyssey of an idea / Paul M. Gaston.

p. cm.

Includes index.

ISBN-13: 978-1-58838-225-2
ISBN-10: 1-58838-225-7

1. Gaston, Paul M., 1928- 2. Civil rights workers—Alabama—Fairhope—Biography.
3. Utopian socialism—Alabama—Fairhope—History. I. Title.
F334.F35G37 2009
323.092—dc22
[B]

2009033432

Edited and designed by Randall Williams
Printed in the United States of America
by the Maple-Vail Book Manufacturing Group

FOR MARY

Partner All the Way

Contents

Prologue

HOMEWARD BOUND

I n the summer following my fiftieth birthday I took the risk of going home again. Thomas Wolfe had planted seeds of doubt in all of us Southerners, one of whom I counted myself to be, even if more by preference and profession than by birth and rearing. I was born and reared in Fairhope, Alabama, deep down in the Deep South, but my hometown was created by non-Southerners with some very un-Southern ideas. Indeed, some very un-American ideas. Apart from my father and my grandfather, the two men whose ideas had shaped my town's reason for being and set my own moral and intellectual compass were two Yankee radicals, Henry George and John Dewey.

Fairhope's founders thought of themselves as practical idealists, people who knew how to make good theories work. Like many restless critics of America before them, they withdrew from the larger society to establish a model community of their own that would be a practical demonstration of how the right kinds of public policies and private commitments could foster a just society. With a fair hope that they would succeed, they would point the way to a world with less of the injustice, poverty, misdirected education, and blunted lives that they believed made a mockery of the American credo of democracy.

Fairhope had been in existence a third of a century when I was born in 1928. By then it was a small but thriving center of idealism, reformist and radical thought, artistic and literary expression, and free-spirited individuals, all in a setting of uncommon charm and beauty. The hand of Henry

George rested firmly on the community. His eloquent and passionate indictment of American individualism gone amuck first appeared in his 1879 magnum opus, *Progress and Poverty*. It electrified a generation of dissidents around the world, sending them on missions to confront what he identified as the great enigma of their time, the association of poverty with progress. George's central reform proposal—"*we must make land common property*"—was translated by his followers into a proposal to abolish all taxes save a tax on land values. Coupled with this "single tax" was a modest form of municipal socialism calling for the public ownership and operation of most "natural monopolies."

Trying to make George's "good theory" work was not easy, but the single-tax colony, as it was called, became a place where men and women of modest means could find free land for homes, businesses, and farms. The Georgist principle that land must be made common property, available for use and never for profit, became a reality and was Fairhope's distinguishing feature. It was the magnet that drew hopeful and enterprising men and women to it. By the time I entered the world Fairhope was known as the nation's (indeed, the world's) oldest and most famous single-tax community. Others had emerged, in Delaware, Massachusetts, New Jersey, and one in Spain; all, I was to learn, had been inspired by Fairhope, sometimes called, if a little grandly, the mother of colonies.

John Dewey's influence on Fairhope came with the 1902 arrival of Marietta Johnson, a charismatic Minnesota school teacher with energy and her own vision of a better world. She soon started a progressive school in the Dewey mold, open without charge to everyone in the area. Calling it the School of Organic Education, she meant for it to address the needs of the whole person—body, mind, and spirit: "a sound accomplished body; a reverent spirit; an intelligent sympathetic mind." Dewey himself visited in 1913, returning to write glowingly of what he saw. The school, he believed, showed "how the ideal of equal opportunity for all is to be transmuted into reality." Mrs. Johnson believed her kind of "organic" education provided the palpable democratic experience that was an essential companion of the colony's reshaping of the material world. Together they would be invincible.

I grew up with a special Fairhope status. In 1936, when I was eight years old, my father was elected Colony secretary, basically its executive director and most influential leader. The thoroughly democratic constitution required annual elections for the secretary's position, but my father won thirty-six consecutive contests, always without opposition. He retired in 1972 when he was eighty, loved and revered throughout the community. As a child of Fairhope I identified the colony with my family and saw my father as its chief personification.

Family identification went beyond him. My grandfather, Ernest Berry Gaston, an Iowa journalist and Populist Party officer, had conceived the idea for the colony, written its constitution, and recruited the first settlers. He led the small founding party to Alabama in 1894, oversaw the creation of the community, and rode astride its history for four decades. He was the first secretary and except for two years (1905 and 1913) held that position until his retirement in 1936. He stepped down in favor of my father when he was no longer able to carry on. When he died the next year the newspaper which he had edited from the beginning, *The Fairhope Courier*, the voice of the colony, was taken over by his children. My Aunt Frankie became editor, Dad associate editorial writer, and Uncle Spider business manager and linotype operator.

I think my father would have retired well before he was eighty had I been in the wings, ready to take over from him. Like his father before him, he could almost surely have designated his son as his successor. As a very young man I considered being around for that to happen, perhaps settling in as editor of the *Courier*, until it was my time. The idea may have taken hold because I was an only child (and none of my Gaston cousins seemed likely successors) but I think it had more to do with my belief in the colony's mission and the way in which my father's wisdom and integrity permeated my view of the world. It just seemed the natural thing to do.

After a stint in the Army followed by four years in college, however, my future became less clear to me. I wrote a paper on Fairhope in my political science course and one on Henry George in an economic theory seminar. But now as I read through the many letters my father and I exchanged during those years I see my interest and intentions broadening beyond Fairhope

My father and I kept discussing the single tax and the affairs of the colony, and I always read carefully his well-crafted annual reports. There was never a trace of pressure from him for me to continue thinking of being his successor. But there was no clear decision that I would not. That remained in my mind a possibility. I was no longer a literal single-taxer—believing that all government expenses could be met by a single tax on land values—but the belief that land was our common inheritance, to be held for use and not for private gain, was strengthened by study and experience. I looked on land speculation as the worst of infidelities and regarded capitalistic land reform programs as both ineffective when tried and misunderstood by the historians who later wrote about them.

Time passed. I married, attended graduate school, had three children, launched a career teaching Southern history at the University of Virginia, and found an active life in the Southern civil rights movement. Never making a break or even a conscious decision not to return to Fairhope, I planted roots elsewhere, both physically and spiritually—physically in Charlottesville where I lived and taught and spiritually in a small but energizing community of like-minded persons scattered about the country, activist scholars and teachers, movement people, and Southerners confronting the burden of their history. In all of those years Fairhope remained a jewel of beauty and enjoyment to which my family repaired every summer so that our children might have some of the Shangri-la experiences I had as a child. My mother—loveable, sociable, and fun—died from heart complications in 1968. I was forty, she sixty-eight. My father carried on as colony secretary, living alone in the small home they had built in 1921, the year of their marriage. Our Fairhope visits took on a different hue with my mother's joyous energy and infectious ebullience absent.

In the spring of 1977, working on a book on the Southern civil rights movement, I took up residence in Durham, North Carolina, to be a research fellow in Duke University's civil rights center. At the end of my second day there, Larry Goodwyn and Bill Chafe, good friends and co-directors of the center, took me to a local tavern for beer and conversation. We spoke of Larry's recent brilliant book on the Populist movement. As the conversation moved along, our waiter bringing a second round, I remarked that my grandfather had been an Iowa Populist. In fact, he was a colleague of General James B. Weaver, the 1892 Populist presidential candidate about whom Larry had written. Both of my companions wanted to know the story of Fairhope. When I had finished an abbreviated account they turned on me in unison: I must write that history, starting immediately. I protested that I was in their center to write about the civil rights movement. Larry shot back: "Fairhope is about freedom, too, isn't it?"

I telephoned my wife that night. Writing Fairhope's history was what I had always wanted to do, she told me, but somehow I could never give myself permission to do it. Now my Duke friends had liberated me from whatever it was that restrained me. My father, whom I telephoned next, was measured and circumspect, as was his wont, but he would be there to help if that was what I decided to do. There was a slight reticence, I thought, perhaps some unease, in his voice, but in my euphoria I pushed it to the back of my mind, reckoning that his declining energy and what I believed to be mild bouts of depression explained his mood. He was eighty-five and had been living alone for nine years.

Early in the next year, worn down by anxiety, but never pushing his needs, he said yes when I asked if he would be happier coming to live with us. And so he did. Not long after his arrival, however, Mary suggested that we all go to Fairhope for a year. Dad would be happier in his own home with us for company and care. Gareth, our remaining at-home child, could have a Fairhope experience. Mary and I could begin work on the history. We would sleep in my old bedroom. I would be home again.

A quarter century had passed since I moved out of that room. Fairhope had grown and prospered during the interim. Between my birth in 1928 and leaving home in 1952, the town had grown from 1,500 to 3,500; now, in 1978, there were 7,000 residents. I had noted the arrival of the new people and watched the many physical alterations on my frequent visits. But what struck me most forcibly on my return was how familiar the place both felt and looked. In many ways it seemed that I had been in a time warp.

The bayfront gave the surest feel of continuity. Fairhope's setting on table land overlooking Mobile Bay remained uniquely beautiful. When my grandfather first arrived he wrote rapturously of what he saw. I copied his

With my father on his eightieth birthday.

description of it and read it aloud to myself once, standing where he had stood eighty-three years earlier:

> Here we have a short strip of sandy beach, then a narrow park ranging in width from 100 to 250 feet and covered with almost every variety of shrub and tree which flourishes in this locality—pine, live oak, magnolia, cedar, juniper, cypress, gum, holly, bay, beach, youpon and myrtle. On the east side of this "lower park," as we call it, a red clay bluff rises up almost perpendicularly to a height of nearly 40 feet. Along its serried edge tall, arrowly pines stand like sentinels looking out to sea. . . .
>
> From the top of the cliff, looking out over and between the lower rooted trees, the bay spreads in all its beauty, with here and there a white sail or over in the channel toward the western shore, the smoke of a steamer or the bare poles of a ship. . . . On an ordinarily clear day the western shore may be plainly seen and in the background to the northwest the spires and smoky chimneys of Mobile.

THE BEAUTY OF THE high bluffs, the beaches below, and the long pier extending out to deep water (where as late as my early childhood ferry boats from Mobile tied up) had cast a spell over Fairhope from the earliest days. As a small child as well as an adolescent, I had spent countless hours fishing, crabbing, swimming, sailing, wandering through the sand-bottomed gulleys, picnicking—and daydreaming—in what seemed a vast public park. It belonged to all of us, every Fairhoper, because we were a special community where no individual could own or monopolize scarce colony resources and where "keep out" and "private property" signs would have violated our sense of community.

The bluffs and the beaches below were still public parks, a fact in which a returning son could take pride. The entire eastern shore of Mobile Bay, winding for twenty miles from Spanish Fort in the north to Weeks Bay in the south, was seductively appealing but only in Fairhope could the Bay actually be seen. Unknowing travelers, driving along privately owned land where both view and access were prohibited, were suddenly startled when a great vista opened up to them in Fairhope—a vista that vanished as quickly as it had appeared once the barricade of private property was reached again in Battles Wharf and Point Clear, the neighboring villages to the south.

Not everyone in Fairhope in 1978 shared my enthusiasm for the parkland heritage. Many old acquaintances spoke of refusing to allow their children to swim in the Bay and complained that they could no longer enjoy the breakfasts on the beach that had once been a special pleasure and a distinctive community activity. Some worried that the Bay was polluted. The more frequently cited trouble, however, was the blacks. They were said to be overrunning the place, especially on the weekends, coming from all parts of the county as well as from Mobile. Such lamentations, sometimes laced with racist folklore, tempered my enthusiasm for the return home and reminded me of my mother's deep anguish over the appalling power racial myths and fears had gained in the years of the civil rights movement. Fairhope was "Wallace country," she used to snort, disgusted that its utopian heritage had not been a shield.

But that heritage was never free of segregation or the racial assumptions underlying it. In fact, my Shangri-la was for people of my race only. The intense pleasure that had shaped my childhood in a colony founded to abolish special privilege was itself special privilege, a privilege denied to all of my black contemporaries. Now that privilege was no longer denied. But it wasn't thanks to the liberated vitality of the Fairhope spirit; instead, it was to the spirit and strength of the black liberation movement that had driven the federal government to make the Fairhope practice of segregation illegal.

Through the summer and into the early fall of 1978 I frequently made estimates of the numbers of whites and blacks in the beach park, marveling at the fact that Fairhope was now a bathing Mecca for people of both races, especially those with modest incomes. With the only public bayfront in the county of any size, Fairhope now provided a working example of how integration could work. During the week, when locals predominated, blacks were a minority. On the weekends, especially in the afternoons, large crowds from Mobile and other parts of Baldwin County arrived. On these occasions blacks generally outnumbered whites, but seldom by much.

My family and I came for Sunday breakfast on the beach, much as we had forty years earlier when I was a boy. My brother-in-law, the novelist and short-story writer Lawrence Dorr, noted at one of these gatherings how he felt he was participating in an ancient religious rite: the clan gathered for renewal and affirmation as we sat about after the meal, under the trees close to the water's edge, speaking of the vagaries of colony politics and the enduring relevance of Georgist philosophy and progressive education. Swept up in his poetic insights, my astute brother-in-law failed to see that our family and a very small number of our friends were the only ones still practicing this tribal rite.

Community leaders, including nearly all of the colony members, had long since abandoned the beach-front ritual celebration of the marriage of nature and ideology. But at many of our numerous social gatherings, on the beach and in the homes of friends, we found lively, interesting people—artists, writers, and mavericks who seemed precisely the kind of idealistic and curmudgeonly people proving the ongoing vitality of the Fairhope spirit. Almost none of them, however, was supportive of the putative custodian of the Fairhope experiment. I thought most of them were hostile to what they viewed as the quisling-like nature of the current colony leadership, scoffing at the single-tax corporation as a rapacious landlord in the pocket of the powerful and the privileged, people making a mockery of Henry George's—and E. B. Gaston's—radical commitment to equal rights and economic justice. Similarly, but with less vigor, they dismissed the Organic School as an interesting anachronism long since corrupted.

Jangled by such hostility to my childhood holy grails, my emotional barometer set in troublesome gyration, I looked for signs of continuity and symbols of affirmation. The beach and the bay were the easiest places to find them, the familiarity and the beauty still there. The bay was not as clear as it had been when I was a boy and I recalled the outrage my friend Craig Sheldon had expressed at what he called the "pollution crowd." He threatened on one occasion to blow up an offending dredge in the bay, but settled for colorful testimony before state investigating commissions and extravagant broadsides and letters to the editor. Even in its impure form, the bay was still beautiful and nurturing. I visited it regularly, alone in the mornings, just as I had as a boy, finding rare peace and a sense of harmony swimming along the bottom or resting quietly in its buoyancy.

Sailing also confirmed old attachments. Soon after we arrived, I bought a Lightning, a nineteen-foot sloop, which I moored in the public marina. Except for the cold spells in the winter months, we sailed regularly at the end of the day, often taking friends, drinks, and supper along, returning to harbor with the glow of a sunset in our wake. Far enough out in the bay that only the trees and cliffs were visible, little seemed changed from the time I had viewed the shoreline from the sixteen-foot sailboat my cousin Tommy and I bought for ninety dollars when I was fourteen. My father, now eighty-seven but with renewed energy and agility, accompanied us on many of these sails, occasionally taking the tiller. He may have remembered the legendary sailing canoe he and his friends had crafted and sailed before I was born.

To experience again the intensity of Fairhope's sensual pleasures established a vital link to my childhood sense of security and uniqueness. That was critical to the work ahead, or so it seemed at the time. Mary, who had first visited Fairhope when she was twenty-two, in the summer before our marriage, understood this instinctively. She responded much as I did to the beauty around us but she also understood the context in which it had flourished. In a Christmas letter to our friends and family she captured the essence of what we were feeling. "Each time one misses a sunset over the Bay," she wrote, "or neglects to go running across the pine-needled bluffs in the morning or have time to stop and gather morning glories still in profusion in December or go sailing when the wind is from the southwest, or spend several hours gathering pecans to send to friends, or spend another hour picking out crabmeat from the large pail of crabs just caught and donated by a cousin it seems as if one is allowing life to be diminished." And then she added: "Living in a place that was founded by people searching for the public organization and private commitments that would produce a good society for all makes us spend a lot of time thinking about what we really value in life." Here was the reason, she believed, that I had decided to write the book, "probably a typical mid-life concern, but one that we feel lucky to be able to attack in this way."

But along with the good luck and well-being that she expressed was

Mary gathering morning glories by the beach.

some bracing realism that kept clawing for attention. "One has to deal with the diminishments and losses of age that are all around us," Mary wrote. And, "more importantly," she added, we had to face "the failure of many of the original hopes and ideals that this community symbolized but didn't bring to fruition and the reflection of those failures in ourselves." That was an arresting thought that, in the heady first months of research, I found hard to absorb fully. It would later become a major theme in my writings about Fairhope.

Meanwhile, the research began. Almost as soon as we arrived, I climbed the steep stairs to the second floor of the office of the Fairhope Single Tax Corporation (FSTC), the formal title the colony had assumed when it incorporated under Alabama law in 1904. It was in this structure, now called the Gaston Building, that I would find a place to work. The upstairs offices had been abandoned for thirty years or more and were heavily coated with dust. My father, a chiropractic physician before he took over as colony secretary, had his practice in one of those upstairs rooms. My grandfather had written his last editorials in another. That was the one I selected. I was soon grimy from heat and dust as I wired my new room for lights and an air conditioner, scavenged boards and bricks for a bookcase, and hauled my manual typewriter and an old desk and chair up the stairs. I was ready for work. From the windows I could look out on Fairhope Avenue and the town center below and wonder about the history that had been made there and what it meant.

The colony archives, carefully stored in the vault on the floor below, were a historian's dream. There was a score of large boxes of letters along with minutes of every meeting of the colony council, financial records, land books, maps, all but a very few issues of the weekly newspaper, and numerous photographs and memorabilia. After a quick inventory, I sorted out the very early materials and plunged in. Each day I walked the short distance from our home to the colony office, just as my father and grandfather had done before me for three-quarters of a century. I was finally following in their footsteps—literally and, I hoped, with something of the same spirit.

Perfectly situated, my hideaway did not remain a secret. I soon began receiving visits from curious friends and relatives. What was the book to be about, they wanted to know. Was I going to reveal scandals and ferret skeletons out of long-locked family closets? Some of my visitors had secret histories of their own they hoped I might tell. Others generously agreed to be interviewed, wishing to be part of the story, or offered to supply photographs and to search their attics for bundles of letters.

One visitor had a very different mission. Lester Boone, husband of one of my favorite cousins, climbed the stairs one morning to ask if I had really come back to write a book. Perhaps, he coyly suggested, I had something else in mind. "What might that be, Les," I asked him. "Well, my friend," he answered, "not everyone believes your book is what brought you here." Even before I asked him who had such doubts I knew there was only one person in Fairhope given to such dark turns of the imagination. Les confirmed my unspoken suspicion: "Mr. Sam doesn't believe you've come home to write a book; he thinks you're here to try to take over the colony."

"Mr. Sam," a term of sycophancy I was a little surprised to hear Les use, referred to Sam Dyson, the recently elected president of the Single Tax Corporation. Twenty years my senior, Sam was a Fairhope native. His wife Helen, a pretty woman with an engaging accent, had been my kindergarten teacher. Both were Organic School students—school sweethearts who married after the dissolution of Sam's brief first marriage—and they were intensely loyal, in their peculiar way, to Marietta Johnson's memory and legacy.

Both Sam's mother and his father, an English socialist émigré, had been valued friends of my grandparents and were among the most respected champions of the colony and school. My childhood memories were of a cordial, perhaps close, relationship between my parents and the younger Dysons; and, judging from the 1930s letters I found in the archives, my father looked on Sam as a man worthy of his support and encouragement. All of that had changed over the previous two decades, friendship and approval giving way to my father's politely restrained scorn and unspoken but deep distrust. My uncle Marvin, who served on the colony council with both of them, later told me that Sam had made my father's last years as secretary a hellish burden. More than anyone else, Sam had eroded my father's life-long faith in the demonstration that his father had begun and Sam's father had faithfully served.

Ideology was only part of the problem, but it made for a deep rift. On the few occasions when I saw Sam during my college years he struck me as the antithesis of the Georgist radical I associated with Fairhopers. None of his indignation was directed toward the maldistribution of wealth or the penalties visited on the poor because poverty accompanied progress, the enigma that George believed to be at the heart of the problem societies had to unravel to survive with any semblance of justice. Sam was vigorously indignant over many things but his special objects of scorn, as I recall them, were New Deal liberalism, the growing power of the federal government, the intrusive influence of the Supreme Court, growing threats to white supremacy, and the insidious influence of "creeping socialism." I found it hard to believe a Fairhoper could be comfortable with these beliefs.

The rage against socialism was shocking but not totally surprising. Sam, along with many national single-taxers, had come to define Georgism as an antidote to socialism, not its spiritual ally, pursuing a different route to the same end. During my undergraduate years I attended a national Georgist meeting in New York only to be startled by the apparent affluence of the delegates. One of the leaders, with a diamond stickpin in his necktie, typified the lot. They seemed an unlikely group to unravel the enigma of poverty amidst plenty, and I doubted if I would uncover much sympathy for socialism in their midst. In fact, as I was later to learn, the national Georgist movement was moving away from the "cooperative" side of "cooperative individualism," stressing instead the supremacy of individualism in a society in which government would play an increasingly minor role. Single-Taxers easily moved into the Libertarian camp or joined the Republican Party.

I began, after college, to pay more attention to Georgist literature and movements. In 1961 I helped to found an organization of academicians sympathetic to land-value taxation. I discovered, however, that many single-taxers placed primary emphasis on means rather than ends. And, in fact, there were varieties of interpretations of what contemporary Georgism should be; but, the strongest current running through the stream of writings and meetings was that the single-tax program was appealing because it would offer freedom from burdensome taxes (including the progressive federal income tax), and diminish the role of government generally, ergo the appeal to libertarians.

Thus, by the time I returned to Fairhope in 1978 I had shed much of my earlier naiveté. My father had shielded me from his own disappointments, but now spoke of them freely, remarking several times that not half a dozen members of the colony understood or were committed to the founding principles. One of the things he said, out of a deep sadness, I believe, was that the tradition of Fairhope radicalism which he had inherited from his father and, in turn, had passed on to me, had been wiped out, was now bereft of defenders in the very colony founded to spread it. As I thought about the book I planned to write I knew that one of my several challenges would be to explain how an egalitarian faith grounded in cooperation and equal rights had been transformed into a reactionary defense of laissez-faire capitalism now overlaid with racist myths. It would be a complex, multilayered story, but, at the outset, caught up in the flux of immediate tensions, I tended to see particular individuals, Sam prominently among them, as the personification of what had gone wrong. Once distanced from immediate concerns, I would begin to unravel the many structural and human conditions that made it impossible for even the best of men to make their good theories work.

By 1978 Sam sat firmly astride the colony's two pivotal institutions. He had long since become the single power over the Organic School through both the force of his personality and his control over a widow's endowment earmarked for the school. His determination to keep it alive seemed to strengthen as others, including my father, decided it had outlived its usefulness and that its shrunken size, lack of community support, and absence of vision meant it was no longer the demonstration of progressive education that had been its *raison d'être*. Many of the old forms (such as folk dancing and arts & crafts) were maintained but a rigid authoritarianism spoiled their educational effect. The long hairstyles of the hippie era were fiercely prohibited, and when integration finally came to the public schools many fearful whites found a segregated haven in the Organic School, giving it the monetary injection it sorely needed, received apparently with no pangs of conscience. By the time we arrived, the fleeing whites had decided that integration was not as bad as they had feared and that folk dancing was worse than they had expected, so they returned to the Fairhope public school. Our fourteen-year-old son Gareth assumed he would attend the Organic School because he had heard (probably ad nauseum) of my joyful experiences in it. He opted for the public high school. I think we all knew the Organic School he might have attended was nothing like the one that had given me such joy.

Control over the FSTC was slower in coming, but after Dad's retirement in 1972 the way was cleared. In February 1978, before our summer arrival, Sam was elected president. Colony politics were at a pivotal point and Sam appeared to believe he was the only person who could manage the crisis. I had watched it billowing from afar for almost a decade and on one occasion had been drawn into it, writing a letter to Governor George Wallace to urge him to oppose legislative and judicial assaults then being mounted. Despite that one modest entry into the political maelstrom, I came to Fairhope in 1978 determined to remain aloof from the struggle, hoping not to compromise my integrity as a historian. I could not hope to be regarded as a neutral—enemies of the colony would obviously identify me with its defense because of my family history; corporation members, for the same reason, would expect me to join the battle on their side—but

I hoped to establish as much independence as I could.

Les's report that Sam looked on me as a threat to his power was an added complication. I did not regard his news as a warning, although perhaps I should have. My relationship with Sam continued to be correct, but it was never easy and there were a few times when I wondered whether I ought not put the book aside in favor of the contest I was already suspected by him of having in mind. Such musings were never more than that. The research remained an absorbing passion and increasingly I saw its completion as the only fulfilling way in which I could satisfy my role as a Fairhoper, the one sure way I could discharge the sense of family obligation I had come to feel deeply. As it turned out I was eventually drawn into colony politics, never deeply but enough to compromise the independence I had hoped to maintain. My involvement seemed to me then, as it has since, to have made no difference whatsoever to the course of the struggle.

The political struggle into which I was drawn threatened to engulf my energies and strain my loyalties. In many ways, what happened in 1978–79 was inevitable and, in fact, had surfaced, albeit in different and milder forms, in the earliest days after settlement. From the outset, the colony restricted membership to those who professed belief in the single-tax program and followed their application with a $100 membership fee. Members then both owned the colony land and elected the governing council that set the rental charges levied for use of their land. With the rental income the colony paid the county and state property taxes of its lessees, thus (at least before the income tax) simulating the single tax. The excess of rental collections over taxes paid was directed to public improvements.

Almost from the outset, lacking an adequate membership, the colony opened its lands to nonmembers. My grandfather believed, quite wrongly as it turned out, that they would see the virtues of the good theory and become believing members. Instead, they enjoyed the benefits of free land without becoming members. In time, a very large class of nonmember lessees emerged, dwarfing the membership that set the rents. Complaints of high rental charges were lodged early in the twentieth century but after the Depression of the 1930s vanished as an issue, not to recur again until the early 1970s.

The 1970s saw the beginning of a land boom that swept across the eastern shore of Mobile Bay. Colony leaseholders watched their neighbors on freehold sites garner huge profits (what Georgists call unearned increment) from the sales of their land. But colony policy stood in the way of those of its leaseholders who were bitten by the same quick-riches bug. To transfer their leaseholds they could accept a payment of no more than the value of their improvements. Thus, when one of the country nonmember lessees might be offered $100,000 for his barn the colony blocked the sale. The barn itself was worth no more than $10,000 and the land was not his to sell.

Faced at the same time with rent increases, a policy that spiked their get-rich quick ambitions, and a colony council increasingly unsympathetic and autocratic, dissident leaseholders launched an assault that was efficiently led and zealously supported. Claiming that the lease-transfer provision was a "socialist" violation of the American right to control one's own property, the dissidents won the support of local legislators and powerful figures in Montgomery, the state capital. They filed lawsuits, instigated a state-commission investigation, and drafted legislation threatening either to dissolve the corporation or take it over by becoming members and assuming control.

Now under attack, the FSTC was dangerously small and deeply divided. The tiny membership had been a problem for many years. The $100 membership fee, even though it could be paid in installments, was part of the explanation, but more important—according to several nonmember colony sympathizers I interviewed—was that there was no compelling reason for them to join. As one said to me of my father: "Cornie looks after us; why should we become members?" But Dad was no longer there to look after them. Even during his tenure, in fact, he had been unable to block the subversion of the founding principles. Increasingly, members—including members of the Council—acquired multiple leaseholds, built or renovated homes on them, and charged large enough rents for the homes to reap the unearned increment from the land. Land speculators running amuck in the houses of George and Gaston. Thus, by the time we arrived in 1978, the most compelling reason to become a member of the Fairhope Single Tax Corporation was to look out for one's individual property interests, not to make good theories work. At the other extreme, members such as my Uncle Marvin had kept the faith, but for the most part they were aging and had no workable plan for making their theory work. Saddest to me was that no such workable plan was possible.

By 1978, none of the dissidents' efforts had been successful. Still, the community was tense with rumors. The dissenters appeared to be well financed and emotionally prepared for a long struggle. Their membership meetings, pointedly scheduled for the same nights that the Council met, were well attended by aroused and confident men and women who competed with each other in telling of their mistreatment by the corporation officers. At the first of their meetings I attended I entered with a nervous stomach, feeling like a vulnerable outsider. I knew many of them, including their chief officers; some had been friends or acquaintances of many years while those I didn't know bore names familiar from my boyhood. Partly for this reason, but more because I was my father's son, I was greeted with respect and cordiality. "If Cornie had still been secretary," one of them said of my father, "we would never have been in this mess. He would have treated us with respect." I knew this dissenter spoke the truth just as I knew that he would have respected and trusted my father even though they would differ over what was to be done.

Most of the dissidents were plain people, woefully unversed in the subtleties of land-value taxation. They were, on the surface at least, the perfect symbols of an exploited class. Rudy Rezner, whose name would become attached to the climactic lawsuit, was a unique individual but also a prototype of the aggrieved farmer on the march. With gray hair set off by a ruddy face and a warm and appealing manner, Rudy was a born orator. At one meeting of the dissidents that I attended he explained how he was a simple man of the soil who had worked hard all his life, planted his pecan trees ("and you know pecan trees take a long time to grow") and now that he was ready to reap the rewards of his patience and hard work the colony raised the rents so high he would be forced to move off the land, the labors of a lifetime lost. The impersonal corporation was grinding down the honest man of the soil. There were moments that night when my imagination leapt back to the 1890s when my grandfather sat among throngs of aroused farmers, helping them to form the Peoples Party.

However much I might have sympathized with the people leading a charge, I could not see them as heirs of the Populist tradition that had nurtured my grandfather and inspired his creation of Fairhope. Instead, I agreed with my friend Craig Sheldon when he said they were "land-grabbers," drawn to the fight by the prospects of quick and unearned riches. I sensed, too, that they were also spurred on by the excitement of bringing down a powerful corporation whose leader was the perfect target for a popular uprising. I published a letter in the local paper, criticizing their tactics and assumptions and defending the underlying principle of public confiscation of land values, but also discreetly admitting that there had been an unfortunate misunderstanding partly because of the colony leadership's failure to lead. I urged both sides to talk. No such conversations took place. I was foolish to think a few well-chosen words might be influential.

Sam bowed out as president in February. Frequently in the corporation office, he now introduced secrecy as the hallmark of his behind-the-scenes management style, ordering the combination to the vault changed. Shortly after the combination was changed he coyly told me that some people, never identified, thought I was the one who was "leaking" secrets to the opposition. I could be told the new setting, he said in a way meant to be a warning, knowing he could not be brazen enough to keep it from me. There were few "secrets" to leak but Sam's imagination seemed to be fueled with dark suspicions. And I became wary of Sam in ways I find unattractive, even if compelling.

Some time after the vault incident I found a way to have our paper, *The Fairhope Courier,* microfilmed. With only a few missing issues, the vault contained every number from the first, published in Des Moines on August 15, 1894, through 1963, when my family sold it. It was the most comprehensive and revealing history of Fairhope that existed, a precious resource. And now many of the issues were crumbling. Each time I touched one of the older papers and watched flakes of yellowed newsprint drop to the floor I felt our heritage breaking into pieces. This could not be. After making some inquiries I found a firm in Mobile that would microfilm the entire set for a manageable cost that would be borne by my Gaston cousins and me.

The colony office staff offered full support but warned that Sam would not approve. Some said he feared anything that might stir up knowledge of his past; others simply feared he would oppose any project such as this one if he did not control or originate it.

I took the cowardly route. Some called it prudent. When Sam was no-where to be seen, and not likely to show up, we moved the volumes, a few at a time, from the vault to my car. I took them to Mobile to be filmed, brought them back, and then repeated the process. After a month or so the project was complete. Only then did I feel comfortable making it public. Several of my cousins joined me in a ceremony where we announced what we had done. We made a gift of one copy of the microfilm to the Fairhope library and one to the colony library. Later, I advertised their availability for purchase by university libraries, an offer several accepted. This much of my heritage was preserved.

The final two episodes in the colony saga before we departed Fairhope left me feeling both uneasy and, in time, ashamed. A busload of colony supporters journeyed to Montgomery to attend a hearing before a com-mittee of the state legislature considering a bill supported by the dissidents. Norborne Stone, the colony attorney, asked me to speak in opposition to it and I agreed. Norborne thought my family connection, knowledge of colony history, and my professorial status might make a difference. They didn't. One black legislator seemed to understand the founding principles, recognizing a voice for equality when he heard it. I enjoyed a friendly con-versation with him at the hearing's end. The other legislators, well-primed by the talking points supplied them by the dissidents, saw only red: socialism and an un-American attack on property rights.

There was a knot in my stomach as I rode to and from Montgomery with that busload of ready-for-battle single-tax colony members. The knot wasn't caused by worry over what I would say to the legislative committee. I knew the land-grab legislation was wrong and I was obliged to say so. But in opposing the dissidents' bill I was bound to be perceived as defending the colony leadership, a leadership that I mistrusted and had come to see as rivaling the dissidents as betrayers of the founding principles. For my Uncle Marvin and a goodly number of the colony faithful, opposed though they were to the Dyson regime, the dissident assault was such a blatant threat to what the colony was meant to stand for that they suffered none of the ambivalence gnawing at me.

Not long after the hearing in Montgomery the dissidents filed a lawsuit aimed at either securing membership and voting rights for themselves or directly abolishing the lease-transfer provision or both. Norborne, the colony attorney, was calm, but Sam grew anxious and soon let the membership in on his scheme for a clever defeat of the dissidents. He would have us dissolve the corporation, incorporated under the laws of Alabama since 1904, and then reconstitute it as a Delaware corporation, which he believed would put it safely beyond the reach of our enemies. Fevered discussions preceded the day of the membership vote on Sam's proposal. Overwhelmingly, members seemed to favor it. The anti-Dyson contingent reluctantly saw it as a way of defeating the dissident cause without undermining the constitution.

Mary and I went along with our friends. My agreement, however, was accompanied by a deep sense of unease and a worrisome feeling of inadequacy. Sam's stratagem insulted the honor and integrity that had long been the hallmark of my father's and my grandfather's leadership. I knew that. But I lacked the imagination and the courage to oppose it or to propose an alternative. On the day set for the vote, my father, my wife, and I walked in silence to the colony office to mark our ballots. Dad's jaw was set, his face stern, his stride purposeful. After we voted and returned home, but before all the members had marked their ballots, the police arrived with a court order to shut down the proceedings. Apparently the judge had agreed with the dissidents that the attempt to dissolve the corporation was illegal. Sam's bubble of secrecy was punctured, his scheme of deception foiled. The out-for-blood dissidents, their imaginations running on full throttle, now spread the rumor that our aim was to dissolve the corporation in order to divide the vast assets among ourselves. Once again they would be denied what they believed to be theirs by right.

On a drive some days later, Norborne and I discussed the balloting and its significance. Of all the ballots cast, he told me, only one person had opposed Sam's stratagem. Of course I knew who that was. I remember sitting still, unable to speak for a while, overcome with a sense of pride in my father.

He knew wrong when he saw it. He would never be intimidated. And I felt even smaller, the son who had understood, but lacked the courage to act on what deep down he knew to be right.

Thomas Wolfe was correct. You can't go home again. I couldn't. My home no longer existed. It had vanished. But there had once been a home. A home with a spirit, a mission, and a fair hope for a better world. I could revisit that home to discover what it had meant to my grandfather and to my father—and to explore its force as it shaped my own odyssey.

Chapter One

Roots

C oming of age in the 1930s and early 1940s, I learned that most Americans, at least most white Americans, believed that ours was a uniquely blessed country. History books were full of accounts of what their authors called American exceptionalism, the belief that we were different from and superior to the world's other countries. Their histories had been marred by monarchy, feudalism, political and religious persecution, terrorism and torture. Our nation, spared these crippling experiences, had a birthing document that declared all men to be created equal, with inalienable rights to life, liberty, and the pursuit of happiness. Our constitution, the greatest document ever struck off by the genius of man, as the British statesman William Gladstone flatteringly assured us, included an iron-clad bill of rights that no government could violate. No wonder, then, that we saw ourselves as the beacon of liberty—as Emma Lazarus and our Statue of Liberty put it—for "your tired, your poor, your huddled masses yearning to breathe free."

As a Fairhoper, I was an exception to the exceptionalism myth. Deep down in my bones I knew we were not the innocents our self-image reflected. Flawed from the beginning, my nation had never been one in which economic, political, or educational justice existed, let alone racial and gender equity. If the "Creator" had endowed all men with inalienable rights to life, liberty, and the pursuit of happiness, I wondered why he placed on earth so many persons so powerfully endowed with the ability and the will to rob their fellows of that endowment. Deeply embedded in its economic march to progress was its twin creation of poverty, grotesquely evident in the years of the Great Depression. Woven into its proud commitment to universal public education was its child-warping pedagogy. And on my bedroom bookshelf, placed there by my father, was a book with the ominous title *Chain the War Gods*. Even our heroic wars for liberty might have been rooted in ignoble ambitions.

I absorbed these un-American beliefs during my childhood. They were part of my family's values, handed down to me by my father and mother, who had received them from their fathers and mothers. I embraced them without question not because I took pleasure in exposing hypocrisy and denial—that was not part of my family heritage—but because Fairhopers believed their experiment in cooperative individualism and organic education showed how American ideals might become practical realities instead of elusive hopes. There was nothing wrong with the ideals but their implementation left a huge amount to desire. As he set forth to found his model community, my grandfather wrote that "they that shall make good theories work and prove the value of proposed social solutions by practical demonstration will do far more to move the world than the wisest and most brilliant theorists."

I

Many years would pass between my youthful absorption of Fairhoper values and my learning of their origins. My quest for that knowledge began in 1978 with my search through the colony archives and a subsequent visit to Des Moines, the seat of Grandfather's rearing and young manhood and the place where the dream of Fairhope was born. Along the way, guided by genealogical searches, I traced our family back as far as a rebellious noble ancestor named Jean Gaston, le Comte de Foix, a French Huguenot born in 1600. Victims of persecution by the regnant Christians of the time, my Protestant ancestors fled to the British Isles and eventually migrated to Pennsylvania. From there many funneled down the great valley of Virginia to settle in the Carolinas. My branch moved west to Illinois, where my grandfather was born on November 21, 1861. His father, James Estep Gaston, tutored by the famous Alexander Campbell, was a minister in the newly revived

Church of Christ. Preacher Campbell described him as a man "distinguished for good sense, good talent and unfeigned piety." Great-Grandfather had virtually no schooling, but he was admired as a student of Latin and Greek and was hailed as both a good writer and compelling orator.

I have neither the skills nor the evidence to explain why Grandfather became distraught by the widespread poverty and inequality of his generation or why he became a passionate advocate of their abolition. I know that he grew up in the Midwestern villages and towns where his father's preaching took the family and that, before he was very far along in school, he was settled in Des Moines, where his father pastored at the newly formed Central Church of that city. Only scraps of evidence remain. He once wrote that his childhood behavior was less than exemplary, especially for a minister's son. "I readily acquired and easily held the reputation of being one of the worst boys in school," he recalled in an 1887 speech, "and achieved the high honor of being suspended three times in a little more than a month, to say nothing of the minor punishments which were almost of daily occurrence." It would take a bold psycho-biographer to build a character portrait out of this lonely surviving snippet. I am not that biographer.

The story does suggest that he had a rebellious spirit, a fact he confessed in the same 1887 speech, remarking that he "longed for a change." The context suggests it was personal change he sought but it is possible that he was inclined toward some larger social cause. In any case, "still longing for change," he had not found whatever it was he was seeking. He wrote fondly of his adventure as a tenderfoot on a Texas cattle-buying trip, but the life of a cowboy held no appeal. At twenty-one he entered Drake University, in the Des Moines suburb of University Place. His student career was interrupted by periods of employment in Minnesota and Kansas, the student magazine describing him once as "a businessman of Minneapolis." He graduated from the commerce department at the top of his class in 1886, at the age of twenty-four.

He was married the next year to his classmate, Clara Mershon, a gifted music major. They soon began a family, became popular members of the University Place social set, and on the surface seemed poised to have a conventional life with Grandfather as a successful young businessman and civic leader, Grandmother a warm hostess, and both of them popular singers at ice cream socials. Then something happened. First, in August of 1889, not yet twenty-eight, Grandfather bought *The Suburban Advocate*, a small newspaper serving University Place. A month later he brought together a few friends to form what they called the Des Moines Investigating Club. They met weekly throughout the winter to discuss the country's social and economic condition. It was no ordinary book club devoted to sampling the classics or enjoying the newest fiction. Their choices came instead from the list of the most trenchant works of social criticism of the time, including Edward Bellamy's just-off-the-press *Looking Backward, 2000–1888* (1889), Henry George's *Progress and Poverty* (1879), and Laurence Gronlund's *The Cooperative Commonwealth* (1884).

The formation of the Investigating Club marked the beginning of a four-year intellectual and political odyssey for Grandfather, a search to discover why the country's great wealth, power, and noble ideals left so many of its citizens in poverty and despair. By the summer of 1893 he thought he had discovered both the cause and a practical cure. That was when he drew up the plan to demonstrate his ideas in a model community that would be called Fairhope. The path to that decision, however, was not a straight one and there were moments when he must have wondered if he would ever find the answers to his questions.

Much influenced by Bellamy's utopian novel, with its sweeping indictment of the workings of the American capitalistic system, Grandfather urged the famous author to come to Des Moines to meet with his group. Pleading poor health, Bellamy declined the invitation but praised Grandfather as one who was "looking for the morning," and counseled him to do "all you can for our common cause personally and in your paper," assuring him that "you can in no other way serve your country better."

Bellamy's letter, one of scores from the period I found in Grandfather's files, helped me to get some feel for the energy and excitement that must have driven his quest. Even more captivating was the large book in which he kept copies of the letters he wrote to like-minded reformers in distant parts. Water-damaged during the 1906 hurricane that swept through Fairhope, it survives, with a few scribblings from children—my father, aunts, and uncles. I also found his own copy of Bellamy's novel, turning the pages speedily hoping to come across revealing marginal comments. Alas, there were none, revealing or otherwise.

Apart from the books they read, Grandfather and his colleagues spent much of their time discussing several of the communitarian experiments that had been a distinctive part of the American past. Communities like New Harmony and Brook Farm, internationally famous in the antebellum period, demonstrated the ideas of Robert Owen and Charles Fourier, the two most prominent theoreticians of communitarian socialism of the age. The promising idea of reform by example attracted the Investigating Club members. I don't know if they read the pre-civil war writer Albert Brisbane's description of the hope of communitarianism; but, if they had, they would have liked it. The communitarian experiment, Brisbane wrote, would "change quietly and by substitution what is false and defective. . . . It can moreover be tried on a small scale, and it will only spread when practice has shown its superiority over the present system."

Now, in the 1880s, a new burst of communitarianism seized their attention. Grandfather corresponded with the secretary of one of the communities, the Kaweah Cooperative Colony Company of Tulare County, California. It advertised itself to be "a practical democratic co-operative commonwealth" founded on the principles of Bellamy and Gronlund. Grandfather hoped to visit the colony, whose plan he described as "admirable," but he could not raise the money for train fare. When he later read of the quarrels and material failures that destroyed the colony he wrote of its founders as "men of pure and lofty aims," leading him to observe that "the mind capable of planning is not always capable of executing." Young though he was, Grandfather thought of himself as the kind of practical idealist who could both plan and execute. That faith would now meet its first test.

By the summer of 1890 he and his friends had drawn up a blueprint for their own communitarian venture. In July the Des Moines newspapers carried long descriptions of their proposed "National Co-operative Company." Before the month was out press notices appeared in perhaps a score of other cities, most of them announcing a new attempt to institute the "Bellamy Plan," with E. B. Gaston of Des Moines as the secretary to whom interested persons should write for information. In response, cards and letters poured into Grandfather's office. The many he kept had turned yellow, some of them brittle, by the time I got to them ninety years later. It was easy to see how they had both buoyed and moved him.

Some, like the one from a Russian immigrant living in Kansas, told of a man deep in debt, "cracked" in health, who looked to Grandfather and his associates as friends of mankind who might give him the "chance to associate with you in this great movement for delivering humanity from beasthood to humanity." Among a few letters from abroad was the assurance of a German that "warm enthusiasm" would come from "thousands of efficient industrious Europeans, slaves of the capitalists who are thirsting for freedom." Another European immigrant, who told of his home being burned down by the Jesse and Frank James gang, wrote from New Orleans of his struggle to maintain his socialist principles. He hoped he would receive his "reward by getting a chance to work with you." Letters from these immigrants, who had come to America to find greater freedom and opportunity, underscored the ironic fate America held for them.

By October, upwards of a hundred persons from twenty-one states had written to express interest in the proposed colony. All but two or three were men. Some wrote eloquently; some had difficulty spelling or forming their letters correctly; a few were veterans of other cooperative colony ventures; and some wrote learnedly about the advantages of competing economic doctrines. In varying ways all wrote of the failure of the United States to become the land of opportunity its resources, mythology, and history intended it to be. Grandfather replied to all of his correspondents with courtesy and empathy. Deciphering his water-damaged letter book, I copied all of the legible letters. As I did—typing in the room where he wrote his last editorials—I could feel how moved he was by the stories he read and how those stories deepened his resolve to find a way to ease the grief and disillusionment of which they told. I understood better how the suffering and injustice of which he read became a call to leave the comfortable life he had created for his family and to enter one that might address these American shames.

Seeing himself now as a reformer in the making, he wrote to one his correspondents to say that "our present competitive system" allowed men to live "without regard to the needs of the community." To another, one of the more desperate of those who contacted him, he wrote of how "the present system" had "robbed you of all confidence in . . . humanity." And he added: "you are by no means alone in this condition." Human nature, he was sure, "is not essentially devilish." Once freed from the "present accursed system . . . truth, justice, brotherhood, and true liberty will spring up and flourish." Lofty words, I thought, for this twenty-eight year-old idealist who would be a practical reformer.

No copy of the detailed plan he and his colleagues drew up for replacing the "present accursed system," has survived. The correspondence, however, contains enough detail for me to form a reliable picture of what it was to be like. For one thing, Grandfather often made it clear that his was not to be, as the newspapers declared, a Bellamy colony. He rejected what he called Bellamy's "extreme socialism." He also found problems with Henry George's more individualistic philosophy. This came as something of a surprise to me because the Fairhope I knew, the colony which my father directed, and the stories I had been told, were all about Henry George and the single-tax panacea. In 1890, however, Grandfather was not the Henry George disciple he would later become.

Surviving descriptions of the National Cooperative Company tell of a plan to purchase a large tract of land in Louisiana that would be the common property of all the members. Collective decisions would determine what specific tasks would be performed by which workers; a uniform wage scale would be adopted; and the Company would devise a system of credit and distribution that would free it of reliance on the outside world. The construction of homes and public buildings was also to be a communal undertaking, with community values reflected in the structures in which people lived and worked. Schools and intellectual and artistic endeavors would be collectively planned and implemented, reinforcing the members' sense of common purpose. In all of these activities, women and men would stand on an equal footing, thus aligning Grandfather's colony with the struggle for women's rights at a time when women everywhere were disfranchised and denied positions of leadership. With all this, Grandfather wrote, the company would "propagate and extend in the world at large the idea of universal and just co-operation."

For six months, beginning in the summer of 1890, Grandfather was totally absorbed in recruiting members for his new venture. Frequent letters from enthusiastic potential colonists must have bolstered his natural optimism, but as time wore on disappointment piled on disappointment. By December only four persons had actually sent in down payments on a membership. He wrote then that "we have given up for the present our cherished plan." Characteristically, however, he added: "I have never been more determined to put our plans into execution and I will never give up until I see them tried." Admitting defeat did not come easily to my grandfather. Reading through his correspondence of these discouraging months I began to see a man whose ambition rode right along with his idealism. On the day after Christmas he wrote to one friend that "prevailing hard times" explained why so few had joined, but he hoped to renew his effort "ere long." Five months later he wrote to a fellow communitarian explaining that his effort had failed because "the kind of people who are attracted to such an enterprise are . . . poor and suffering from existing conditions"; but, he added, he was "still determined . . . to 'seek refuge' in a Cooperative Society."

II

Meanwhile, there was the matter of earning a living and finding creative outlets for his zeal to make a difference in the world. Income from *The Advocate* was not enough to support a family and I noted that he spent a good part of the winter months in Nebraska and Kansas, selling medical publications from D. Appleton publishers. While the winter snows were still piled high my grandmother became pregnant with her third child. I like to think that this baby boy on the way, who one day would become my father, was conceived partly as solace for the failed experiment but also as confident affirmation of life to come.

What came next in his life unfolded to me as a revelation. Traces of the National Cooperative Company story have survived in Fairhope history, albeit dispatched to the margins, more often explained away than explained. Nowhere, however, had I read or heard of Fairhope's origins in the Populist revolt of the early 1890s. Yet all of its founders were Populist Party members and the revolt of which they were a part shaped its values and character. As early as March of 1891 Grandfather had become secretary of a Citizens' Alliance that would soon evolve into the Peoples Party. Former Nebraska Senator Charles H. Van Wyck, featured speaker at the Alliance's first rally in Des Moines, said "We have been taught to believe we have a superior civilization" with "greater education, equal privileges to all, free and universal suffrage," and "that every citizen, however humble, is sovereign; that our government is of, by and for the people." None of this was true, the speaker roared, to be greeted by echoing roars of approval.

The cause that Grandfather now took up was about to become one of the great mass movements for social change in American history, with a recruiting power far beyond the reach of the small and isolated colonies of communitarian reformers to whom he had so recently committed himself. It must have been exciting for him to find that the very center of the coming revolt was in his home town of Des Moines and that its head was General James B. Weaver. An abolitionist as a youth, the fifty-eight year-old Weaver had been a Congressman and a Greenback candidate for president. He would be the Populist Party's candidate for president in 1892. He was also editor and co-owner of *The Farmer's Tribune*, the voice of the insurgency. Grandfather soon became part of the *Tribune* staff where he met like-minded writers and reformers. Sitting around the office stove they must have spent many hours dissecting their country's problems and mulling over solutions to them.

Weaver was an inspiration, both in his person and for his understanding of the American dilemma. In his first book, *A Call to Action*, published in 1892, the General wrote that "the spirit of the corporation is aggressive and essentially warlike." It had seized the "sovereign functions" of government—"a shameful betrayal of a sacred trust"—and had used them "for the accumulation of vast and overshadowing private fortunes." The "melancholy contrasts of wealth and poverty, of individual happiness and widespread infelicity" were part of a huge contradiction of the great promise with which the Republic was born. These had been constant themes in Grandfather's own writings; they would continue to be in the future. They echo in my world of today.

Accompanying the demands for a more just economic order, the Populists strove for an expanded definition of democracy. As they denounced the corruption and class-based character of the existing government they proposed democratic reforms, such as the initiative, referendum, and direct election of senators, reforms that would give ordinary people power to control their government. When a Kansas Populist declared that "we are emerging from a period of intense individualism, supreme selfishness, and ungodly greed to a period of cooperative effort" he expressed the essence of the Populist hope and creed. His words must also have affirmed for Grandfather his own reading and writing of the past few years and given him assurance that his commitment to the Populist revolt was right for him.

For two-and-half years he was a central figure in the life of the new party, at least in Iowa. As he traveled with Weaver to St. Louis for the founding conference, Grandfather wrote of "the homes of the wealthy crowning the hilltops of our beautiful city." But soon came "the wretched hovels, which in every city mark the abode of poverty." The visible contrasts of wealth and poverty reminded him forcibly of the enigma he had been struggling to understand—and to do something about—since he formed the Investigating Club over two years previous. Now, he believed, he was part of a new political departure for the country that might yield answers. The people he met in St. Louis fortified his optimism. There were leaders of all the country's progressive organizations, including what he described as "a galaxy of noble women, the peers in ability of any men."

He found the oratory thrilling. Ignatius Donnelly's speech, which would gain immediate and lasting fame, would later become the preamble to the party platform. Long before I knew of my grandfather's connection with Populism or that he had been there to hear the speech, I included it in the required readings for my American history class. The fiery Donnelly began with the assertion that "We meet in the midst of a nation brought to the verge of moral, political, and material ruin." After reciting a litany of the insurgents' beliefs, he concluded with the dire warning that "from the same prolific womb of governmental injustice we breed the two great classes—tramps and millionaires."

In addition to the oratory, there were numerous personal satisfactions. One of Grandfather's *Tribune* colleagues, for example, won wide applause with a whistling performance. Following that Grandfather himself came on the stage to join his colleague in singing an emerging favorite, "Good-Bye, Old Party, Good-Bye." He returned to Des Moines to write a long account for the *Tribune,* and to enter fully into Populist Party politics. That summer, at the Omaha Convention, Weaver was nominated for president. Grandfather then took over as editor of the paper while the General carried the Populist message to the country.

Historians reckon that the Populist revolt of 1892 played a pivotal role in loosening the grip of the so-called Robber Barons and other captains of industry on American political and economic life. Shaking up the conservative political order, it nonetheless faded away after the 1896 election. Some of its liberalizing ideas, however, were absorbed by the Progressive Movement that, under Theodore Roosevelt and Woodrow Wilson, culminated in measures to curtail unregulated capitalism and to expand national power in a polity made more democratic. With the New Deal, the Populist goal of expanded government power to exert greater sensitivity to the lives and fortunes of ordinary people seemed to many to have been significantly advanced.

Weaver won more than a million votes—8.8 percent of those cast—and carried four states with twenty-two electoral votes. A dozen Populist Congressmen were dispatched to Washington while Populist governors were elected in Kansas, North Dakota, and Colorado. But in Iowa the results were dismal: Weaver was favored by only 4.7 percent of the voters. Clearly disappointed by the state results, Grandfather stuck with the party, becoming its state secretary, traveling widely to build up interest, raise money, and establish new Populist clubs. According to one report in the *Tribune*, he traveled with the "silver glee club," singing and speaking at fifteen meetings in three counties, "creating the wildest enthusiasm."

His own enthusiasm, however, was waning. His hope that reform politics might usher in a cooperative society based on justice was difficult to sustain. He wrote privately of his doubt that the things he believed in could be established in his lifetime through the political process. Through the spring and summer of 1893 his restless mind and churning ambition brought him back to the idea of communitarian reform, but this time with a new and bold twist. In August he sent out a batch of letters, written on the stationery of the People's Party State Central Committee, to men with whom he had corresponded three years earlier about the National Cooperative Company. He enclosed an essay he entitled "True Cooperative Individualism."

One of his recipients replied: "I gather that your purpose is to apply to a colonization scheme the principle of the single tax together with other economic principles." This man had it just right. Grandfather had returned frequently to *Progress and Poverty* and had been stimulated by frequent meetings with the members of the Des Moines Single Tax Club, including his fellow Populist, James Bellangee. The club, formed in 1891, summed up its mission in two sentences: "We favor raising all public revenues by taxation of land values. We hold that every business in its nature a monopoly should be owned by the government." Hamlin Garland, a Georgist himself and already a prominent author, thought Grandfather was the right person to show why "all social experiments have started on a wrong foundation" because "there has been no clear perception of the relation of the land question to social experiments." E. B. Gaston was the man to make that relationship clear.

III

On January 4, 1894, Grandfather called twelve of his Populist Party comrades to his office to read to them his cooperative individualism essay. When he began by denouncing the existing social and economic order for its "hideous injustice and cruelty" he was preaching to the choir. When he warned that "the slow movement of majorities" would likely mean the victims would go before the injustice, he was calling upon them to do as he was ready to do, to abandon electoral politics as the engine of reform. He was persuasive. Before the meeting broke up the group agreed to draft a constitution for a model community. Grandfather and four of his colleagues assumed the task of drawing it up. They did their work quickly. Their draft was approved and officers elected by the group of thirteen, meeting on the 31st of January. Grandfather took the office of Secretary, his familiar role. Two weeks later the *Tribune* announced the creation of the Fairhope

Industrial Association that was "organized by a number of leading Populists of this state . . . to make a practical demonstration of . . . the principles we have been advocating as a party."

The term "cooperative individualism" was Grandfather's unique contribution to the lexicon of reform. What it addressed, however, was a perennial concern of political philosophers and statesmen from Plato onwards. How, he and they asked, should rights and responsibilities be defined and allotted in a just society? How should one establish the balance between the power and duties of the state, on the one hand, and the freedom and obligations of the individual on the other? I would not claim, and Grandfather would have been mightily embarrassed if any of his contemporaries had suggested, that he was a world-class political philosopher or an eminent statesman. But as he drew from the writings of such authorities and more immediately from his Populist colleagues and the writings of Henry George, he struggled with the same problem and then fashioned a blueprint for a society he believed would offer a workable resolution of that conundrum.

He described his constitution as "the only plan of co-operative colonization ever proposed which secures the benefits of co-operation and yet preserves the freedom of individuals." He believed his model community would fall between the excessive government direction of socialism and the corrupting influence of his country's largely unfettered individualism. Now a firm follower of Henry George, he agreed with the author's plan to "reach the ideal of the socialist, but not through government repression." To curb the excessive individualism eating at the country's vitals, and to promote the reality and spirit of cooperation, he designed a model community that would own and operate "natural monopolies," supplying "water, light, power, telephones, transportation, etc., by association control and operation at cost." No individuals would profit from control or ownership of what the constitution called "public necessities."

The anchor of his plan rested in its land policy. Fully persuaded by this time of George's belief that the solution to the enigma of poverty amidst plenty was to make land common property, Grandfather's constitution provided that no private ownership of land would be allowed within the community and that all of its land would be owned in common by the members. Understood broadly, land meant all natural resources, all those factors of production and necessities of life that, as Fairhopers frequently said, were gifts of God or gifts of nature, not the creation of individuals. It followed that no individuals should reap profit from their ownership. And, equally important, all members would have free access to land on which to build homes, businesses, and farms. The land speculator would become extinct. Opportunities once denied would appear and multiply.

Notices of the Fairhope plan spread across the country through the Reform Press Association, an effective creation of the Populist Party. Once again letters and cards came to Grandfather and, once again, he replied to every query. Copies of the constitution along with the cooperative individualism essay accompanied his replies. From February on, he worked furiously to publicize his venture and to recruit members for it. Until August his comrade Alf Wooster's newspaper *Liberty Bell* served as the voice of the proposed colony. On August 15 the first issue of *The Fairhope Courier* was published in Des Moines, with Grandfather as editor and the Association as its owner.

As I sat in his old office, reading those early issues of the *Courier,* I began to have an uneasy feeling. Not many people were sending in their down payments on the $200 membership fee. Was this to be a repeat of the earlier colony venture, doomed to failure for lack of sufficient interest and money? There was much more interest this time, but little money was coming in. I began to sense—what later became very clear—that Fairhope was falling between two stools. To reformers tilting toward individualism, primarily single-tax purists, its cooperative dimension seemed too close to socialism. To socialists it smacked too much of individualism. There was an active national single-tax movement at the time but its wealthier members, of whom I thought there were quite a few, were reluctant to lend significant support. In part, I believed, their chariness stemmed from Henry George himself. He had earlier written (not in reference to Fairhope) that he did not favor a communitarian experiment to demonstrate the virtues of his ideas. He feared such a venture would fail and bring discredit to them.

Despite the lack of funds, members, and support from single-taxers and George himself, Grandfather gave no sign of discouragement. The council sent two of its officers, James Bellangee and Shuah Mann, to search for a site. They spent much of June and July looking over possibilities in five Southern states. The South appeared to be chosen because of both climate and cost. Bellangee found one fault or another with most of the locales they examined. Then, on the eastern shore of Mobile Bay, in Baldwin County, Alabama, he found a site that he could recommend with enthusiasm. "We viewed the land & country over the hills and along the shore," he wrote to Grandfather. "It is lovely indeed. . . .The view from the shore is magnificent. . . . If we could secure a mile frontage on the bay and good body of land running back to the table lands we would be nicely fixed." Adding what must have been a special inducement, he wrote that Henry George himself had recently visited a friend in the village of Daphne, close by the favored site, who believed "that if we go there we will be able to get George's endorsement . . . and make it a big single tax enterprise." I was saddened reading these letters knowing that neither the hoped-for extent of land nor George's endorsement would be realized.

But Grandfather pushed on. In the August 15 first issue of the *Courier* he reported the location committee's findings and recommendations. The September 1 issue proudly listed a "roll call of honor" of members, and announced a forthcoming membership vote to select a site. This would be the Association's maiden referendum. The results of the balloting were announced in the October 1 *Courier.* A western Tennessee possibility was favored by eight of the members. The Baldwin County site was the overwhelming favorite, with twenty-six first-place votes. Fairhope would be built on the shores of Mobile Bay, deep down in the Deep South.

But could it really be done? Sitting there in Grandfather's old office, poring over the pages of the *Courier*, reading the large batch of letters and his carefully kept minutes book, the bold, clear hand exuding confidence, I imagined myself struggling along with him in the autumn of 1894. When he announced that the Association had an option on a good parcel of land and that the roundup of settlers on the site would take place on November 15, I felt uneasy. Were there enough members to make it work? Was there enough money to purchase the needed land? The Association had been formed in January with nineteen men taking part either as participants in the first meeting or as officers elected on January 31. Only ten of those nineteen made the required partial payments to be members in good standing. The full membership fee of $200 was being paid in small installments by those who wanted to join; full payment was beyond the reach of most. Undaunted, Grandfather kept calling for help. "Friends," he wrote in the October 1 *Courier*, "your membership and your money mean more to us now than they ever will again. We cannot buy land or goods or make public improvements with your promises, hopes or good wishes. They encourage us but we cannot 'realize' on them." Still short of what he needed, he wondered two weeks later, "shall we ask in vain?"

I feared that he did seek in vain. But he was determined. He had waited long enough. His powerful combination of ambition and idealism allowed him to ask others to take the great risks he himself had no doubt about taking. With that confidence, he set off from Des Moines on the evening of November 12 with his wife and four children, the eldest five, baby Leah walking but still in diapers. I was shocked, probably a little angry, too, to

Grandfather Gaston and his family on the eve of their departure from Des Moines.

discover that Bellangee, his closest Association comrade and forthright advisor, was staying behind, running for state auditor on the Populist Party ticket. The president, vice president, five of the six councilmen, and the three trustees also opted to stay at home. From the group of founders and officers only council member Jimmy Hunnell would be at the roundup. Strange doings, I thought. Bellangee and a couple of others would eventually join them; most never would, declining the challenge of making their good theory work. So, setting off that evening on the southbound train with my grandfather and his family were only Jimmy Hunnell's parents, neither a member of the Association. Their son, already in Alabama, was seeing to the safe arrival of the Gaston and Hunnell family possessions, including Grandfather's cow and his mare, Dolly.

Twenty-eight persons showed up at the November 15 roundup at `s, the settlement just south of the chosen site—seven couples, nine children, five single men. They came from Iowa, Nebraska, Minnesota, Ohio, Missouri, California, and Pennsylvania. Before the end of the year five additional adults arrived. The colony's numbers, however, were quickly depleted. A January 22, 1895, report on "members in good standing," that is, those who had kept up with their five-dollar monthly payments, listed only eight locals. Before long half of them would drop out. Some had returned whence they came; some stayed in the area but abandoned the colony to buy and settle on land they would own. My friends Paul and Rocky Alyea, in their 1956 history of Fairhope, indulged a taste for understatement when they headed their chapter on these events "An Inauspicious Beginning."

IV

Discouraged though I was by these desertions I was impressed—amazed might be a better word—by Grandfather's determination and energy. He built two small homes himself, one for his family, one for his mother-in-law, kept up his correspondence with Bellangee, urging him to come as soon as possible, and managed to bring out regular issues of the *Courier*, dispatching them to likely members and contributors around the country. Most importantly, he negotiated the first land purchases.

That first one would be the most important. For six dollars an acre, the colony acquired 135 acres, running 2,800 feet along the waterfront. Ominously, however, a swath of land nearly 500 feet wide running from the Bay about 2,000 feet deep divided the new purchase in two. Its owner, a putative Georgist, refused to sell to the band of Georgist followers. The privately owned tract continued for decades to divide the heart of the colony into a south and a north division, requiring for a while negotiations to permit crossings from one colony section to another. Most of it remains in private hands today. My grandfather's half-sister, Clara Atkinson, purchased a substantial section. According to family lore she never believed the colony would succeed, but, because she loved her brother Ernest, she moved to Fairhope partly to protect him from the consequences of failure. A little land speculation to that end was apparently not beyond her.

The next purchase came a month after the first, 200 acres in the interior, adjoining the first purchase, at $1.25 an acre. By 1900, after five more purchases, the colony had acquired a total of 1,200 acres. By 1906 the acreage had climbed to 4,000, most of the money for the additions coming from Joseph Fels, a wealthy Philadelphia soap-manufacturer and ardent single-taxer. The land, however, was not in solid, contiguous blocks but dotted about the countryside. And the first purchase and the adjoining land behind it—the area that would become the colony (and later town) center—remained divided into two parts and adjacent to privately owned lands. This patchwork of landholdings, which did not increase significantly in size in later years, was, as the Alyeas correctly write, "grossly inadequate" for the establishment of the kind of model community my grandfather and his colleagues had envisioned.

Still, people did come, attracted by the free land, by the site on the Bay, and some by the idealistic mission that underlay the community. By 1900 the census enumerator found one hundred people living in the Fairhope area. Not all, however, were members, or even believers, though they might be living on colony land. This unanticipated circumstance resulted from Grandfather's recognition that there were too few members to occupy and develop even the small amount of land the colony owned. His optimism and confidence once again rising to face a setback, he proposed that colony lands be opened to nonmembers, arguing that once aware of the colony's advantages, nonmember lessees would seek membership. Bellangee strongly disagreed. As early as mid-1894 he had written to Grandfather to say that he was "more than ever convinced that we must take great pains to get single taxers only into it. Otherwise we will wreck the thing by dissension." He repeated that view after the settlement. Grandfather's will prevailed but his prediction did not. In time the class of nonmember lessees would constitute a disturbing element within the colony. Many turned out to be happy with their advantages but saw no reason to pay the $100 (reduced from the original $200) to become members, putting their faith in my grandfather and, in later years, my father, as wise and trustworthy stewards.

EIGHTY-FOUR YEARS AFTER THE colony's founding, I sat quietly in my office, wondering what would have happened if Bellangee's view had prevailed. What would the future have been like if the colony's lands were occupied exclusively by advocates of the mission. Would that have been a better way? Even as I ruminated, hostile nonmember lessees were in the midst of the most serious attack ever launched. Bellangee's words—"we will wreck the thing by dissension"—rang ominously. But perhaps Grandfather was right. Perhaps no community, model or otherwise, could have emerged in the 1890s if single-taxers were to be its sole occupants.

A second compromise Grandfather reluctantly favored was to deny membership to African Americans. There was no discussion of this in the run-up to the founding although Bellangee and Grandfather had both written harshly of Southern racial practices. Four years after the first settlers arrived, a prospective supporter wrote to say he could not contribute to a colony that denied membership to Negroes. Grandfather replied directly in a *Courier* editorial. "The criticism of our friend," he wrote, "illustrates anew the difficulties and differences of opinion arising in the effort to determine how far we can practically go in the 'application of correct theories' within a general condition of applied incorrect ones, over which we have no control." Racial discrimination—especially when it thwarted access to the land—was wrong, he wrote. "We believe in 'universal equality'—equality of rights"; no man had "more moral or natural rights to any particular portion of the earth, the common heritage of mankind, than any other of his fellow men." But, he asked, did this mean that the colony should "follow the naked principle of equality unreservedly, regardless of conditions existing?" He could not recommend it. To make Fairhope a racially mixed community at that time in that place would result in "self-destruction" he wrote. To make his good theory work, to provide an example for the world at large of what a just society might be, he consciously endorsed what he knew was a course of action that violated the principles of his good theory. I expect he reflected on how hard it really was "to make good theories work."

The compromise of principle may have been easier to make because of Grandfather's belief that, at bottom, racial prejudice was a function of economic injustice and that, insofar as the Fairhope demonstration might help to point the way to a better economic order, it was hastening the day when racism might diminish if not disappear. The only remedy for such tragedies as race riots, he wrote after one of them, "is economic freedom." On other occasions he stressed the common predicament of those white and black Southerners ensnared in economic exploitation as sharecroppers, denied free access to land, dependent for their lives on a landlord. He continued throughout his life to speak out against racist excesses and uphold standards of decency and fair play. "We shall certainly vote against it," he wrote of the proposed 1901 Alabama constitution that would disfranchise African Americans and most poor whites, "and advise everyone else to do likewise." Lynchings brought outrage to his editorial columns. They showed "how thin is the veneer of civilization." When the Ku Klux Klan appeared in Fairhope in the 1920s he attacked and ridiculed it. Lecturing the Town Council on the "Invisible Empire," he said that the "creator had not endowed men . . . with invisibility" and there was nothing American in an Empire, "invisible or otherwise."

Growing up in Fairhope, I had absorbed Grandfather's basic faith in democracy and fairness in much the same way that I took for granted the bounties and freedoms of Mobile Bay. Yet somewhere along the way, still a young boy, I also learned that all of these blessings were neither accidental nor the natural order of things. I have strong memories of my father reading to me the constitution of our community, written by his father, declaring that Fairhope was to be "a model community . . . free from all forms of private monopoly" where its citizens would have "equality of opportunity, the full reward of individual effort and the benefits of co-operation in matters of general concern." On other occasions my father read to me his father's declaration that Fairhope was designed "to establish justice, to remove the opportunities for the preying of one upon another." In one of his letters, he wrote: "We close the gates against injustice; we open them to unselfishness. Society can do no more." These and other colony aphorisms became part of my early learning and consciousness so that I came to feel that we not only had an obligation to struggle for justice but that we were armed with special insights in how it could be achieved. Our lives seemed to be lived with high purpose.

Ned Cobb, a fellow Alabamian of my father's generation, a black sharecropper and a radical far removed from the Fairhope scene, once said about the evils surrounding him: "I was big enough and old enough to stretch my eyes at conditions and abominate what I seed." For most of my youth my eyes stretched to conditions outside our community where I abominated what I saw: wide divisions of wealth, power, and privilege; hierarchies and exploitation; regimented, outcome-obsessive education; and an excessive individualism that everywhere unraveled bonds of community. We were confident critics of American values and practices and sure of our hold on the answer to these abominations.

When I was twelve years old, however, I stretched my eyes for the first time at the conditions at home, in my Shangri-la. I didn't exactly abominate them, lacking Ned Cobb's circumstance and wisdom, but I was shaken, taken aback.

It happened on a summer morning in 1940. I walked from my home, only five minutes from the Bay, to the wharf, our community recreation, fishing, and gathering place, stretching 1,800 feet out to deep water. I often kept my sailboat moored there and we all swam from one of the two swimming and diving platforms.

This day, as I approached the wharf, I noticed a large, unfamiliar sign where before there had been only empty space, an open view of the blue-green water. Up closer I read the large-lettered words:

For White People Only

My first thought was: "has this been here before and I am just now noticing it?" Afterwards, I began slowly to wonder at its meaning and the affront it was to my internalized belief in the just society. That puzzlement and anger—rising and falling in intensity over the rest of my life—worked itself out in many ways, leading me eventually to study Southern history, to teach in a Southern university, and to enlist in the Southern civil rights movement. It also led me, in a strange and unexpected way, to write one of the three stories that became my 1984 book, *Women of Fair Hope*.

I came indirectly upon the link between, on the one hand, my grandfather's idealism, and on the other, his suppression of principle for the sake of practical survival. At the outset, I had no idea of where it might lead or of how it might seize me. I had no notion I would eventually connect it with the sign on the wharf.

I had begun my research for what I then thought would be a big social history of the Fairhope experiment. Poring over the colony's well-kept minute book, I was brought up short by a puzzling entry. The date was January 22, 1895. The colonists had been on the site for two months and were negotiating an important land purchase from the estate of a deceased man named John Bowen. The entry betrayed concern over a claim a woman named Nancy Lewis was apparently making to part of the land the colonists were about to buy. She and some of her family were living there, firmly disputing the claim that it was not theirs.

Several entries followed, each making me more curious. I was rooting for Nancy Lewis, but she was clearly losing her battle. Soon I read that she had given up her claim and had agreed to sell all of her improvements to the colony for $100. My grandfather then recorded in the minute book the "purchase of 200 acres of Bowen land including 40 acres claimed by Nancy Lewis . . . for $250.00." Mention was made of a written contract sealing this agreement. That sent me searching through the colony's file drawer of deeds where I found it, near the bottom of the pile. It was singed (charred, I learned from my father, by a 1951 office fire), but Nancy Lewis's well-formed signature, there by my grandfather's, was still legible. Her improvements are enumerated—"houses, sheds, fences, orchards, clearings"—and she was given sixty days to move. A month passes before we hear from her again. Her loss is now complete and the poignancy of it upon me: one of the colony's officers is preparing to move into her old home, to make it his new home.

Why had this happened, I wondered. How ironic that the Fairhopers, who believed in making the land common property, should anchor their utopia on the morally dubious act of evicting an honest farmer and home owner from the place that warranted her freedom and security. I thought I knew why they did this and when I asked my father the answer he gave me confirmed my suspicion. Had he ever heard of a Nancy Lewis, I asked. "Oh, yes," he replied; "she was the colored woman who was squatting on the land the colonists purchased." Once again—but this time at the very heart of my own heritage—I was to learn that nothing happens in the South without race somehow testing, defining, and illuminating values and assumptions, shaping personal behavior and public policies.

The colonists were not unaware of the South's peculiar racial beliefs and habits when they decided to start their experiment in the Deep South. One of them wrote bitterly of the way in which Southern whites "regard it as an essential that the negroes should be kept down." The way in which this was done, he believed, was "the most pathetic evidence of the injustice of the conditions under which they live that could be afforded." My grandfather, agreeing with these sentiments, believed the remedy lay in Georgist principles of cooperation and free land. Before he left Iowa, he wrote that "use gives the only right to the control of land," and he thundered out his belief that legal titles to land were "no more evidence of moral right than the bills of sale in which the unfortunate blacks were held in bondage but a few years since in our land." Nancy Lewis, the honest land user, could hardly have said it better: human slavery and private ownership of land were both offenses against justice.

Awareness of such realities, however, did not move the Fairhopers to take on racial injustice as one of their causes. They had their reasons, their justifications. Economic justice, which they believed would follow from the example they wished to set, would in time wash away irrational racial prejudice. Meanwhile, they reckoned there was no way they could successfully challenge the racial assumptions surrounding them.

Three years after the first encounter with Nancy Lewis, my grandfather addressed the question head on. A potential contributor had threatened to withhold his support if the colony continued to exclude blacks from it. "The criticism of our friend," Grandfather stated, "illustrates anew the difficulties and differences of opinion arising in the effort to determine how far we can practically go in the 'application of correction theories' within a general condition of applied incorrect ones, over which we have no control." Racial discrimination—especially when it thwarted access to the land—was wrong. "We believe in universal equality," he wrote, "equality of rights"; no man had "more moral or natural right to any particular portion of the earth, the common heritage of mankind, than any other of his fellow men."

What, then, was to be done? Should they follow what Grandfather called "the naked principle of equality unreservedly, regardless of conditions existing?" He could not recommend it, sure as he was that "the naked principles of equality" was the one sure thing white Southerners would crush. Thus, to preserve his colony and make possible its otherwise radical experiment, he sadly agreed that it must be for whites only. Doing this, however, he made it clear that the "whites only" policy was a fundamental contradiction of the "good theory" Fairhope existed to demonstrate.

Like my grandfather's first two compromises of principle, his third was also fashioned as a means of survival. Increasingly, starting about 1905, the colony came under attack from nonmember lessees, whose numbers had increased in greater proportion than members. Some, like the socialists who had moved from the failed Ruskin colony in Tennessee, seemed to hanker for a rebirth of their failed experiment. Many more, without ideological axes to grind, raised the specter of an undemocratic single-tax corporation denying to its lessees both the right to vote and a say in setting rents and determining expenditures. As I read these complaints I heard once more the echo of Bellangee's warning that, failing to fill the colony lands exclusively with single-taxers, "we will wreck the thing by dissension."

There was dissension aplenty. Once again Grandfather faced a difficult and unanticipated dilemma. The dissenters' cry of taxation without representation raised sharply the issue of democracy about which he cared deeply. The colony constitution was a model of democratic rights but it applied only to members of the colony. It was drawn looking toward the creation of a "model community" made up of believing members. The reality was now very different. To give the complaining lessees the right to vote in colony matters seemed to Grandfather to be a sure road to corruption of his demonstration. As anger and protest arose around him, with a few of the members themselves—Bellangee ironically prominent among them—urging one plan after another to grant the nonmember lessees some of what they wanted, Grandfather thwarted the opposition by supporting an alternative plan—the formation of a municipality in which all adult residents (but, under Alabama law of the time, only male adult residents who could meet the property-ownership requirement) would have the right to vote, hold office, and determine town policy. Such a move, he believed, would take the sting out of the dissident movement, keeping the colony free to hold to its principles.

The Town of Fairhope was incorporated in 1908. The town itself, fronting on and spreading back from the Bay, covered an area of about one and a half square miles. An unofficial census found 569 persons (466 white, 103 black) living within the town limits. Three-fourths of the land within was privately owned. Of the colony's roughly 4,000 acres, all but 521 (including park lands) lay outside the new town. The municipality did not then, nor did it ever, seek a home-rule charter that would allow it to raise revenue exclusively from a single tax on land values. With two different land-tenure and revenue-raising arrangements as well as two different governing bodies with different rules for elections and office holding, Fairhope became an anomaly difficult to explain to outsiders and not always understood by insiders. Sitting there in my grandfather's old office, I almost wept, wishing it could have been different.

As I pored over the correspondence, minutes, and *Courier* files it suddenly struck me that it might have been different. There had been a chance. In the run-up to the election of a mayor and councilmen a straw vote of residents (most of them lacking the required property ownership to be qualified voters) favored Grandfather by a vote of 69–13 over Dr. H.

S. Greeno, a bitter and outspoken opponent of the whole single-tax idea. Many urged Grandfather to run. Joe Fels, Fairhope's influential wealthy supporter, wrote to oppose the idea. Bellangee strongly opposed it, virtually accusing Grandfather of caring more about power than about democracy. He was not persuasive. Grandfather announced his candidacy. Bellangee voted against him, carrying three other colony members with him, giving a 21–19 victory to Greeno. The town of Fairhope thus began with one of the most outspoken colony critics at its head. "I have not been and am not now in sympathy with what is known here as the 'Fairhope Plan'," the mayor stated shortly after his election. Without what I now came to consider Bellangee's apostasy, Grandfather as leader of both colony and town might well have had the clout to lead the new municipality to acquire a home-rule charter and through this means spread the single-tax idea to the town. Bellangee, who was elected to the town council, apparently never proposed such a course of action.

Thus, the creation of the town made virtually impossible the realization of Grandfather's carefully drawn plan—a plan Bellangee had helped to shape—for a model community featuring the Georgist philosophy bound in the principles of cooperative individualism. The hostile editor of a neighboring newspaper believed he had pronounced the epitaph for the FSTC when he wrote that "Fairhope will be known hereafter as a town, and the name 'colony' will go out of use, except to describe certain local usages, such as 'colony rents' and 'colony lands.'"

None of this was clear to me in my youth. In graduate school I published a review of the Alyeas' 1956 history where many of these first problematic years were discussed. What I read, however, did not sink in until I began my own research in 1978–79. As I grew up in Fairhope, the great compromises of those early years were deep background events. In the foreground were the ongoing uniqueness and special reformist qualities of my home. These shone more brightly for me as my heritage than the reverses and disappointments my grandfather faced in his struggle to make his good theory work.

And with good reason. As I pursued my research in 1978–79, I found abundant evidence of the continuing vitality of Fairhope as a single-tax colony. For one thing, the "cooperative" features envisioned in the constitution were visible in the parklands, especially at the Bay, with its long beach and pier, bath houses, and swimming platforms. It was also evident in the colony-owned waterworks; a new telephone system; the building and maintenance of wide streets and sidewalks; a unique library presided over by the author and communitarian reformer Marie Howland and stocked with the large book collection of her late husband Edward; and Grandfather's short-lived Peoples Railroad, designed to haul freight from the wharf to the railroad line eight or ten miles away. It may not have been the model community envisioned by the founders, but it was a unique community, with the FSTC playing a major role within the town.

The special quality of life that Fairhope residents celebrated emanated from the colony. As time passed, the ownership of its public services were transferred to the town. Thirty-nine acres of streets were the first to be handed over, in 1909. The parklands, including the beach front and the pier, became city property in the early years of the Depression, but with a proviso that they must remain parklands in perpetuity on penalty of the title reverting to the FSTC. Ownership of the library, the last public service to become city property, was transferred in 1964.

Despite these divestments, Fairhope continued for many years—certainly all through my youth—to attract idealists and reformers drawn by the founding vision. Creative writers, artists, and craftsmen were attracted by the congenial spirit of the place and the companionship of its inhabitants. Men and women of modest means found in the free land the answer to their hopes and the foundation of economic well-being and recovered self-esteem. Fairhopers might disagree on many subjects, as early settler Alice Herring wrote, but there was a "spirit of comradeship" she had never seen elsewhere. It gave meaning to life and direction to one's actions. No amount of "personal love," she wrote, "can take the place of the comradeship that unites a community."

Fairhope was hardly a united community during the years of controversy that brought the town into existence but versions of Herring's testament continued to be pronounced for years to come. During those years, the town achieved modest coverage in the national press because it was a "single-tax town." Notables like Clarence Darrow, a member of the Chicago Single

Tax club, visited on several occasions in the 1920s and '30s, frequently chewing over the virtues of Henry George's writings with my grandfather. Upton Sinclair and after him Sherwood Anderson found secluded spots to live and write for brief times. Wharton Esherick, eventually to become one of the nation's most esteemed craftsmen, attributed his artistic start to his time in Fairhope. Scores of persons, up to and including my friend Craig Sheldon—maverick columnist, sculptor, and builder—wrote or spoke of how single-tax land transformed their lives. As Fairhope grew, the land within it that was most intensely developed, including all of the downtown area, was single-tax land. By 1930 Fairhope edged past Bay Minette, the county seat, to become the largest town in the county. Most observers attributed its standing to FSTC policies.

V

Fairhope's modest fame was broadened and its attraction to northern intellectuals and progressives was enhanced in the years immediately after the incorporation of the town by Marietta Johnson's School of Organic Education. The school would shortly become a virtual equal of the single-tax colony in defining Fairhope's unique virtues and Mrs. Johnson would soon stand beside my grandfather as his co-equal rebel leader. Marietta and Frank Johnson came to Fairhope in 1902, moved briefly to live in Mississippi, and then returned for her to start her school in 1907. There were six children in a one-room cottage when it opened. Seven years later it occupied a ten-acre campus provided rent-free by the colony. Enrollment had reached 150, including two-thirds of the town's school children as well as the offspring of a number of northern visitors and others attracted by organic education and the progressive spirit of the community.

By organic education Mrs. Johnson meant that "education is growth," a definition that John Dewey, the most influential American advocate of progressive education, was to emphasize and plant firmly in the lexicon of progressive educators. Both of them meant by the term that schooling should not be training or preparation for future demands but the proper nurturing of immediate needs of the whole person. Mrs. Johnson called her idea organic education because she believed that no part of the student's

Mrs. Johnson and students, from frontispiece of Dewey's Schools of Tomorrow.

development could be isolated from another without endangering or warping the child. The spiritual, physical, and mental requirements needed to be kept in balance.

By 1913 she and her school had achieved a national reputation. Persuaded of its significance, Dewey came to Fairhope that year to see for himself and to enroll his young son during their brief stay. Two years later he published his findings in *Schools of Tomorrow*, a study of the leading experimental schools of the nation. He found the Fairhope school a "decided success," praising every aspect of Mrs. Johnson's work and placing a photograph of her with her students on the frontispiece. Students, he wrote, progressed "bodily, mentally, and morally . . . without factitious pressure, rewards, examinations, grades, or promotions, while they acquire sufficient control of the conventional tools of learning and study of books . . . to be able to use them independently." Natural, unselfconscious growth was the key, he believed, and he saw it happening in Fairhope.

The joy of learning that he observed and that so charmed his son was evident in the school activities he noted: "physical exercise, nature study, music, hand work, field geography, story telling, sense culture, fundamental conceptions of numbers, dramatizations and games." Comparing Organic

School students with pupils in conventional schools, he wrote that the Fairhope pupils were "apt to be stronger physically and are much more capable with their hands, while they have a real love of books and study that makes them equally strong on the purely cultural side of the work." The "freedom from self-consciousness" unleashed initiative and enthusiasm, and increased the pupil's "power to indulge his natural desire to learn, thus preserving joy in life and a confidence in himself which liberates all his energies for his work."

Dewey ended his study with the sweeping claim that to educate the "whole individual" was a revolutionary proposal with dramatic consequences for American society: "The democracy which proclaims equality of opportunity as its ideal requires an education in which learning and social application, ideas and practice, work and recognition of the meaning of what is done, are united from the beginning and for all." The Fairhope school was of critical importance for the way it facilitated the holistic growth of its students. But in addition, it showed "how the ideal of equal opportunity for all is to be transmuted into reality."

For Mrs. Johnson, and for the Fairhope community, these braided strands of organic education were critical. She was drawn to Fairhope in the first place because of the single-taxers' commitment to economic equality and the generally progressive spirit of the community. Shortly before she opened her school she wrote to my grandfather to say she looked on Fairhope as a community built on the idea that American society must be shaken up, wrested from its old fetters, and given new direction. Fairhope, she believed, could be the antidote to the ills of society. But changes in the economic structure of society, vital though they were, required for their success an educational system in which democracy was a daily reality, something children actually experienced, not a form of preachment within the context of rigid structures and results-oriented pedagogy.

From the beginning, the colony supported Mrs. Johnson with financial contributions and the free use of the spacious campus. Each institution—colony and school—came to see how the other advanced its mission. Throughout her Fairhope life Mrs. Johnson made a case for the link between the between the two, partners working in tandem to create a just society, a point she made often in public as well as in the unique course she taught on the single tax. Her speeches and letters frequently testified to her commitment. Typical was the letter she wrote to a friend and former student a short time before her death: "I do hope you . . .are studying Henry George. . . . Do . . . use your influence for fundamental justice in economics."

Even before Dewey's rave review in 1915, Mrs. Johnson had achieved a remarkable cachet in the expanding world of progressive education. Developing personal contacts through women's clubs, single-tax groups, civic organizations, and educational associations, she spent every summer from 1910 into the 1930s on the lecture circuit. In 1911 she conducted a demonstration school at the University of Pennsylvania before setting off for engagements in New Jersey, New York, and the Midwest. In 1913 she met a group of progressive women in Greenwich, Connecticut, who persuaded her to conduct a demonstration school there. A reporter for the *New York Times* came to observe. "A woman of quite remarkable personality," he wrote, "has been brought from a little Southern town and asked to try out her ideas in this community of rich New York suburbanites." The Greenwich women were impressed. It was they who persuaded Dewey to visit Fairhope. Women of means and action, they established what became an ongoing Greenwich summer school, to be directed by Mrs. Johnson. More important for her Fairhope school, they created in 1913 the Fairhope League, renamed the Fairhope Educational Foundation in 1920, which raised money for the mother school.

Emboldened by the flow of endorsements, she set out to convert the nation to what she now called "The Fairhope Idea in Education." By the end of the 1920s she had been midwife to at least nine organic schools, staffing most with teachers she had trained. Her scrapbook and the *Courier* files are rich with accounts of her "semi-annual flights to the north," one report noting twenty-three public addresses in twenty-six days. She was a charismatic personality and persuasive speaker. Full of confidence, she came to see progressive education as the wave of the future and to believe that her own vision could become the nation's vision. In 1918, she approached Stanwood Cobb, a zealous progressive educator and influential organizer, asking him to endorse the "Fairhope Idea" as the model for the American progressive education movement. That commitment was more than Cobb thought wise to make, but when she amended her proposal to suggest an association that would encompass several visions of progressive education he came on board. The result was the Progressive Education Association, founded in 1919 with Mrs. Johnson as one of the four speakers at the inaugural banquet in Washington.

Her fame led to requests by some of her Northern friends to give up the Fairhope school in favor of moving her permanent operations to Greenwich. She could easily see the material advantage but that was hardly enough. "I could never feel quite willing to do this," she wrote in her memoir, *Thirty Years with an Idea*. "The simple environment of Fairhope, the fact of charging no tuition from people of the vicinity, gave a freedom to work out an idea which could not be approached in the more sophisticated community." It was also true that what she and Dewey viewed as the social reconstruction aims of the school would better be demonstrated in a community founded with that aim as its *raison d'être*. Upscale, wealthy Greenwich was hardly that community. She was happy, however, to make Greenwich the northern base of her Fairhope movement, returning to it regularly in the summers. She trained and recruited teachers there; she demonstrated her teaching philosophy there with young children. And the Greenwich connection with its Fairhope Educational Foundation remained strong through the 1920s, keeping her school afloat.

Not merely afloat. It was during the 1920s that the school reached the peak of both its appeal to outsiders and its influence in Fairhope. At the beginning of the decade, enrollment rose to 220, with 72 (mostly Northerners) from out of town. Attendance numbers varied through the rest of the decade, from a low of about 100 to a high of about 200. Fairhope children were divided more or less evenly between Organic and the public school. A new dimension was added in 1921 when Mrs. Johnson introduced a six-week winter course to bring together parents, teachers, and social workers from around the nation to join Fairhopers in studying her school and its philosophy. *The New York Times*, still keeping Fairhope before a national audience, wrote approvingly of the winter course: "to be the fit environment of childhood, the Fairhope School . . . believes all adults should have special courses in school work." Seventy persons attended the first year. In 1930 the *Courier* reported that people from thirty-one states, Canada, and South Africa enrolled.

For the people of Fairhope the winter course seemed always to bring a buzz of excitement. One woman I interviewed, lamenting her presumed inability to get across to me "the interaction, the free-flowing feeling of the community and the school," explained that "all sorts of people came here: artists, Theosophists, philosophers, scientists, just marvelous people from north, south, east, and west." Clarence Darrow, who came more than once, spoke to a large assembly in 1927 explaining that crime would be reduced if the single tax and organic education were to spread. They were heady times.

VI

Mrs. Johnson died in 1938, two days before Christmas. It was a month before my eleventh birthday. My memories of her are both dim and few. Her school I remember in vivid detail. But of its founder and director I can conjure up only hazy images of an older woman in flowing skirts walking across the campus. On the other hand, I was devastated by the news of her death because I feared it would mean the end of the school. I did not know then about the fading Greenwich support or other reasons for the severely worsening financial condition but I did know, from often overheard conversations in my home, that money was scarce and survival uncertain. That was frightening. When I heard that Mrs. Johnson had died the fear mounted and I broke into a torrent of tears. One of my fellow students, a few years my senior, recalls that my father came to speak to a school assembly shortly after Mrs. Johnson's death. The school would survive, he assured them. It did. Teachers, parents, friends, and faculty rallied. My fears eased.

I am deeply indebted to Mrs. Johnson for creating the educational environment which I treasured and in which I thrived. The roots of my belief in what Dewey called "the school and society" were deeply planted in the school she created. But I owe her an additional debt of a different kind: without her forceful intervention, my mother and father would never have met. In 1919 my mother's father, Paul Nichols, came to Fairhope for a visit—a visit during which he met Mrs. Johnson. She was so impressed by him she insisted that he move immediately to Fairhope to become the principal of her school. Like many another person who fell under her sway, he found her irresistible. With his wife and five grown children, he moved to Fairhope as she had commanded. My father and mother met shortly after her arrival, fell in love, and were married on April 4, 1921. He was twenty-nine, she, twenty-one.

My father and his four siblings—two brothers, two sisters—came from a warmly supportive and caring family. My Aunt Leah (who had taught in both the Organic and Greenwich schools) spent part of her adult life in Fairhope but most of it in Spring Hill, a suburb of Mobile. The other four

My parents shortly before their marriage.

lived nearly all of their married lives in Fairhope, close by their parents' home. My grandfather used to make the rounds in the evening, to sing to his grandchildren. I recently read through hundreds of letters that deepened and validated my youthful impressions of the closely knit family.

In 1997, Mary and I sold our Fairhope home, the house my parents had built seventy-five years earlier. Great piles and boxes of letters, photographs, and dusty memorabilia lay in the attic. Among this historian's treasure were two boxes of letters that had once sat in the attic of my Gaston grandparents, later to be moved to my parents' attic and then to my study in Charlottesville. The boxes contained few letters from Aunt Frankie and Uncle Jim for they were seldom away. Aunt Leah wrote frequently from Greenwich and Uncle Spider from his Army encampments during the First World War and later from Nebraska during an extended visit there. Both wrote lovingly not only about their parents but about every one of their siblings.

Dad's letters, invariably beginning "Dear Folks at Home" and signing off "Lovingly, Cornie G," came first from Panama, then Peru, and then from the Pacific Northwest. Shortly after he graduated from high school (two graduations, actually: one from the public school, a second from Organic), not yet settled on a career and his family lacking funds to send him to college, he tried to enlist in the Navy to be part of the Great White Fleet, the fourteen-month voyage of sixteen white-hulled battleships Teddy Roosevelt sent around the world to show off American sea power. Recruitment ads promised educational courses onboard ship. Disappointed that he failed the physical examination, and still full of wanderlust, Dad took a job in 1912 as printer on a passenger ship of British registry out of New Orleans. Wearying soon of that life, he jumped ship in Panama, looked up a man he had known only through the *Courier,* and through him got a job as a drill hand on the Panama Canal construction crew that lasted for two years. "Then I got the gold bug," he recalled in a 1972 interview. "I went into the jungles of Central America to find gold—and went broke prospecting." After another stint working on the Canal he joined a friend to explore Peru. There he was hired by the Cerro de Pasco Mining Company, high up in the Andes.

At the end of 1917, convinced that Germany must be defeated and that he had a duty to help that happen, he sailed home to join the army, arriving just in time to be with his family for Christmas. Luckily for me, he left behind the Peruvian woman to whom, he once told me, he had formed a strong attachment. His brother Arthur (my Uncle Spider), had enlisted and was readying to ship overseas when the armistice was signed. Dad joined up early in 1918 and was sent to Washington state where he was assigned to a lumber company. Somehow this was meant to contribute to the war effort. Early in the new venture he was told he must pay—out of his own pocket—for certain needed equipment. He wrote home, objecting to the idea that a soldier must pay for equipment needed to be used to further the war effort. The problem appeared to be that the army had leased the men out to a private logging company. "We are working in the capacity of civilians employed by a private corporation," he explained. He found the corporation's demand unacceptable, but was also apparently troubled by what to do, or at least by how to do what he knew he must do. His sister Leah, writing home from Greenwich, said she was "distressed about Cornie." She found it "hard to understand his situation" which was so unfair to him, especially after "he went to so much trouble to enlist."

The combination of strong principles and stubborn character that would distinguish my father throughout his life set him up against the corporate power. He refused to obey the order. The logging company quickly dispensed with him, returning him to the army. The army, finding nothing heroic in his actions, put him on duty as a night watchman for the next six months. With no other assignment, he found free time to study French and to write more frequently to his parents and siblings, occasionally about political matters. Among other subjects, he was critical of the minimal self-sacrifice he believed most Americans made for the war effort and he wrote disapprovingly of his two Alabama senators "who voted against the woman's suffrage bill." Finally, in November (a few days before the armistice) he wrote to his sister Frances to tell her "I have ceased to be a watchman." He had begun "to work at the warehouse here in town but I guess I can stand it after loafing for six months." Before long he was discharged and back home in Fairhope. Not long after that he met and began courting Margaret Nichols. He once told me that, one afternoon while he was in the army, he and friends were drawing in the sand. Asked to write the initials of the woman he would marry, he wrote "MN." Always a man of logic and rationality, never superstitious, he nonetheless kept this story in currency throughout his life.

On his return, Dad found a job at the shipyard in Mobile, but soon went to work for his father, operating the *Courier's* brand-new linotype machine. That employment ended in 1924 when, influenced and guided by his father-in-law, he set off for Chicago and a new profession. My grandfather Paul Nichols—"Pop" to his many friends, Grandpa Nichols to me and my cousins—was a man of many parts. Widely read with a large storehouse of information on esoteric as well as conventional subjects, he charmed and instructed those who knew him. He took a law degree at Vanderbilt University but never practiced law, moving about, instead, as a schoolmaster through Arkansas (where he met his wife), Tennessee (where my mother was born), and Kentucky. Alternative approaches to good health ranked high among his many interests. Sensing that Dad wanted more out of life than a career setting type, he spoke to his son-in-law of the virtues of chiropractic and together they began a search for a way to follow up that interest. Selecting the National College of Chiropractic as the best place to train, Dad moved to Chicago in 1924 to begin his studies.

Among the hundreds of letters I retrieved from my parents' attic were 150 or so detailing the three years they spent in Chicago. They were happy ones, except perhaps for the months Mom remained in Fairhope, teaching at the Organic School. (As I was to discover, she kept the letters he wrote to her, scarcely a day passing without him writing to his "love girl.") For most of the time they were together in Chicago, up to their return in late 1927. Both held part-time jobs, Dad usually working in a print shop, Mom as a clerk at Marshall Field department store. In 1978, just starting out on my Fairhope research, I found their last Chicago home, on Bittersweet Place. They once told me they often walked from there to a nearby tennis court, carrying their own net with them, and, a little farther on, to the shores of Lake Michigan to swim. I was conceived in that home, my arithmetic telling me that event very likely took place on their sixth wedding anniversary.

Chapter Two

LIVING THE DREAM

I have read a fair number of Southern autobiographies. Several years ago I taught a seminar on coming of age in the South in which we read novels, short stories, and memoirs. It seemed to both my students and me that all of the best, the most famous and widely read, works portrayed childhoods full of dark struggle, misery, injustice, and a lot of just plain meanness. Coping, enduring, and triumphing were familiar themes. It almost seemed as though childhood misery was a prerequisite for creativity, wisdom, and a life interesting enough to write and read about.

My childhood fit none of these patterns: no misery, no dark struggles, no rebellion against family or community. The problems would come later. In my late fifties, seeking a better understanding of some concerns about both my personal and professional life, I met with a psychiatrist. I don't know whether this doctor was a Freudian but in all of our early sessions she kept digging into my early childhood to unearth my unresolved traumas. She never found any. Reluctantly—or so it seemed to me—she eventually agreed with my own feelings about my childhood. I grew up blissfully happy in a home, school, and community where I was nurtured, respected, admired, and loved. And I loved, respected, and admired my parents. My friendships were numerous and enriching and I thought of my school and my community as models of perfection.

But she wouldn't give up. Somewhere in my utopian childhood there was bound to be a fault line. Finally, taking a new tack, she found it. The discovery brought an unaccustomed smile to her lovely but generally too serious face. My school and community, but most of all my parents, were all the things I had told her they were, she now conceded, but they were something else as well. I was the town's fair-haired boy all right: affirmed, admired, and liked. The problem, one that could have been headed off by more astute parenting, was that my parents were insufficiently critical. They did not prepare me for life's inevitable hard knocks, reversals, disappointments. Most of all, they did not prepare me for disapproval or disdain, for the stress and strain I would encounter in the big world outside Fairhope where my values would be met with snickers rather than smiles, amusement rather than affirmation; where success would be measured by markers I had been reared to disdain. In fact, she seemed to be saying, they almost ensured that when these problems came my way I would have difficulty coping with them. There was truth in what she said, but not enough to make me wish that my childhood had been different.

I

My father helped with my delivery into the world on January 31, 1928, at ten minutes before noon. When he returned from Chicago with his chiropractic degree he learned that he would have to pass the state examination for medical doctors before he could practice in Alabama. There were no separate examinations for chiropractors. Dad read quickly to prepare and passed with good marks. His highest score was in obstetrics. I don't know whether he told this to Dr. Skinner but he was there with him to deliver me, his first and only demonstration of what he had learned from the books.

My mother, a few months past her twenty-eighth birthday, must have been in good health. According to the story I have heard many times she was a regular on the tennis courts, playing every winter day that weather permitted, right up to the day before I was born. On that day of my arrival, so the story goes, her friend Mildred cranked up her telephone to give the operator Marge's number. Instead of ringing through, the operator said, "Mildred, is that you? If you're calling Margaret to ask her to play tennis I think I just saw her going over to Dr. Skinner's to have her baby." It was a small town.

It was, indeed, a small town. In the 1920s the population had jumped by more than 80 percent, from 853 in 1920 to 1,547 in 1930. During the Depression years, the years of my childhood, the rate of growth dropped to 20 percent, the 1940 population reaching only 1,845. Everyone knew my family and so I suppose it didn't seem totally strange when, according to another often-told family story, I walked uptown at age three-and-a-half to ask someone, "Hey, where is that Organic School?" When I arrived on campus I am said to have asked, "Hey, where is that kindergarten?" Finding it, I enrolled myself, a year earlier than I was meant to begin. The school archives bear out at least part of that story, showing me in kindergarten for three years, not the usual two, which were to begin at age four. My cousin Eloise, who began at mid-year, was my only rival for early enrollment honors.

Once enrolled, it seems unlikely that I walked to kindergarten by myself, but perhaps I did. The distance from home to school was but a half mile. There were few automobiles cruising the unpaved streets and horse-drawn wagons would not have been a cause for my parents to worry. I might well have walked with my father to his office. I would have been more than halfway there then, with only two more dirt streets to cross before I reached the campus. The town that I remember from these early childhood days seemed so safe, open, and easy to navigate—with a cousin, aunt, uncle, or friend of the family in sight on nearly every route—that I would never have been lost or frightened.

While I do not remember precisely how I got from home to kindergarten, I do have many lasting memories of my three years there—long nature walks through the nearby woods; pressing leaves onto litmus paper to form their delicate images; building tepees with pine needles for their floors; listening with fascination to Miss Helen, my teacher, read to us or tell stories; singing; and sometimes acting out stories we had heard. We also played with large wooden blocks. I remember the pleasure I had in handling and building structures with them. Miss Helen (she would become Mrs. Sam Dyson) was a recent graduate of the school; Claire Totten (she would become Mrs. Judson Gray), her assistant at one point, had graduated the year I started. Many years later one of Claire's granddaughters would become my daughter-in-law. Both Claire, now 95, and Helen, 100, continue to live in Fairhope as

I write. In October 2007 Claire was out of town but "Miss Helen" attended the 100th anniversary celebration of the founding of the school, a three-day event that attracted about 150 former students and teachers.

The kindergarten building, at the bottom of our ten-acre campus, also housed our First Life classes, what elsewhere were called the first and second grades. My recollection of First Life is blurrily merged with kindergarten memories, but it was in First Life that I met Barbara, my first "girlfriend." When she and I were in our sixties, we reminisced about our romance, the chief feature of which we both remembered as the time I wrestled her to the ground for a kiss. Barbara's sly remark was, "My, my; it's a good thing I moved away: think of being pregnant at eight!" For Second Life I moved up the campus to the Bell Building, the school's first permanent structure. Third Life and Junior High were also housed in the Bell Building, each of the three groupings having a good-sized airy room. By this time I was riding my bicycle to school. By this time, too, I had a new girlfriend. Everyone called her Little Sister, I suppose because she was the second born in her family. I often rode her home after school on the cross bar of my bike, her mother meeting us with cookies and milk. Sometimes on the weekends I would take her to the movies.

I entered Third Life in 1938 at age ten. The "senior class history" that appears in our 1946 yearbook records that "Paul began his romance with Edna in Third Life, and kept the love light burning until high-school." I would later jokingly explain my transfer of affections from Little Sister to Edna by saying that while Little Sister would let me pay her way into the movies she would not let me put my arm around her. Edna, however, would not let me pay her way into the movies but she would let me put my arm around her. That lucky circumstance may have been a factor: I have never forgotten the thrill of feeling her hair brushing against my bare arm, the arm I cautiously slid across the back of her seat. When Edna moved with her family to a farm two-and-a-half miles out from town, I sometimes rode my bike out to visit her. On many a Sunday, with her on the cross bar, her hair blowing back on my cheeks, I would pedal to town and the picture show. I must have had very strong legs to support my ardor, traveling that distance with balloon tires over rutted sandy roads.

Whatever ignited my "romance" with Edna, it deepened into a rare friendship rooted in shared values, similar likes and dislikes, and an easy enjoyment of each other's company. Young though we were, we felt a special kinship because our two families were comrades in the Georgist and progressive education movements and their Fairhope demonstration. Edna's father, Reuben Rockwell, was a member of the colony council, a friend of my father, and a warm admirer of my grandfather. His wife, Helenbelle, was one of the pioneer settlers; she knew how to make young people feel welcome and good about themselves. With her infectious laugh and happy ways she always lifted my spirits. Edna and I were inheritors of the reformist zeal that gave Fairhope its reason for being, but we did not spend much time discussing the intricacies of rent calculation, the desirability of Georgism over both Marxism and unfettered capitalism, or the superiority of our ungraded, student-centered school over the regimentation of the public schools. It was more that we knew we were part of an important historic experiment, that our parents were living lives of high purpose, and that they had answers to the world's most difficult questions. Our conversations flowed easily, but on other subjects.

At Christmas 1940 my cousins Tommy, Eloise, and Carolyn gave me a diary in which I wrote faithfully every day from January 1 until June 5, when the entries unfortunately and without explanation cease. Edna figures prominently in my record of daily events, beginning with my January 1 entry: "Edna is still my girl. (I hope.)" I recorded her bouts of chicken pox and tonsillitis; her absences from school; when she returned; the dates we had to go to the picture show; my bicycle rides out to her home; our trips to Fly Creek, Fish River, and the Gulf; and her visit to my house after a scavenger hunt. In nearly every entry her name is underscored, as in my Baldwin County Day note where I listed the names of all the folk dances we performed for the public and ended with "I danced with *Edna* in everything but Newcastle and the girls' dances." Or, again, of a group outing to Burkel's roller-skating rink: "We really had a lot of fun. I skated with *Edna* a lot."

Edna and Little Sister both attended the 2007 weekend 100th anniversary celebration. Both confirmed the accuracy of what I had written about our "romances" some sixty-five and seventy years previous, Little

I'm facing the camera at the upper left, with Little Sister to my right, Edna to my left.

Sister adding details I had forgotten, Edna giving me permission to print what I have written here about her. At our Saturday night folk dance party I held the hand of each of them in our foursome, coming home the next week to look at a photograph of us in the same configuration during our high-school years.

The diary is filled with details I have long since forgotten, but the picture it gives of my activities in the month before and the four months after my thirteenth birthday is wholly familiar. My life in these pre-high-school years was crowded with activity. Scarcely a day passed that I was not playing one sport or another: basketball; touch football; softball; high jumping (record height 4'6"); pole vaulting (record height 7'6"); marbles; or tennis. My mother beat me 6–4 in the one tennis set I recorded. The next year, according to memory, we were tied at 6–6 when she quit and, with a chuckle, said she would retire before I defeated her. I was an obsessive record keeper, writing down the scores of games I both played in and watched as well as the baseball games I listened to on the radio. Our junior basketball team, a regular loser, never played a game without me recording the results along with the number of points scored by every player. I faithfully reported our team's loss to Loxley, 29–1, with me scoring our only point. And two weeks later I noted that my three points were team tops in our 61–6 loss to Robertsdale. We did win one game that season, beating Foley 19–16, "believe it or not," I wrote in my diary, also writing that my eight points were high for our team. Both the team and I would do much better in years to come.

Throughout our years of losing basketball seasons, which lasted through my sophomore year of high school, we made a point of emphasizing the school's credo that what mattered most was not who won but how the game was played. Were we good sports? Did we do our best? Those were the things that mattered. The Organic School's disapproval of excessively competitive activities and attitudes was surely something we carried with us. However, given the lopsided defeats we suffered, it must have been comforting to have standards other than winning by which to measure ourselves. Still, when we did win honors and a respectable portion of our games in my junior and senior years we, and those who wrote about us, emphasized sportsmanship and cooperation alongside our winning ways. However imperfectly I may have exhibited the non-competitive lifestyle, I know that I internalized it so that it existed right alongside my competitive urges and nature. In my mature years I regarded the Vince Lombardi mantra—"winning isn't everything; it's the only thing"—as a form of mental sickness.

My diary entries lack reflection and seldom show emotion; they are mostly a recording of the events of the day. Even so this terse March 26 entry startles me: "We gave Mappo away to a man named Chico who had lots of other pets." Mappo, a spider monkey, became part of our household in 1937. On a trip to Mobile with my mother and her sister, my Aunt Lorena, I spied Mappo in the pet-shop wing of Van Antwerp's drug store. My initial pleadings that we purchase her were rejected, but later in the afternoon, after the cocktail hour, Mom relented, forking over $35, a huge sum in those Depression years. For at least three years Mappo was my treasured companion. We built a house for her on the back of ours and fixed a wire from her house to the sycamore tree twenty-five feet away. A chain from her collar reached down to a pulley on the wire so that she had an abundance of climbing freedom, as well as freedom for visits to the ground. She often was allowed in the house, snuggling up against the fireplace in the winter time. Eventually, however, she started biting people, including me. My parents made the decision to get rid of her when the right chance came along. Chico, with his traveling menagerie, was that chance. I felt the loss and wonder that I did not say so in my diary.

Other diary entries report on the frequent meetings of the Dramatics Club, and the plays in which I took part. Dramatics was tightly woven into the Organic School curriculum from kindergarten through high school. Theatre was also a lively part of the Fairhope ambience, with Shakespeare plays performed in a natural amphitheater cut out of the bluff, facing the Bay. My parents were regulars in the summer performances. Singing, as important in the school as drama, was also a part of our school curriculum from kindergarten through high school. Despite my considerable difficulty with carrying a tune I was never one of the quiet ones. By the time I graduated, thanks to fifteen years of practice, I could sing so that others could recognize the tune. My musically talented cousins, after many years of indulgence, noted the achievement with some pleasure—and considerable relief.

I was more adept at piano, marveling at the sounds it could produce. I started taking lessons from my Grandmother Nichols when I was eight. Her home was a five-minute walk from mine, with a commanding view of the Bay. She was gentle, comforting, and encouraging. She died during the summer when I was eleven. I associated everything about the piano with her and shied away from continuing to play after she was gone.

On the summer day in 1939 that Grandmother died I was sitting in the stands at the local baseball field to watch the Fairhope Cardinals, our men's team, play a county opponent. At some point, perhaps before the game began, the manager called to me to tell me I would play right field. Apparently they were short one man. I was both thrilled and frightened. I have no idea how I fared at bat. I feel sure that if I had had a hit (or even hit the ball) I would have remembered. I remember only one play. A fly ball was hit to me. My hands shook as I positioned myself to catch it. I caught it, hands still shaking. Racing home after the game to tell everyone that I had played with the men's team, I arrived to learn that my grandmother had died. All the Nichols family gathered at her home. The thrill of my adventure would not subside. I was going through pantomime motions of throwing, catching, and hitting when one of my older cousins brought me up short: "Paul! Grandmother has just died. Stop that." I did. But Grandmother would have understood. I can still see her gentle smile, as she listened to me tell her how I had caught that ball.

II

Warm weather came early to Fairhope. By March, the grass began to grow. I spent several hours a week mowing lawns, again reporting the details in my diary, as in "this afternoon after school I mowed Esther Young's lawn; it took me an hour and a half so I got 30c"; or, "this afternoon after school I mowed Aunt Frankie's lawn. I got 50c for it." When scuppernongs were ripe I sought shade under her arbor and gorged on the grapes. I reckoned that I earned $6.40 in that month of May 1941, a handsome sum that gave a measure of the financial well-being I would have throughout my Fairhope years. In addition to mowing lawns I had a paper route, taught swimming, babysat for a neighbor's child, and occasionally served as an overnight sitter for Mrs. Swift, the night watchman's wife. Sometimes during these early years I was allowed to work, or pretend to work, at a filling station, pumping gas and visiting with customers; on other occasions I accompanied the ice man on his deliveries around town, sometimes carrying the lighter blocks into the homes on our route. The smell of the wet gunny sacks covering the ice has remained with me, one of the many remembered scents that take me back to my childhood.

Fairhope's springtime magic enveloped us all. I recall the adults reveling in the azaleas and I suppose I knew our town was remarkable for the profusion of its flowers and plants, its pine, oak, and magnolia trees. I took it all for granted, absorbing it but never consciously aware of it. I doubt that much had changed since the April a quarter-century earlier when Marie Howland had written of "how glorious is Fairhope now with its gardens of roses. . . .The amaryllis, the Chinese primrose, the exquisitely fragrant Chinaberry tree, and hundreds of others are nearly at perfection. The grancillium jasmines have been in bloom and other jasmines and clematis are just opening."

The gulleys were a special attraction. Several ravines snaked through the town, opening up at the Bay. There was Big Head Gulley, a mile or so to the south of our home. It was a popular site for family and school picnics. Its brownish sand base was wide, flat, and solid. The reddish clay walls were ideal for climbing, miniature caves providing perfect retreats for games of hide and seek. My favorite gulley, Sand Hill, was beside the park across from Grandmother Nichols's house. It had a narrow base with an intriguing passageway leading to the Bay. The sides of light-colored sand were wonderful for sliding down. Sand Hill, a frequent gathering place for us youngsters, found a special place in my subconscious. For years—at least until I graduated from high school—I had dreams of flying over it, from one side to the other, and then through it on to the Bay. They were always happy dreams, never the kind where you are seeking escape from a menacing pursuer.

Not all of nature's springtime gifts were to my liking. I especially disliked the sandspurs that sprouted everywhere. Their sharp, spiny points were a warning to us youngsters to keep our shoes on, something few of us did in warm weather. One spring, however, I was ready for them. The previous November, when the temperature dipped down into the fifties, I persuaded my parents and, with their agreement, the school principal, to let me go without shoes throughout the winter months. All went well until December when we had our first freeze. My feet opened up with large cracks. My amused but sympathetic mother had me put them in a pan of hot water while she gently rubbed camphor ice into them. The softening balm allowed me to persevere and before long my toughened feet seemed almost immune to the cold. I may have been inspired by the example of Henry James Stuart, the hermit of Montrose, whom we saw in town often, a dignified, bearded, shoeless man. Whether inspired by him or not I do not know, but I was joined with him in literature many years later, identified as the boy who went to school all year without shoes in Sonny Brewer's *The Poet of Tolstoy Park*, a novel inspired by Stuart's life. When the sandspurs popped up in the spring my schoolmates walked gingerly to avoid them. I smashed them flat with my bare feet. Mission accomplished. I hope that Sonny will insert the story of my triumph in the movie adaptation of his book.

Apart from the coming of the sandspurs, spring in Fairhope brought for me, my cousins, and my playmates a cornucopia of unending outdoor pleasures. My April 14 diary entry reports that after school, "I hitch hiked out to the creek and went swimming, the first time I have been swimming this year." Fly Creek was a little more than a mile from the school and we often walked there, through the woods along the bluff above the Bay, but, as this entry suggests, hitch-hiking was a common means of more rapid transport. Two days later, on the 16th, I reported that "our room went on a picnic to fly creek. . . . We walked out and back. We sure did have fun."

A winding stream flowing for more than a mile, Fly Creek opened up as it approached the Bay. On its way it meandered through banks of marsh, reeds, and a variety of water trees. Snakes, especially water moccasins, could sometimes be spied if you ventured upstream in a canoe. Where the creek widened to form our swimming hole there was solid land on either side. From a high bluff, the branches of a substantial oak tree hung out over the water. We would swing out to jump into the water from the rope we had tied to one of its limbs. Sometimes we would turn upside down during the swing out, knot our toes in the rope, and perform a graceful, or less than graceful, dive. The fresh water was cold in April and refreshingly cool even in August.

Pictures of my father in an old family photograph album show him as a young man paddling his canoe in the same creek. My own album has several pictures of my mother, father, and me as a toddler. In one I am standing confidently on the end of a diving board, my father smiling behind me. In those days there was a bridge across the creek as well as the diving board. I have no memory of either. Other photographs remind me of the close companionship I had with my cousins on my mother's side of the family. Six of us lived near each other and grew up together. Joy was the eldest, five years my senior; Tommy, the youngest, was eight months my junior. His sisters Carolyn and Eloise and Joy's sister Marian completed our group. A 1940 photograph of a barge moored in the creek brings back memories of the times all six of us practiced our diving off the high ladder rising up from its deck. Joy was the undisputed judge, awarding points after each cousin's dive.

Fish River, four or five miles east of town, flowed southward to empty into Weeks Bay. It was wide, deep, and cool; and, unless the rains had been heavy and frequent, it was clear beneath its dark surface. Occasionally we hiked there for picnics. An album photograph from the spring of 1941 shows my schoolmates Peggy and Aline drying their socks on the end of long sticks held over a fire. My diary tells me we had walked out and back to the river that day and that when we returned "I was really tired." I recall a few times when some of us rode our bikes to spend the night beside the huge kiln at Clay City Products, where the tile for many Fairhope homes was fashioned. It warmed us through the night. More often we went to Buell's Island, owned by a relative of Edna's. There we found a long cable to which was attached a pulley, chain, and bar that would take us from one riverbank to the other. Even more frequently we went for picnics and birthday parties to Harold Graham's camp, a rustic building surrounded on three sides by a bend in the river. Temple Graham, Harold's wife and my classmate Dorman Porter's mother, was an energetic entertainer for all of us.

The Gulf of Mexico, thirty miles distant, was too far to reach on foot or by bike, but trips to it became one of the great adventures of my youth. There were times when one of the grownups would say, "Let's go to the Gulf." And we would go, taking along a picnic supper. I'm sure I was grateful, although I probably took it for granted that Johnnie, my Aunt Lorena's husband, or one of the other adults, would have time to take us on a moment's notice. It was much later when I realized that, during the Depression, some of them had no jobs to keep them at home. They might as well take us to the Gulf. There were also school trips, family outings, and, most memorably, excursions in Mr. Stimpson's truck. Mr. Stimpson's son Owen, a few years my senior, would often drive. His brother George—we all called him Big Boy—was a year ahead of me in school and one of my favorite companions. Owen would load several of us on the truck bed. Once to the beach we would sometimes deflate the tires so the wheels would not sink into the soft sand, and drive for miles up the water's edge, stopping occasionally to swim.

My photographs recall a Gulf coast that has long since been desecrated by condo culture. In the years up to and including World War II—all of my growing up years—there were miles of unspoiled white sand beaches, sand dunes, the occasional frame cottage set well back from the water, and a pavilion in the state park where we danced. ("We must have put at least $3.00 in the nickelodeon," I wrote in my diary after a class picnic.) We swam in always clear, unpolluted green water. Sometimes, when the wind and surf were up, we dog-paddled out far enough to catch the crest of a large wave to ride it into shore. On the beach we collected shells; built sand castles; played follow the arrow; built fires for roasting marshmallows and wieners, sitting by them after dark for storytelling; and slept overnight in the lee of a sand dune. Moonlight walks, the water gently lapping on the beach, the wind helping to soothe and cool the day's sunburn, provided a magical setting for both budding and full-blown romances and the deepening of friendships.

Fly Creek, Fish River, and the Gulf of Mexico were deeply influential parts of my coming of age experience, permeating nearly every aspect of my sense of self and my unconscious sense of how the world ought to be. What was true of them was doubly or trebly true of Mobile Bay. Thirty miles long and ten miles wide, the Bay was fed by two freshwater rivers flowing into it from the north and, from the south, the salt water of the oceanic Gulf of Mexico. Well before I was born, the Bay had become the center of both Fairhope's commercial and social life. With no easy overland access to Mobile and the outside world, the Fairhopers quickly built a pier running eighteen hundred feet out to deep water where ferry boats might dock. The steamer *Fairhope*, built on the Fairhope beach, was unfortunately uninsured when it burned in 1905; it was succeeded by other ferries that made regular crossings to and from Mobile, carrying both freight and passengers. A causeway across the head of the Bay was built in 1927, making it possible to reach the city by a twenty-five mile automobile route. Ferry boats continued to ply the waters for several years, however. My memories of boats docking at the pier head are few and dim but I do remember the time when my father, fully clothed, dived into the water to retrieve a lady's

The 1800-foot pier, 1920s.

hat that had blown off her head as she stepped from the ferry.

From the very earliest years, Fairhopers gathered on the wharf to meet the boat, stroll, swim, fish, visit with their friends, and watch the legendary sunsets. In the early 1930s, when I first became a regular on the wharf, the "big chute" and the "little chute" were still standing, one on each side of the wharf. You climbed up a ladder to slide down a tin chute into the water. On the "big chute" side there were two swimming platforms with diving boards and, for a while, a giant wooden wheel. We held on to wooden crossbars as the wheel rotated, turning it by our own human power. Both the wheel and the chutes were removed before I was seven, but they gave me happy memories while they were there.

What my grandfather had called "the lower park" in his first description of the area below the bluffs was, like the pier, a center of Fairhope social life. The sand beach, light brown, not the pure white of the Gulf shores, stretched back from the water's edge for fairly short distances, from ten to thirty feet, the length varying both with location and the passage of time.

The tree-shaded land on the eastern edge of the beach measured from thirty to fifty feet or more before it ran up against the base of the bluffs. It was here that groups and families met for both formal and informal occasions. My family and their friends gathered there frequently, especially for Sunday morning breakfasts of pancakes, bacon, and eggs. Evening suppers, climaxed by the setting of the sun over the Bay, were also common. At both morning and evening gatherings we children swam, built sand castles and, where a small freshwater stream ran out into the Bay, constructed dams to make small ponds in which we launched tiny boats made of reeds. Meanwhile, back at the picnic tables, the grownups told jokes, swapped stories, no doubt talked about us, and always spent much of their time in serious conversation about the state of the world and what the Fairhope experiment might do to improve it. I remember more than one occasion when my father read passages from *Progress and Poverty*.

During the warm weather months the Bay was an almost daily presence for me. Our home was but three short blocks away, a five-minute walk if I didn't dawdle. At the beginning of the summer when I was eight years old I was allowed to go there by myself. I had learned to swim well by then and the Bay itself was not a cause for parents to be concerned. The tidal changes were slight and there were no strong currents or undertows. The firm sand bottom held no dangers and the water deepened very gradually. The mixture of gulf and river water gave the Bay both a clarity in the summer months and a low-enough saline content so that the eyes would never sting when you opened them under water. I learned to swim stylishly, with Johnny Weissmuller's Tarzan as my model, but my lasting memories are of swimming beneath the surface, examining the occasional shells, the variations in the patterns of the bottom, and the fish that sometimes swam near me. Even now, as through all of my adult life, I find a rare sense of peace and harmony when I bring to mind those underwater swims. I try to blot out the knowledge that man-made pollution has destroyed the possibility of that experience for my granddaughter, already a good swimmer by the age of nine.

Another pleasure my granddaughter will be denied is the search for soft-shell crabs. Many a weekend morning my father would take me to the

Bay to follow behind him with a bucket as we walked carefully through the grass beds where the soft-shells could usually be spied scurrying along the bottom. With his long pole, net on the end, he would scoop up the makings of dinner for that night's family gathering of aunts, uncles, and cousins. I enjoyed the cool and quiet of the early mornings, the dimpled surface of the water, the clear view of the sand bottom, and the excitement of watching Dad's expert use of the crab net. My only regret is that, at that time, I did not like to eat crabs, soft- or hard-shell. I have long since made up for that deficiency.

Still another Mobile Bay experience she shall certainly miss is swimming nude with her cousins in the early mornings, hanging on to her grandfather while he, floating on his back, instructs her in the healthful effects of nude swimming. My Nichols cousins and I have vivid memories of our grandpa orchestrating such outings. At a recent gathering we traded stories about how natural and unexceptional we found it that his genitals floated peacefully. Besides risking an infection from the pollution, grandfathers leading such an expedition today would be scolded by friends and families or arrested by the beach-cruising police for indecent exposure and for contributing to the delinquency of minors.

I DID NOT KNOW the meaning of the word hedonism when I was a boy but I was acutely aware of the sensual pleasures of the Fairhope environment. From the earliest days the colonists had celebrated the vital nexus between their egalitarian mission and natural beauty, writing about it in the *Courier,* holding their public discussions and social gatherings in places of beauty. Cooperative outings in the first couple of decades were devoted to the planting of magnolia and oak trees and the landscaping of Knoll Park. Almost from the beginning the streets, widening as they moved toward the Bay, were laid out so that as many residents as possible could have a bay view. All of this was based on the fundamental principle that scarce natural resources should never be privately owned or controlled and that the places of unique beauty, such as the bay front, should belong to all members of the community, always beyond the grasping reach of money, power, and privilege.

Only gradually did I become aware of the theoretical underpinnings and public policies that created my Shangri-la. Before I reached high school, when I would write papers about the Fairhope philosophy, I took my good fortune for granted, including especially the fact that we lived where there were no such things as "keep out" signs and felt safe and welcome wherever we went. We grew up—at least I grew up—with the sure sense of our right to be wherever we wished to be. The world around me seemed not only to belong to me but to everyone else as well. This may have been a version of what my grandfather called "cooperative individualism" or what Henry George envisioned as making the land common property.

To have experienced it virtually every day of my life was to implant in me both a visceral and an intellectual loyalty to the idea on which Fairhope was built and to the mission of my grandfather and my father. The form of the loyalty would shift, but its core remains to this day a constant guiding force.

III

High school years did see an end to my romance with Edna. We had been "going steady" for almost five years when we started dating other people. The deep friendship we had forged, however, endures to this day. For most of my last two or three school years Joyce attracted my romantic impulses. A perky blonde, she won my heart and came near to breaking it more than once. We were a star couple on the dance floor; went on hayrides (in Mr. Stimpson's ubiquitous truck) to the county fair in Mobile; spent many hours in the swing on her screened porch; and she held my bleeding head in her lap as we drove from Mobile to Fairhope to attend to the injury I had sustained in a district tournament basketball game.

During one of my uncertain periods, when it seemed Joyce would be promoting a reunion, my cousin Eloise handed me a stern note, one that somehow survived among my papers. "Paudie," she commanded, "don't let her talk you into coming back. She is fickle and you will only be hurt again." My mother would have sympathized with her niece's counsel, but for a different reason. Joyce, Mom thought, was not the right girl for me and I suspect she worried that my virginity would be a casualty of our relationship. She was right on the first count but not on the second. The relationship endured, with frequent breaks, until after I returned home in 1948 from my stint in the Army. Joyce married shortly after that and we did not meet again for nearly forty years, when I gave a speech in Atlanta, where she and her husband lived. Cousin Eloise and her husband Gale came to hear me. We all gathered at Joyce's in the evening. On her marbled foyer floor we danced just as we had in our salad days—or so I fantasized. This time, however, Eloise had no reason to send up warning flares.

All through high school our classes were small, rarely numbering more than ten. Mrs. Johnson died in 1938; the outside funding that had kept the school afloat, and sometime thriving, as in the 1920s, had dried up. The war, declared on December 8, 1941, sucked away some of the young men who might otherwise have been available to teach. There was much talk in my home about the school's mission and future. My parents' fierce determination not just to keep it alive but also to attract the faculty who would understand, approve, and be able to impart organic education was constantly on the fringes of my awareness. Gradually, I realized how much the "Fairhope Idea in Education," as it had come to be called, had permeated their sense of how the world ought to be. And it became my idea as well. With Dad as president of the school and Mom a teacher of short hand and typing, we were all involved. It was our school, a school with a mission—a democratic, egalitarian mission.

Somehow Dad and his colleagues managed to secure outstanding teachers. Grandpa Nichols, who served as principal and also taught sporadically in the 1920s and 1930s, had moved to Pascagoula for supervisory work in one of the Mississippi shipyards. S. W. Alexander, a former public school teacher who had taught Latin and mathematics at Organic since 1930, became principal in 1935. His firm convictions and gentle manner made him a sound leader and sympathetic teacher, though he lacked Mrs. Johnson's charisma. In the middle of my freshman year Dad and his board succeeded in persuading William E. Zeuch to take Mrs. Johnson's old position as director of the school.

Dr. Zeuch, as we all called him (pronouncing his name Zoyk), came out of a radical background that fit him well for becoming a Fairhoper of an earlier type. An Iowa native with a University of Wisconsin Ph.D. in economics, he gravitated early to involvement in labor and cooperative enterprises. He wrote a stinging defense of his friend Kate O'Hare, a 1919 victim of the Sedition Act; he had ties to the Ruskin socialist colony in Florida and the New Llano colony in Louisiana; and he was a co-founder, with Mrs. O'Hare and her husband, of Commonwealth College in Mena, Arkansas. Commonwealth, where Zeuch was director from 1923 to 1931, was designed as a worker's college. It was hounded by the usual right-wing forces, including the American Legion which charged it, according to William H. Cobb, the college's historian, with "Bolshevism, Sovietism, communism, and free love." Zeuch himself was a Debsian socialist keen on labor education and communal living, distinctions lost on the Legionnaires. Their slur stuck, however; and Commonwealth became known as the "Red" college. An internal squabble forced Zeuch out of the directorship in 1931 and he left for Europe to study on a Guggenheim fellowship. The college itself closed in 1940. Zeuch found employment in Washington with one of the New Deal agencies during at least part of the 1930s. He would be a great subject for an enterprising biographer.

Shortly after arriving in Fairhope in early 1943, Dr. Zeuch set out to create an endowment fund, to attract boarding students, and, in other ways, to save the school from sinking further toward financial collapse. I knew of his efforts, but like most of the students I sensed no immediate danger. We carried on happily, confident that our school was the best, and our teachers, for the most part, outstanding. One, Professor Goodhue, was Dr. Zeuch's fellow teacher in the 1920s at Commonwealth College. At the time, none of us had any idea of his radical antecedents. We knew him as the kindly, sometimes amusing, teacher who walked with a cane and whistled through his teeth as he spoke.

In contrast, Dr. Zeuch impressed me from the start. He was short and bald (dubbed "curly" by some of us) and authoritative. There was a kind of mystery about him, too. I had the sense that his life had been intriguing but he didn't talk about it and I never knew the particulars. He was also an excellent teacher, probably the most stimulating I had in high school and the one from whom I learned the most. I recall especially giving a report on some aspect of the virtues of the single tax. After I remarked about something being "a generally accepted fact" Dr. Zeuch fixed me with a half smile and asked, "By whom is that fact generally accepted?" It was the best lesson in the need for evidence I was ever taught.

He seemed to take a special interest in my education almost from the start. When I was a sophomore he asked me to read and then write a paper on Hemingway's *A Farewell to Arms*. That choice did not sit well with Mom. Dr. Zeuch called me in a few days later to tell me that I was to read another book, *Young Man of Caracas* by T. R. Ybarra. I asked why. "Your mother doesn't want you to read *A Farewell to Arms*," he replied. I did read the assigned book, and have absolutely no memory of it; but, as Dr. Zeuch may well have guessed I would, I spent several afternoons in the public library reading *A Farewell to Arms* and, after that, *For Whom the Bell Tolls*.

I liked school. I liked it from my first day in kindergarten. Nothing ever happened to make me change my mind. For one thing, I liked my fellow students, or at least most of them. Some of us had been together for many years, giving us a strong sense of community. New students coming in our high school years were quickly and easily welcomed. Shaw Smith came for our junior and senior years. Her parents had sent her to Ashley Hall, a private girls' school in Charleston. It wasn't for her. She was wishing, according to our senior class history, "to be rid of gloves, stockings, no lipstick, and chaperones." Shaw's parents ran a bookstore in Provincetown in the summer and another in Key West in the winter. John Dewey was one of their Key West customers. When it became clear that Shaw was not a good fit at Ashley Hall, her parents asked Dewey where he thought they should send her. The eminent educator recommended the Fairhope Organic School. And so she came. A year later, for our senior year, Shaw's Key West friend Sesyle Joslin joined us.

Ses and Shaw were great additions to our school and to my life. Both had literary ambitions, coupled, I thought, with talents to justify them. Both had written articles for *Seventeen*, becoming the only published authors in our student body. They seemed to thrive in the relaxed and stimulating atmosphere of our school and in the variety of our classes, from folk dancing to English literature, from silver smithing to American history. Both have been special friends ever since our school days, Ses in Rome and now

London, Shaw in Minnesota, California, and now Florida. Shaw and I were partners during our junior year in a class project typical of our school. We had asked our American history teacher, Dell Gregg, why we in Alabama required payment of a poll tax as a prerequisite of voting. How could that be justified? Dell responded by sending us out to interview townspeople about their views. Shaw and I teamed up for the assignment. Dell was one of our favorites: eccentric, impulsive, sympathetic, smart. She and I kept in close touch until her death, more than fifty years after my graduation.

When Charles Rabold came to Organic from Yale in the 1920s, he introduced English country, sword, and morris dances to the curriculum. He had previously studied with Cecil Sharp, father of the folklore revival in England and founder of the English Folk Dance Society. When Sarah Gertrude Knott started the National Folk Festival, an event that attracted dancers and singers of many ethnic backgrounds from most parts of the United States, our school sent a team to the spring event to perform English folkdances. I danced with our team in 1943 in Washington and 1946 in Cleveland. Because of the war there was no festival in 1944 or 1945. A news clip in my scrapbook tells me that over a thousand performers, from twenty-five states, were present in Cleveland. It was at the Cleveland festival that I gathered one of my early insights into how racial discrimination might be undermined. In the evenings after the performances many of the dancers gathered in one of the halls for social dancing. On one of those occasions my cousin Tommy, a star jitterbug, walked in the hall, surveyed the dancers, and cut in on a black couple. The girl, he judged, was the best jitterbug on the floor. Tommy was no crusader for racial justice. His only interest was in dancing. Racial prejudice could have no place when the issue was talent.

I liked nearly all of my school courses but Spanish was my favorite. For one thing, even though it had been many years since Dad had lived in Panama and Peru, he could still speak and understand the language. As I started to learn it in junior high school, we made it our secret language. By the time I was a sophomore in high school my teacher was Rafael Davila, the Venezuelan consul at the port in Mobile. I visited his family's home for dinner in nearby Montrose and had a strenuous language workout. Early

Our cheerleaders, from left: Little Sister, Eloise, Joyce, Edna, Phyllis.

in the second semester Mr. Davila, with the approval of my parents and Dr. Zeuch, arranged for me to visit some of his relatives in Caracas. I was to take a steamer out of Mobile and be away for a month. I was excited by the prospect and eager to improve my language skills. Then a problem arose. On February 11 our basketball team defeated the Fairhope public high school team 18–15. On the 25th we lost 16–22, with me scoring ten of our sixteen points. The playoff game for the city championship was set for March 10. I was booked to leave for Venezuela a week before then. What was I to do? I stayed and played. I led our team in scoring, with eight points, but to no avail. We lost, 19–21. I have yet to live in a Spanish-speaking country. Alas.

My passion for sports remained throughout my high school years. In addition to playing one game or another year-round, I followed major league baseball closely. One summer Big Boy Stimpson and I hitchhiked to Washington and then took a bus to New York to watch the Yankees play. In the fall of 1944, Mr. Alexander gave us permission to hitchhike to St. Louis (and arranged for us to stay with his sister) to watch the first three games of the World Series between the two St. Louis teams, the Cardinals and the Browns. We arrived at the stadium early in the morning to get bleacher seats. I knew the records of almost every player, had my favorites (Marty Marion, the Cards' shortstop, high among them), enjoyed watching batting practice, and was thrilled by the three games we watched.

In my junior year our basketball team finally overcame its losing ways. We won ten of our twenty games, captured the city championship, and went to the semifinals of the district tournament where we lost to Murphy, the large public school in Mobile. Murphy defeated McGill, a Mobile Catholic school, to win the championship. We had a smashing victory over our town rival in the consolation game. The Mobile paper reported that we "overpowered Fairhope High, 41–21, making the third victory in four games for the little Organic squad with Fairhope this year." Ending the season on such a high was a refreshing novelty. I was thrilled to be named to the all-tournament team along with four of the Mobile players, two each from Murphy and McGill.

During the following summer, when I was seventeen, I was a regular on the men's baseball team. Military service must have captured many of the town men because three high schoolers were in the lineup. We were seventh, eighth, and ninth in the batting order and ended the season with very low averages. We didn't do much damage, however, since we won eight of our eleven games. My most thrilling experience came when we played the Brookley Field air force team in Mobile. Their pitcher, whose name I have forgotten, had pitched in the major leagues. We scored no runs against him and lost by a lopsided score. After striking out twice I came up in the top of the ninth inning. My cousin Henry, twelve years my senior, a regular on our team, and always good for a laugh, handed me a beer from the tub. "Try this," I remember him saying; "maybe it'll make you hit a home run." I took a big swallow, my first taste of beer, and luckily felt more relaxed than woozy as I walked to the plate. I hit the first pitch deep into center field. I was halfway to first base when the back-peddling fielder caught it. I may have been out but I returned to the dugout with a wide grin and to thunderous applause.

IV

High school years were also marked by continued remunerative work so that I never came to feel like a poor boy despite the very modest salaries of my father and mother. When I was fourteen and about to enter high school, Kirby Wharton, the president of the bank, happened into my father's office while I was typing, a skill I had acquired in school with my mother as the teacher. Kirby needed someone to type transit letters that accompanied checks drawn on out-of-town banks being sent back to their locales. He cleared it with my father and then asked if I would like to work at the bank. I said yes immediately. In my first month or so of employment I served as a janitor as well as a typist. Soon, however, I was devoting all of my time to white-collar tasks. The promotion was apparently occasioned by my inability to recognize and remove dirt when I saw it.

For the next four years, I was a bank employee after school during the school year and full-time in the summer. On the Monday afternoon that I began work my task was to sort the currency taken in that day—deposits from merchants' weekend's business—and then smooth and wrap it in bundles of fifty bills each. I had never seen such huge piles of money. It must have taken me two hours or more to complete my assignment. My hands were filthy, giving new meaning to the term "filthy lucre."

Before long I was promoted to teller, receiving deposits and cashing checks. On Friday afternoons we stayed open late to cash the checks of the shipyard workers returning from their jobs in Mobile. In a back room of the bank I kept a white shirt and a tie that I put on when I came in from school. Since the counter hit me just above the waist, I reckoned that what I wore below would never be revealed. One memorable afternoon a woman I knew presented her husband's check for cashing but asked for something—I have forgotten what—that caused me to move away from the counter. "Paul," she shouted for all in the lobby to hear, "you have no shoes on." It was true. My secret was out. Thereafter, I was known as Alabama's barefoot teller.

Our banking was sociable and easy going. We took breaks on summer afternoons to eat watermelon brought in by one of the local farmers; we journeyed together to the Gulf once a year for a day of swimming, sunning, and feasting; and we kept up with, and made many comments on, the personal and business lives of our customers, all revealed through the checks they wrote or the loans we made to them. One of my most vivid memories is of a Catholic priest's Saturday night drinking binges. Every Monday morning the Riverside Night Club would bring in its Saturday-night checks. Among them was nearly always a series of five, six, or seven written by the priest, with his handwriting getting shakier and shakier as the evening wore on.

In my work at the bank, as in every other aspect of my childhood and youth, I experienced the admiration and, especially, the trust of those with whom I worked or was associated. One afternoon, for example, we were staying late to balance the books. We were $25 short and we couldn't go home until we found out why. As the afternoon wore on, Henry Bishop, the cashier, told me to go to the drug store next door for sandwiches. Apparently we were to stay on into the night trying to solve the problem. "Do you have money with you for the purchase, Paul," Mr. Bishop asked. I would, of course, be reimbursed when I returned. I reached into my pocket and our problem was solved. I had taken $25 out of the till but the check I had written to cover it had remained in my pocket. "Well, Paul," Mr. Bishop said, with a warm smile following, "let's go eat at home; you'll remember not to let it happen again, right?" There was feeling of regret on my part, but not guilt. No recrimination came from Mr. Bishop.

During my four years at the bank I drew a salary that gave me not only a sense of financial well-being but also the ability to buy my first car—a used 1932 Ford V-8 coupe with a rumble seat—for $225 from my older cousin Jimmy Gaston. It was shiny green with elegant brown leather seats. I drove it to school and back regularly and occasionally to nearby towns for our basketball games. The rumble seat was especially prized by my male friends, eager to double-date with me. Maintaining the Ford, however, was not easy. I could manage to get where I wanted on the four gallons of gasoline a week allowed by war-time rationing, but flat tires and rubber rationing were a real problem. I quickly learned how to patch flats and keep going.

My first major purchase, two years before I bought the car, was a sailboat—a 16-foot Marconi-rig sloop that my cousin Tommy and I bought for $90. We usually moored it in the Bay by my Uncle Spider's bathhouse. Often, though, we docked it at the municipal pier, ready for nighttime sailing when the wind and moon were right, as they often were. One such evening, when I was sixteen, we met Joanne Kelly and Bebe Betbeze, a blonde and a brunette, over the bay from Mobile. We were all at the Casino, the grand dance hall, snack bar, and bowling alley at the foot of the pier. The four of us danced and sailed and met occasionally afterwards before the summer season broke up and we all returned to school. Several years later, when we were in college, Bebe was crowned Miss America, the first and last of my acquaintances to capture that distinction. A half-century passed after her coronation before we met at her Georgetown home to reminisce about those magical nights of dancing and moonlight sailing.

I sailed often through my high school years, sometimes alone, sometimes with friends and family. The varying rhythms of the boat, the feel of the breeze on bare skin, the sense of oneness with the elements—wind, water, sun, moon—these gave me a sense of peace and harmony. Sometimes I came to the boat not to sail, but to sit quietly in it, especially in the very early morning, the smooth surface of the Bay sparkling in the new sunlight. Other times, during intense summer heat, I would wake up at night on sweat-soaked sheets and ride my bicycle down to Uncle Spider's bath house to sleep on a mattress and be cooled by the breeze coming across the Bay. At sunrise I would swim out to the boat, climb in, and let my imagination, my daydreams, run free.

Not all of my sailing adventures, however, gave such pleasure and reassurance. Three stand out in my memory.

The first misadventure came about on a still and cloudy summer evening when I was fifteen. I had planned a moonlight sail with my new girlfriend, Kitty, accompanied by my friend Marney and his date, Betty (the same Little Sister of my Second Life years). I was dressed in a white silk shirt, white duck pants, topped off with a white naval aviator's smart dress hat, a gift from a friend at the nearby naval air station. Tommy had left the boat tied to a platform jutting out from the pier. The mainsail was up. So was the center board, a fact I did not know, but should have. I held Kitty's hand as she boarded, then Betty's. They moved aft, out of my sight behind the sail. I stepped on board. With all three of us on the same side, and the center board up, we turned over at the dock. That was my last date with Kitty. For years to come, a veteran sailor who had watched us from the pier took pleasure in reminding me of my courting prowess and nautical expertise.

The second adventure was of a very different order. It was September. The prevailing south wind had shifted to the north. The bay was turning from blue-green to brown, an unmistakable sign of the end of the summer season. We had a new student at the school, Michael, and our Lithuanian folk dance teacher, Vyts Beliajus, had recently arrived. I wanted them to see what it was like to sail. Jimmy Rockwell, who knew how to swim, but not to sail, went along with us. The Bay was choppy, the breeze capriciously brisk and shifting. Out a good distance from the shore, I cautioned my passengers to be careful to stay on the high side. Jimmy misunderstood me and moved to the low side just as the wind speed picked up. We turned over.

My father had long before instructed me never to leave a capsized boat. Someone would surely come to my rescue. This day, however, there was not another boat on the Bay. Vyts, I discovered to my horror, could not swim. Michael and Jimmy, however, seemed competent. I was a strong swimmer and reckoned I could get to Uncle Spider's bath house and his motor boat in less than half an hour. So, I told my friends to look after Vyts, making it clear that, under no circumstances, should they sit in the sail or hold on to the mast, risking the likelihood of turning the boat upside down. Hold on to the side, I told them, look after Vyts, be calm; I would be back soon. I swam hard but before I reached the bath house I saw my cousin Tommy coming my way in the motor boat. Passing by my uncle's home on his paper route he had noticed that our sailboat was missing. He ran to the motor boat and started out to rescue us. My father was right. I should never have left the boat.

I had made a near-fatal decision. My passengers had done precisely what I told them not to do. The boat had turtled. The twenty-five foot mast hit the bottom with such force that it snapped and became stuck in the soft sand ten feet below the surface. When Tommy and I reached our boat I gasped. Its bottom was thick with barnacles. Vyts's arms were scraped and torn by them. The waves kept pushing him away from the boat, making him hold tighter to the barnacled bottom. A Roman Catholic, he was deep in prayer, not asking to be saved but for acceptance into the next world. He told me later he was sure he would die.

He didn't, but if Tommy had not come to our rescue, if I had had to swim the entire distance and start up the motor boat, he probably would have. Back at the bath house, one of the adults covered Vyts in blankets and did what she could to comfort him. It was a sign of the times that we not only carried no life jackets on board but that I never felt guilty for having none. I felt guilty enough for having left the boat. My father, as was his way with me, never spoke to me sharply or with anger. He gently reminded me of what I already knew. Vyts recovered from his near-death experience and, remarkably, considered me one of his special friends, right to the end of his life a half-century later. He wrote affectionately of me in his autobiography and recalled me as his savior in the boat incident.

My third and final lesson on how (or when) not to sail came at the beginning of my senior year. The hurricane season was upon us; a major storm was brewing. Tommy and I felt it unsafe to leave our boat tied to a piling near Uncle Spider's bath house. So we set sail for the Yacht Club and its protected harbor in Fly Creek, a mile to the north. With a fierce wind coming out of the south, we planed the entire distance. I recall the excitement of it, even as the bow sometimes dipped under the water. Disaster came when we turned to sail into the harbor. We had to sail on a close reach, more or less perpendicular to the wind. Both of us feared we would turn over. Then we noticed that the current rushing out of the creek was so strong that it pretty much halted our progress. Soon we were blown into nearby pilings and there we did turn over. As we were struggling to clear the boat of the pilings, foolishly hoping to save it from damage, my Uncle Jim arrived in a motor boat and commanded us to get in it, leave our boat, and come to safety with him. I have a picture in my mind of him raising an oar to whack us when we protested that we must stay. He was serious. We abandoned ship.

That was my last sail in the boat I had loved and enjoyed on so many wondrous days and nights. Once the weather eased we somehow managed to get it out of the water, onto a truck bed, and into the school shop. It remained there until the following spring. By then we had made enough repairs to be able to sell it to a friend. I never saw it on the Bay again. Vivid memories of it, however, have been a treasured lifetime companion.

V

Fairhope was my Shangri-la, my place of peace and pleasure. Unlike James Hilton's fictional land of peace and harmony, the Shangri-la of his novel *Lost Horizons*, it was not isolated from the corruption of the larger world. Nor was it intended to be. My grandfather did not lead his followers there so that they could isolate themselves from the injustice and exploitation of the world they knew. They came, instead, to show how that world might be changed for the better. They regularly referred to Fairhope as a demonstration or experiment, not an escape route. People were drawn there to solve social problems, not to escape them.

I have strong memories of learning from my father, mostly during my high school years, what Fairhope was meant to stand for. Its constitution, which I recall him reading to me more than once, said it was to be "a model community . . . free from all forms of private monopoly" where its citizens would have "equality of opportunity, the full reward of individual effort and the benefits of co-operation in matters of general concern." On other occasions Dad read to me his father's declaration that Fairhope was designed "to establish justice, to remove the opportunities for the preying of one upon another." In another document Grandfather wrote, "We close the gates against injustice; we open them to unselfishness. Society can do no more." These and other colony aphorisms became part of my early learning and consciousness so that I came to feel that we not only had an obligation to struggle for justice but that we were armed with special insights into how it could be achieved.

There was a kind of egalitarian spirit in Fairhope that seemed to be borne out in the places we lived and the way we related to each other. The architecture of the community was unpretentious, marked often by tasteful cottages, of which our small home was one. There was only one large, imposing house in the whole of town while I was growing up. During the Depression years the home next door to us, a two-story frame house built by my great aunt Clara Atkinson, Grandfather Gaston's half sister, was lived in by the Prince family. They were poor but not impoverished. Their children (I remember Howard, Annie Ruth, and Myrtle Lee) did not go to the Organic School and their use of the language was not influenced by Strunk and White. None of that, however, mattered. We were neighbors and friends. We played games together in our front yard, shared jokes and tales, and respected each other.

There was a time in my early adult life when my Fairhope stories would stress what I thought of as the town's near classless society. There were no very rich people and no very poor people and money did not seem to be a marker by which people measured themselves or were judged. After about 1932 my parents owned no automobile and my father's income from his chiropractic service and, after 1936, his job as secretary of the colony, was very modest. The Organic School was technically a private school but, like a public school, it was open without charge to all town residents, albeit whites only. Nor was there a conventional private school that might siphon off the children of those who thought of themselves as belonging to the upper classes. We all went to a public school. Even so, as one critic has pointed out to me, there was an aristocracy in Fairhope and I belonged to it—the Gaston family aristocracy. My grandfather was the revered founder and most influential person in the colony; my father, his successor, was likewise trusted and admired; my Uncle Jim, the Ford dealer, was on the county Board of Supervisors; my Aunt Frankie and Uncle Spider edited and managed *The Fairhope Courier,* the paper everyone read.

Still, as a child, I was never aware of my special Fairhoper status. With no class consciousness, I also grew up without any real sense of ethnic differences. The southern portion of Baldwin County was settled by various ethnic groups, lured there in part in the early twentieth century by newspaper advertising and enterprising recruiters of the Southern Development Company and the L&N railroad. Good Georgists can identify the land speculation that facilitated the settlements, but some of their leaders rightly regarded themselves as providing places of refuge for their countrymen. The Greek colony at Malbis, for example, was founded by a man of that name who hoped to provide a safe haven for his fellow Greeks, away from exploitation, while they learned English. The Italian colony in Daphne,

founded by Alesandro Mastro-Valerio, aimed to attract Italians from the
large cities to find a better life as farmers. There were Czechs and Swedes in
Silver Hill; Germans in Foley and Elberta; a small contingent of Poles that
spread out from Summerdale; and a scattering of French and Croatians near
Robertsdale and other hamlets.

Growing up among them seemed normal to me. I had no idea of any
of them being "foreign"—they were just the folks I knew or knew about.
Bohemian Creek, east of town, was a favorite swimming hole. I'm sure I
had no idea where Bohemia was and probably thought little about why
the creek carried that name. Mr. Novak, from Silver Hill, was a music
teacher everyone admired. His daughter Marie played the trumpet in
his small band. I had a crush on her and sometimes, when the band was
playing at the Casino, I would sit nearby until they took a break, leaving
the music up to the Nickelodeon. On a few of those occasions I worked
up my courage to ask her to dance. To this day I think of her when I hear
the trumpet solo in Tommy Dorsey's rendition of "Marie." Lou Svoboda
came from another large Silver Hill family; he was one of the stars on the
men's baseball team; Al Benik, from a Czech family, not only was the star
catcher on the men's team but also the most graceful swimmer and diver I
ever saw; Daphne Allegri was from a large Italian-American family. I never
asked her how she liked having the same name as her town. Frank Manci,
also from Daphne, was one of my early heroes when he starred on the Auburn basketball team. Alice Littletaylor, a fellow bank employee, anglicized
her name but her husband, Joe Kriekerjick, did not. The Casino, where I
spent so many of my free summertime hours, was owned and run by the
Howie family. They were all swarthy but I attached no ethnic significance
to their appearance. Many years later my father told me they were from
Syria. Several Jews were friends of the family but in my youth that aspect
of their identity was lost on me.

Race, of course was a different matter. In my adult life, as a teacher
of Southern history and a participant in the civil rights movement, I was
frequently asked how a fellow like me, born and reared in the Deep South,
could turn out to be a liberal, especially a liberal integrationist. Apart from
the naiveté of the questioners—there have always been liberals, including

racial liberals, in the South—the question was valid. The South that most people know of is the place where bias and bigotry have had a long and vibrant life. More to the point for Fairhope, the culture of white supremacy seeped into our lives, often in ways of which we were unaware. It was, I believe, in constant war with the Fairhope culture.

I was well aware that Fairhope was a segregated community, its blacks living in an area adjacent to town that some of our cruder citizens called "niggertown." I knew that both my Uncle Marvin and my Grandfather Nichols had on rare occasions entertained black guests, but Dad and Mom had no black friends. And, unlike many Southern boys one reads about in memoirs, I never played sports with anyone who lived in the segregated black community. No one that I knew belonged to an anti-segregation group. On the occasions that family discussions turned to racial matters, Dad rarely if ever spoke critically of the colony's whites-only membership or the segregation policies of the City Council, of which he had been a member since 1932. He did often tell me that he believed economic inequality was at the root of racial discrimination—and that the Georgist cause to which he was committed was the surest path to racial justice. I grew up, then, in a family atmosphere in which racial segregation was faulted in theory, understood to be inconsistent with Fairhope philosophy, but not opposed in practice.

My father, like his father before him, accepted segregation as the inevitable if lamentable price the colonists had to pay for survival. Also like his father, Dad spoke out against the racist actions of his fellow Alabamians. In June 1943, for example, he wrote a stinging *Courier* editorial which he called "Home Front Crumbles." Mobile shipyard workers, after a riotous day and more of attacking blacks, had been excused by much of white opinion that was influenced by "wild rumors of exaggeration." He condemned both the attackers and their apologists. They were in striking contrast to "those who bore the brunt of the attack and showed greater nobility and greater worthiness of our democratic endowment."

I did have one black friend in our school. His name was Chester Hilson; he was the school janitor. As a small boy I thought of Chester as a tall man. He was trim, had a kindly smile, gentle ways, and as far back as I can remember seemed to enjoy talking to me as much as I liked talking to him.

Our favorite topic of conversation was baseball. We both made frequent trips across the Bay to watch the class B minor league Mobile Shippers. He sat in the "colored bleachers," I, in the whites-only grandstand. On Monday mornings we discussed the games we had seen over the weekend. I have no memories of feeling angry that the laws kept us from sitting next to each other at the pastime we loved. The memory that survives is of our ease with each other, my eagerness to get to school early enough on Mondays for our conversations.

One other memory survives. I don't know how old I was, probably younger than twelve. I was hitchhiking home from Fly Creek. A car approaching from the north began to slow down as if to pick me up. As it came closer I could make out that its driver and passengers were black. I had never before ridden in a car with black people. I dropped my hailing arm, turned my back on the road, and walked a few steps away from it. I heard the car stop, its motor running quietly in neutral. The driver, Chester Hilson, asked, "What's the matter, Paul; don't you want to ride with colored folks?" I wished for the earth to open up and swallow me. Although I have no memory of what followed I am sure that I accepted the offered ride. Our friendship endured. Chester let me learn from the experience and from him.

VI

Sometime during the fall of my senior year I began to gather catalogues from universities and colleges around the country. I was puzzled when I read that a certain grade average was required for admission. Grade average? What could that be for someone who in fifteen years had never had a grade? Taking my worries to Mr. Alexander, I was greeted by that smile of his that always put us at ease. "Don't concern yourself with that problem, Paul," he told me; "we'll take care of it."

And I didn't concern myself with it. Memories are tricky, of course, but I cannot recall ever worrying again about a grade average. I simply trusted that Mr. Alexander would explain that at our school we did not believe in grades and that he would then write up something favorable about me. Others may not have been so innocent but I can't recall any of my classmates discussing the problems of college entrance. And we did go to college. Shaw went to Bennington, Ses to Goddard; and two or three of the other girls in the class went to colleges whose names I have forgotten. Of the four boys, all went to college; two of us went on to earn Ph.Ds. I shouldn't think that there were many schools in the country where all of the boys went to college and half earned doctorates. Nor, truth be told, was that anywhere near typical of the Organic School.

But we did have grades. It was thirty-three years later when my innocence was undone. In 1978–79, when I began serious research on Fairhope's history, I found in the school's archives the detailed comments on the pupils I had assumed would be there; to my surprise, there were letter grades as well. I was jolted when I read that Mr. Allinson had given me a C+ in Ancient History in my freshman year. Most of my other grades were A's, with a scattering of B's. Shaw and Ses, as I suspected, had an unbroken string of A's. My cousin Eloise, the most vibrant and cheerful member of our class, had received lower grades. We and she knew that her academic skills were modest. But one of her teachers wrote of her: "Slow in getting a point, but once located it's hers!" Part of the genius of the school was that it never broke her spirit. On the contrary. She thrived in the folk dance classes, was outstanding in arts and crafts, drama, and music; and in her mature years she became one of Fairhope's admired painters. Her zest for life endured, inspiring all those who knew her. She was, and remains, a living example of Mrs. Johnson's dictum that "no child may fail."

Chapter Three

SOLDIER AND STUDENT

The combination of a shortage of money and a hankering for adventure led me to postpone college in favor of a year and a half in the Army. In 1946, just a year after the victories over Germany and Japan, one could enlist in the armed services for eighteen months and receive thirty months of college funding through the GI Bill. It was an irresistible offer. I had hopes of joining the occupation forces in Germany, learning to speak the language, studying the history and culture of the country, and watching the reconstruction of that defeated, dispirited nation, now liberated from its Hitlerian scourge. And on the completion of my tour of duty I would have the funding I needed to attend the college of my choice.

Sometime in the spring of 1946, before our graduation, Abe Waldauer persuaded me that I should aim for Swarthmore College. Abe was a Memphis lawyer, an avid Georgist, and a great champion and nonresident member of the Fairhope experiment. He had corresponded frequently with my grandfather and now was a close friend of my parents. He and his wife, Dot, were frequent Fairhope visitors. His son Joe was a Swarthmore student, and that was the place for me, Abe told me. I had already decided that I wanted to go to a relatively small college, one that was both coeducational and outside the South. If it had something of the Fairhope progressive spirit so much the better.

In the summer after graduation I hitchhiked up to Provincetown where Shaw was spending the summer with her parents before heading to Bennington in the fall. I enjoyed her company and that of her parents, and found Provincetown fascinating but the sea unbearably cold. No one reared on the waters of Mobile Bay could endure swimming off the shores of Cape Cod. From Provincetown I hitchhiked home, stopping in New York to visit the Henry George School of Social Science and in Swarthmore to look over the College. I fell in love with it immediately. My conversation with one of the deans encouraged me to think I would be admitted. He told me to keep in touch and to let him know when I was ready to apply.

I

With my college choice thus pretty well decided I entered the army in October, eager for new adventures. Basic training at Fort Eustis, in the Virginia Tidewater region, introduced me to a wide variety of men, including an obnoxious bully and the vulnerable nerd he taunted. One night I foiled the bully's intended prank on the nerd with a gentle push that sent him tumbling over a foot locker. Luckily for me the first sergeant walked in on us before the bully could retaliate. I don't think I would have been a match for him and I had no desire to prove, or attempt to prove, my manhood.

Most of my new comrades were teenagers like me, open to all the new experiences before us. I played tackle football for the first time, achieved a high marksman's score with the M-1 rifle, went on a pre-dawn march to the James River to hear our captain lecture about the founding of Jamestown, and missed some of the drudgery of basic training as the company clerk's assistant. Somehow he discovered my typing skills and enlisted me as his helper. On cold days I appreciated the warmth of our office.

I also had my first experience of interracial socializing which I described in a letter to Shaw. "I was at the service club," I wrote, "and was drawn to the piano by some good duet boog, only to discover to my surprise and pleasure that a colored and a white boy were playing together." They were "forgetting all about race relations and concentrating on music. Black and white hands on black and white keys making music for all colors to hear. . . . And this in Virginia!" Shaw and I had discussed and exchanged letters before on the South's racial problems. She was for assaults on discrimination on every front. I wrote back, pompously and naively, I fear, that "you must get to the ROOT of things; fighting effects and not causes is not the way eventual democracy for all will be established." At the root, I wrote in good Fairhoper fashion, was enforced economic inequality. For my dad, as it was for his dad, the answer was George's single tax. Abolish poverty and you abolish racial prejudice.

Basic training came to an end in December. By then I had learned that Germany was not to be for me. I was given a two-week furlough for a visit home. After that I was to cross the continent by train to board a Liberty ship in San Francisco, bound for Korea. I spent more of my holiday visiting with family and friends, dating my old girl friend, Joyce, and playing basketball than I did reading up on the history of Korea. I did know that it had been occupied by Japan from the end of the Russo-Japanese war in 1905 and that forty years later, in 1945, it had been divided along the 38th parallel with the Russians in charge in the north and the Americans in the south. I was told that our duty would be to secure the peace. I wasn't sure how we were supposed to do that. I didn't know then that our leaders were also unsure of how that might be done. They failed us—and the Koreans—badly.

The voyage was long; the living quarters were cramped. I loved the sea, however, and enjoyed the companionship of new friends and the endless card games. I became adept at poker, a skill that would serve me well later. Before we reached our destination we were told that our ship was in need of repairs and that we would put in at a Japanese harbor. Once on land we were efficiently transported to an army replacement depot, surrounded by barbed wire, where we stayed for several very cold January days while our ailing vessel was patched up. We were totally isolated from the Japanese, cooped up in the army camp, so the interval had no cultural value for us. I remember wondering about the atom bombs dropped on Hiroshima and Nagasaki and had a vague sense of unease brought on, I suppose, by the short, cold gray days. What must it have been like for the families of those killed by what we thought of as our war-ending, life-saving bombing? What must it be like for us to have unleashed, for the first time in history (and so far the only time), the greatest of what we would today call weapons of mass destruction?

In a few days we were back on board ship, bound for Inchon harbor, an inlet off the Yellow Sea halfway up Korea's west coast. The first weeks in my new country were marked by bitter cold weather and warm collegial friendships. At Inchon there were no toilet facilities for us. Bowel movements were managed by sitting on a long plank reaching across a wide pit. I have not forgotten the sight of one of our soldiers losing his balance, falling into the new and frozen excrement below. I don't think any of us could summon laughter.

I soon arrived in Chonju, a city 110 miles to the south, where I was assigned to the mortar section of an infantry company's weapons platoon. My nineteenth birthday came a week or so after my arrival. My new comrades organized a surprise celebration, staged after lights were meant to be out. During a tour of kitchen police duty they had appropriated supplies from the mess hall: bread, jam, and cheese. A block of the cheese, with lit matches inserted into it, served as the birthday cake. I was misty eyed. To Shaw I wrote that "one guy swiped a loaf of bread from the mess hall and another pilfered a can of jam and another had some cheese so we sat around, ate bread and jam and cheese while they sang happy birthday to me." I've rarely had a birthday party to match that one.

The comradeship of these early days presaged months of enriching and enjoyable relations with a wide variety of young men. We played softball in the spring and summer, basketball in the fall, and gave the evenings over to poker, bridge, and conversation. I earned a fair measure of mild teasing from my hut mates as I persisted in explaining the virtues of Henry George's writings about progress and poverty and John Dewey's theories of progressive education. I don't remember many discussions of race, but I know from rereading my letters that there were some. The subject was seriously on my mind, serving there in a segregated army with no black soldiers—or people—in sight anywhere. It seemed unnatural to be living where there were no blacks to be seen. Writing of my only ally on racial matters, I once reported to Shaw that he and I were "the only two in the hut to defend the Negroes," and added: "You should hear the arguments we get into." But I apparently retreated from the fight. "I've decided not to argue race anymore," I confessed. "You just don't get anywhere arguing with prejudiced minds."

In May I managed a transfer to the regimental intelligence service,

Shaw, who kept my letters.

an assignment that seemed to hold out opportunities for learning about the country. I was a private first class by then, serving with a captain. The two of us, along with an interpreter who doubled as a driver, made our way to isolated parts of the countryside. Some of the people we met had never seen an American before. In a letter to Joyce, I wrote that "our job is to report on all civil disturbances, riots, political meetings, etc. . . . We go on patrols twice a week . . . interviewing the mayors and police chiefs. . . . It's really an interesting job."

Soon, however, my interest waned. At all of our stops the captain queried the Koreans about their attitudes toward the forthcoming elections the Americans had arranged for them. Everywhere the answer came in the form of a question: "Will this mean we can keep a larger share of our rice crop?" The captain, who should have been aware of the harshness of Japan's forty-year occupation, seemed not to grasp the importance of the question. I didn't try to discuss Henry George with him, let alone Karl Marx, but I did gently suggest that the bare right to vote was no guarantee of economic well-being. The young captain, like too many Americans, had been taught that the right to vote was a cure-all for every social problem, whatever the economic and cultural ground in which it was to be planted. It seemed never to have occurred to him that it hadn't worked in our own country.

After a few trips like these, where we gathered no useful "intelligence," I became increasingly frustrated with the captain's lack of interest in or understanding of the problem of poverty and inequality. I seized the chance to move with my company to the coastal city of Kunsan and took an assignment at the regimental supply office. The duties there were less than challenging, as our responsibilities consisted merely of supplying goods and services to various postal exchanges. My most interesting adventure was an eight-day train journey shepherding two boxcars loaded with empty Coca-Cola bottles on a two-hundred-mile journey from Kunsan to Ascom City, the American city near Seoul. My companion and I were well-fed with our C rations and found more amusement than frustration in being moved about from one siding to another in various rail depots. We learned the virtue of patience.

My letters to Shaw are full of detailed reports on my athletic activities, reflecting both my passion for sports and my devotion to the keeping of detailed records, an obsession that had not abated. During the spring and summer of 1947 I wrote of our softball games and my batting averages. We won the battalion championship, apparently losing only two games. In November I wrote about being captain of our basketball team. "We win games 72–44, 62–54, 83–29, 59–30 and so on," I reported, contrasting those scores with our low-scoring high school games. "We have one man UNDER six feet. And we won the 'City Championship' yesterday by trouncing the MP quintet 62–54." That was our season-ending game; the weather was turning cold and our games were played out of doors.

Apart from sports, I was seduced by the countryside. "Korea is truly a beautiful place in the spring time," I wrote to Shaw in April. "I spend a lot of my spare time up in the mountains alone—just absorbing the sunshine, writing, reading, and being alone. I've never before found a way to be completely alone before this, taking to the hills." Sailing, my great passion in Fairhope, came my way months later after I had been transferred to Kunsan. Our "house boy" arranged an outing on the boat of a friend of his, a wooden gaff-rigged sloop, sturdy and a bit chunky but a great joy on that day. As we cruised about in the Yellow Sea I took the helm, pleased by the captain/owner's smile of approval.

In that same summer of '47 several of us spent a week's furlough in Shanghai. I was fascinated by the bustle and mystery of the city, totally innocent of its eventual fall to the Communist forces of Chou-En-Lai

With Korean children.

and Mao-Tse-Tung. I bought silk robes for my parents and an elegant silk smoking jacket for myself (my younger son wears it on occasion now). Still missing Fairhope, I was overjoyed to find a bowling alley in an American establishment that served milk shakes just like at home. I remember the sense of total comfort and reassurance I felt as I entered it. Then, in the alley adjacent to me, I spied a familiar face and asked, "Hey, aren't you White from Foley?" Jack White replied, "Yeah, and you're Gaston from Fairhope, aren't you?" We had played basketball against each other in high school. He was stationed in Ascom City, where he worked at the station hospital. We spent enjoyable evenings together later when I arrived to deliver empty Coke bottles.

I was lonely for Fairhope, but its spirit coursed through me frequently. Much as I was enriched by the companionship of my hut mates, I wrote to Shaw that the "American soldier, on the whole, is such a poor ambassador of democracy—slapping down the natives; robbing the stores; raping the women—that the American occupation will be remembered, not only here but all over the world, with bitterness. We may have to pay dearly for our actions someday!" To Senator Lister Hill, a frequent correspondent of my father, I wrote to complain about the relationship between our troops and the Korean people. I did not keep a copy of my letter, but I reported to Shaw what I had suggested. We should have an "on limits" night club. "We could dance, sing, eat American food, learn to converse a little with each other and generally learn a little about each others customs and habits. There could be all kinds of meetings and groups bringing together the Korean youth and GIs. But no, Uncle Sam never thinks of anything like that. Instead we must adhere to a hands off policy. It is even punishable by courts martial to visit a Korean family after eight o'clock at night They can't eat with us and we can't eat with them." I recall a characteristically prompt reply from Senator Hill, full of sympathetic words, family greetings, and no assurance that anything would be changed.

I corresponded fairly regularly with my old high school teacher, Dr. Zeuch, continuing to learn from him. I discovered that he was planning to become the educational director of a group of English and German colonists in Paraguay. They were to operate on a basis of "mystical fraternalism" and pacifism. I wrote back to say I was eager to join him. Could I perhaps come for a month or two in the spring of 1948, after my return? I told Shaw that I might sign on a merchant vessel, just as my father had done as a youth, and then "jump ship" at the port nearest my destination.

Dr. Zeuch replied that he would keep me in mind but he was not enthusiastic about my idea. "The cooperative life and mystic sense of brotherhood among the colonists would seem strange to an extrovert such as yourself and they would think you wicked and worldly if you got to playing around with their girls—à la Fairhope." I kept up my hopes, though, and on a couple of occasions wrote to Shaw suggesting she and I might go together. The following November, however, I wrote that "Dr Zeuch isn't going to South America. . . . Revolution broke out in Paraguay. . . .He is in Los Angeles now." So much for my life of mystic brotherhood.

In March 1948, fourteen months after my arrival at Inchon harbor, we set sail for home. John Parker and I, together since basic training, were mustered out at Camp Stoneman. After a couple of days in San Francisco, we journeyed home together, first by coach to Denver, then by Pullman car to St. Louis to spend a couple of days with my Organic School friends who were there for the National Folk Festival. I was backstage when W. C. Handy, standing alone, played "The St. Louis Blues." I have listened to many renditions of that classic, but none has moved me as much as the solo trumpet performance I heard that day. Blind and shuffling, Mr. Handy came by where I was standing as he left the stage. I reached out to shake his hand. He had a warm, firm grip.

Anxious to get back to our homes and families, John and I flew the rest of the way, he to Birmingham, I to Mobile. As I walked down the ramp from the plane I spied my parents and their close friends, Paul and Bunny Smith, Shaw's parents, smiling below me. Before I touched the tarmac I heard them singing the Korean national anthem, to the tune of "Auld Lang Syne" and with the words which I had spelled phonetically for them months earlier. I knew I was home.

II

Soon after settling back into my old room, checking in with my old flame, Joyce, and shooting a few baskets at the Hall, I wrote to Swarthmore to say I was back and ready to take whatever tests might be required for admission. Almost by return mail I was instructed to take a set of entrance examinations. The nearest administering site was Birmingham, home of my comrade John Parker. He and I visited a few of his favorite bars the night before the exams. I recall being a little sleepy when I showed up at the test site, and less than clear-headed when I began filling in the bubbles. I had never taken such a test before but I doubt that I can blame my dismal performance on either inexperience or the previous night's pub crawling.

Sometime in April a Swarthmore dean wrote to tell me I would not be accepted. The problem was my test scores. I don't think I took my inadequacy terribly seriously at the time, but I do recall some inkling of what I was later to recognize—and rue—as the absence of disciplined hard work that had characterized my school years. I reached judgments and opinions quickly and easily and read enough in the assigned books to fortify my conclusions; but I never became a voracious reader and I never developed the habit of long hours of study. Partly, I suppose, the reason for this was that most things came easily to me so that being less than thorough seemed penalty-free. The letter from Swarthmore was a reminder that it wasn't.

Abe Waldauer happened to be in Fairhope when the letter arrived. He told me and my parents that he could not allow such a decision to stand. He wrote to the dean to demand a reconsideration and assembled a batch of letters from my former teachers, including Dr. Zeuch, whom he reached in Mexico. Apparently he told them they were missing the find of the half-century and he could not allow them to miss that opportunity. The dean replied that he was impressed by the letters and that the admissions committee would reassemble on September 8 to reconsider my application. Abe was a man of force and confidence, as I was to discover many years later when I began to write a book about him. Still, he was prudent. I should gain admission to another college in case his efforts were unsuccessful. My choice, he said, would be Southwestern at Memphis (now Rhodes College), directly across the street from his Memphis home. I was readily admitted, I assume with Abe's help.

I put aside college thoughts for the summer, joining a group of Organic School graduates for a fund-raising trip through the Midwest. Under the leadership of Warren Stetzel, one of the school's new teachers, we danced and acted before audiences we hoped would be drawn to the school's philosophy and would open their pocketbooks to help with its chronic financial woes. We had little material success but the trip was educational and enjoyable and our audiences seemed to like what we did. I played a lead role in Chekhov's *A Marriage Proposal* and performed with Norma Stetzel, Warren's younger sister, in a romantic modern dance we called "La Paloma." The traditional English folk, sword, and stick dances were our mainstay.

Perhaps my most memorable experience on that trip was listening on a car radio to Hubert Humphrey's famous Democratic Party convention speech, calling upon his fellow Democrats "to get out of the shadow of states' rights and walk forthrightly into the bright sunshine of human rights." Southern Democrats, of course, had no intention of taking such a walk. As Handy Ellis of Alabama shouted from the convention floor that "without the votes of the South you cannot elect a president of the United States," the Alabama delegation walked out of the convention hall. His prediction was wrong even though the victorious Harry Truman was not allowed on the ballot in Alabama. Feelings of shame over my home state were to be a recurrent feature in my life.

September came and Abe was in Fairhope once again. My footlocker was packed for departure. All I lacked knowing was whether I would be taking the bus to Memphis or to Philadelphia. The Swarthmore dean had promised to telephone Abe at our home, but when the appointed hour for his call passed the impatient Abe put in the call himself. The apologetic dean reported that there was bad news and there was good news. The committee had voted 4–3 against admitting me, an improvement, I judged, on the 7–0 negative vote of the previous spring. The good news was that the college would reserve a place for me in the sophomore class pending a year of good work at another college. I would jokingly remark in later years that Swarthmore would let me in just as soon as I had learned to read and write.

I did have the requisite good year at Southwestern, earning more A's than B's. I received a demerit only for poor chapel attendance. I took an advanced course in Spanish, was president of the Spanish Club, and played the lead in a Spanish-language play. My most interesting class was a year-long study of Bible history. For a confident nonbeliever like me, reading every word of both the Old and New Testaments, along with a good sampling of Biblical criticism, was a fresh and rewarding experience, one that would fortify me in years to come as I examined my religious skepticism. The most interesting paper I wrote that year was about what I called "The Fate of Korea." In it I predicted that, should the United States withdraw its troops, the North Korean army would invade the south. My instructor praised my analysis and research but he marked the paper down to a B-minus because of two sentence fragments. When American troops were withdrawn and the invasion I had predicted did come I wondered if he reflected on my prescience. I valued the grade, though, and thought of his standards often in the future as I fought against the proliferation of dangling participles, sentence fragments, verb-noun disagreements and other offenses against the language perpetrated with increasing regularity by my students.

My first college experience with grades was managed easily enough. I got off to a rocky start, however, in my European History course. I missed the first class, unable to find the room where it was held. When I arrived late at the second meeting the professor was quizzing the students about the names of rivers, cities, and mountains in Europe. With his long pointer he would indicate on a large map the sites to be identified and ask us to write them down. I knew most of the answers but there were a few I didn't know so I looked on the paper of the student sitting next to me to be sure I had all the identifications right. I was surprised at the end of the class when we were instructed to turn in our papers. As we made ready to leave, Professor Lowry called me aside to explain Southwestern's honor system: you don't look on someone else's paper for answers, he said, not when you are taking a test. I explained to him, with perhaps too much Organic School bravado, that, first, I had no idea we were taking a test and, second, wasn't it important that I should know all the answers? I probably also told him that I had never had grades before so the idea of cheating was a new one to me. He let me go with a kindly smile and a gentle warning. During the year we developed a warm friendship, often meeting in the library where he answered my questions about aspects of European history that especially aroused my curiosity, the "land question" prominent among them.

From the outset, however, I was conscious of my need to do well enough to earn the transfer to Swarthmore. The Southwestern ethos was alien and disagreeable. The political and social conservatism of the Mississippi and Arkansas Delta students; their unreflective acceptance of fraternity and sorority culture; the absurd hazing week of all freshmen; the reverence of the anti-cheating "honor" system; and the pervasive emphasis on rating people according to looks and personality all clashed with my internalized Organic School upbringing. Fairhope was a racially segregated town and there were no blacks in our school, but I grew up knowing both were wrong. At Southwestern I encountered for the first time the internalized white supremacy culture of the Southern elite. That was probably the most valuable learning experience I had as a college freshman.

Even so, I look back on my first semester's political activities with sorrow and not a little embarrassment. The college's mock presidential election came at what was a hugely important moment in American political history. There was Harry Truman, the feisty Democratic president, running for reelection against the favored Republican candidate, the pompous Thomas E. Dewey. To Truman's right was the Dixiecrat white supremacy party headed by Strom Thurmond of South Carolina, with Mississippi's Fielding Wright as his running mate. To his left was Henry Wallace and his Progressive Party. My father was a Truman man. Alabama's racist power elite, banning Truman from the ballot, would prevent him from voting his conviction. My Uncle Marvin was a delegate to the Wallace convention. A photograph of him in what the Mobile paper called the conventional clenched fist salute of the communist left made its way to Uncle Marvin's employers at city hall, and to his firing. The retribution might have been allowed to stand if my father had not intervened. I was never told what he said to my uncle's superiors but I can imagine him speaking with that way he had of being absolutely clear about what was right and wrong without raising his voice or heaping scorn on the perpetrators. He had the kind of reputation for integrity that made it virtually impossible for small men to oppose him.

Despite this family history (and my own values), I did not support either Truman or Wallace. I became, instead, the chairman of what must have been a one-man committee for Dr. John Maxwell, candidate of the Vegetarian Party. He was a frequent presidential aspirant whom my parents had known in Chicago in the 1920s; I opted for a frivolous gesture at a time when serious questions called for answers. The memory of Humphrey's human rights speech and Handy Ellis's defiant secession oration must also have been with me. Ah, well. My recollection of the election outcome has long since departed, but a kind librarian at Rhodes checked *Sou'wester*, the student newspaper, for me. The popular vote was not reported, only the thirty electoral votes. The Dixiecrats won seventeen of those, the Republicans thirteen, a clean sweep for racism and conservatism. No wonder I could not feel at home there.

I successfully tried out for the basketball team to become the only freshman on the varsity squad. Never a starter, I played in all but one of the games, a thriller against Ole Miss which we lost by a whisker. My modest prowess on the basketball court and my Spanish Club presidency apparently garnered merits and I was sufficiently personable and had the requisite good looks to receive fraternity bids. I don't think my would-be brothers ever understood why I spurned their offers. Their self-confidence about the way they lived brooked no doubts. Someone like me had to be understood as a puzzling aberration. A puzzling aberration to them, I felt myself to be an outsider at Southwestern, marked by my Fairhope background and beliefs never really to fit in, seldom really belonging. It was at Southwestern that this sensibility first came to me. It would become a constant and complicated presence as my life in the larger world unfolded.

Abe had suggested Southwestern as a back-up choice for me in large part because the Waldauer home was adjacent to the campus. He and Dot made me feel it was mine, a place to repair to whenever I felt the need or desire. I was there frequently for suppers, enjoyed my visits with Dot and warmed to her constant support. In Abe I found a stimulating and challenging spirit and a measure of approval and even comradeship that enriched my Memphis sojourn. An ardent Zionist, he was full of enthusiasm for the infant state of Israel, just months old when I arrived. We must have had several evening conversations talking about its promise and prospects. Much of our talk centered on our hopes that the new government would come to approve Henry George's belief that land should be common property and then to implement a comprehensive policy of land-value taxation. The thought of a whole state becoming a single-tax colony was exciting to contemplate. To imagine it in the company of one as wise and witty as Abe—and he a friend of Fairhope, my parents, and my grandfather—was a rare experience.

The Waldauer home opened up to me a good deal more than family warmth, support, and stimulation. Joe, a Swarthmore senior, was never at home while I was in Memphis. But his younger sister Mary Alice, a freshman at Earlham, came home from college frequently. I don't recall when we met but I have not forgotten the electricity that surrounded our first meeting. She was, as I described her in my still-unfinished book about her father, a raven-haired beauty of uncommon verve and charm, with much of her father's puckish engagement of life. We dated as frequently as we could. As our relationship became serious I began to back off, announcing one night while we were sitting in her parents' car, parked in their driveway, that I thought we should not see each other for a while. Her reply was a shocker: "Well, my daddy wouldn't let me marry a Gentile anyway so we might as well break up." Marriage was far from my mind as I thought it must have been from Mary Alice's. I had just turned twenty-one, she nineteen. What shocked, however, was her announcement that, because I was not a Jew, Abe would reject me as a son-in-law.

Until that moment I had not thought much about what it meant to be a Jew, and not much more about anti-Semitism. There were few Jews in Fairhope but I actually had no idea who among the several Semitic people I knew were Jewish. The Howie family, proprietors of the Casino, were from Syria, but I didn't know that at the time. Bigotry and prejudice, in my limited experience and undernourished thought, were peculiar to white attitudes toward blacks. It was partly out of my innocence, then, that I could not imagine Abe's Judaism being a barrier. Surely, I thought, the closeness of our families and our single-tax beliefs would not permit that. If I was already like a son to him, why not a son-in-law?

I never learned the answer to that question. At the time I processed Mary Alice's retort as her form of defense against what she took to be rejection. A half-century later, hard at work on the book about her father, I learned a great deal about his understanding of Judaism and his extraordinary work in Jewish causes, but still could only conjecture. With my ego less at stake I was more inclined to think she was right. When I found her in New Orleans for an interview we reviewed our separate lives and reminisced about our brief but intense romance of fifty years earlier, but I never asked her about the truth of what she said to me that dark night in the coziness of her parents' automobile.

June came. My year at Southwestern and my romance with Mary Alice ended. I took a bus to Fordyce, Arkansas, where relatives of my mother turned over to me a 1942 black Chevrolet sedan to be delivered to my parents who had given up their only car, a Model A Ford, fifteen years earlier. I drove it home, my few belongings fitting easily in the trunk. The Swarthmore acceptance letter had come several months earlier but I did not spend the summer reading furiously to prepare myself. It would have been a good idea. Instead, I took a full-time job at the bank. The pay was good and the summer passed happily with sailing, dancing in the evenings at the Casino, playing the romantic lead in a Little Theater production of *Smilin' Through*, and having a real-life romance with my leading lady, Danny Benton, whose mother directed our play.

Until that summer I had occasionally thought of acting as a career. Theater was an integral part of the Fairhope ambience and I had been in drama classes from early childhood through high school. I seemed to have a flair for acting, at least according to some of my teachers, and the *Courier* reviews of my performances. But in that summer of '49, working with my friend Clayton Corzatte in *Smilin' Through*, I abandoned whatever ambitions I may have been harboring. Clayton was a drama student at the University of Alabama and all of us saw in him the makings of a real professional. And our vision was good. He has had a distinguished stage career. I once saw him play the role of Bottom in Washington and remembered with amusement my own amateurish efforts in that role at the school. I was on the boards only once more in my life, playing again the romantic lead with the Carolina Playmakers during my graduate school days.

Sometime during the summer of '49 I met Sam and Liz Hynes at one of our frequent Sunday morning breakfasts on the beach. Sam was related to one of the local families and had visited Fairhope before from his home in Minnesota. He and Liz, a Birmingham native, were but recently married and were readying to go to Swarthmore for Sam's first teaching job. He was still working on his dissertation and was only a few years my senior. Like me, he was nervous about the Swarthmore challenge. During our first semester there we met from time to time in the Commons for mutual support. Sam's brilliance and charm soon established him as one of the college's most popular teachers. He moved on, after I graduated, first to Columbia and then to Princeton and eminence in the field of English literature.

III

Swarthmore would become a great joy for me after a while, but my first rocky semester filled me with doubt and anxiety. I arrived knowing I would meet some of the brightest students in America, products of the elite prep schools and the best public schools, most of them from accomplished, intellectual families. I was eager to exchange the provincial and oppressive culture of Southwestern for Swarthmore's vaunted cosmopolitan and progressive atmosphere. But on one of my first nights there I walked into a dorm room where I found Dabney Altaffer and George Scanlon, pipe-smoking upperclassmen, dressed in tweed jackets, absorbed in quiet discussion of Thomistic philosophy. I probably had some idea of who St. Thomas was, but the level of conversation was far too elevated for me to find an entry point.

Luckily, Dabney soon became a good friend, as did his brother Tom, my future roommate. The fact that they had lived in more than one European country, spoke German and French fluently and perhaps Italian as well, and were sons of an American diplomat, soon became less intimidating. Dabney, in fact, saved me from bailing out of the college after a near-disastrous early semester quiz. It was the first test in my American history course. The essay question—"The freest of the world's colonial peoples were the first to revolt. Discuss"—left me totally baffled. I froze. I turned to some of the identification questions, hoping that writing something, anything, would help. I recall confusing Noah Webster with Daniel Webster. Nothing helped. Adding to my swelling anxiety, the top of the ink bottle in my jeans pocket came loose; red ink flowed down my leg. After twenty minutes I rose, dropping my test booklet on the professor's table as I left the room. I still recall the arched eybrows of my professor, Jim Field, as I strode embarrassedly past him.

I wandered about the campus for a short while, then made my way down Magill Walk, the long tree-lined avenue leading to the bottom of the campus—and to the train station. I was inquiring nervously about trains to Alabama when Dabney happened by. He took me across the street for a coffee and a reassuring chat, persuading me to stay at least until after my next quiz, a few days hence. That was a statistics course test, straightforward and uncomplicated. I knew I had made an A when I finished. When our American history test papers were ready for us to retrieve I asked Tom to fetch mine. There was neither a grade nor a comment on the inside. Jim Field had simply written on the cover 10:20, the time I had left.

I wrote home about the disastrous American history test. My father, sympathetic and supportive as always, wrote to tell me that "we felt as bad as you. You can't win all the time, though. . . .Do cheer up and don't let 'em get you down. Do the best you can and that's as good as anyone can do." By the time I received Dad's letter Dabney's reassurance and the A I made on the statistics test persuaded me to stay. I had a full spectrum mid-term report card: A-B-C-D-F. A few good friendships, growing appreciation of the amazing opportunities Swarthmore offered, a lot of hard work, an A term paper for Jim Field on John C. Calhoun—these gave me the confidence to stay on. My final grades for the semester—two As; two Bs; and a C—were respectable, especially since the C from young and brash Sid Morganbesser in my intro philosophy course was the grade he reportedly gave all of his students that semester. Sometimes, according to legend, he gave nothing but As. Mine was the C year. Recalling what I felt I had learned, I think that was about right for me.

Everything went splendidly after that. I graduated with High Honors (only four of my classmates received Highest Honors), was elected to Phi Beta Kappa, and won a Fulbright fellowship to the University of Copenhagen. Ten years later, when I was teaching at the University of Virginia, Swarthmore invited me to join the faculty. Jim Field was my champion. I declined the offer because the South was where I had chosen to work. Jim and I remained good friends. I invited him to Charlottesville to lecture and later to Fairhope for a weekend gathering of friends. Then, in 2002, on the occasion of my fiftieth reunion, the college honored me with the Arabella Carter Award for community service. On a gorgeously cool and sparklingly bright day in the amphitheater, I gave a five-minute talk, accepting the award on behalf of all the Southerners—mostly black, but some of us white, too—who had helped Swarthmore to become, what it had not been during my time, something the Southern civil rights movement made possible—a racially integrated college.

Intellectual life at Swarthmore, intense and demanding in reality as well as by reputation, nonetheless seemed to me an extension of the Organic School spirit. I suppose some who came there felt a sense of competition, but I did not. What I experienced was an extraordinary comradeship in the seeking and sharing of knowledge. For me, there seemed to be an almost universal recognition that we were there to read, write, and reason. We partied, were not total strangers to drunkenness, had our share of romances, watched our football team on Saturdays in the autumn (usually losing), and had open to us an abundance of extracurricular activities in the arts, drama, dance, sports, journalism, politics, student government, and social service. Sororities had been abolished by the time I arrived, but we did have five fraternities. Instead of harboring campus leaders, however, fraternities were seen as social gathering places but not as representatives of the Swarthmore ethos. Everywhere, in whatever our activities, I reveled in seeing the minds of my fellow students at work. Weekend dances with gatherings around a beer keg were extensions of our intellectual life, not escapes from it.

The essence of Swarthmore blossomed for me in its Honors Program, the college's unique contribution to American higher education. President Frank Aydelotte, who created it in 1924, thought of it as a way of breaking what he called the academic lockstep. During our junior and senior years we studied in small seminars, in my case ranging between six and eight students. Two seminars a semester was the norm. Aydelotte modeled his program on the Oxbridge tutorial system but, wisely I have always felt, prescribed seminars instead of individual tutorials. Our seminars, like the Oxford tutorials, had plenty of room for individual expression and development, but within a framework of collaborative effort. We wrote and distributed papers that formed the take-off point for our discussions. If you managed your schedule carefully enough you would write one paper a week. I once reckoned that I wrote more than fifty such essays in my junior and senior years, all of them analyzed by my fellow students and my teachers. At the outset I would write careful outlines before composing one or two rough drafts, then type up the final paper with carbon copies for the seminar. By my final semester I threw paper and carbon in the typewriter at the outset and, with notes at my side, composed the final draft straightaway.

At the Organic School we internalized the belief that learning was to be pursued for its own sake, not to meet standards or expectations of the surrounding society or to be better than somebody else. If anything, we felt we had an obligation to question society's standards. Good Fairhopers knew that some had to be subverted. About the last thing we could believe was the popular American notion that schools existed to be socializing institutions, preparing pupils to enter, fit into, the world as it was. It was the same at Swarthmore. I cannot imagine a freer, more conducive atmosphere for creative and uninhibited thought than we found in our seminars. The role of our professors was crucial to this. They did not sit in judgment on us and we received no grades on our work—two more un-American approaches to learning. There was an abundance of constructive criticism, both written and oral, but it was never undermining and it was always balanced with understanding of what we were trying to say. At the end of our junior year we took trial exams over our four seminars of that year. The faculty used those to decide whether we should continue in the program (a negative decision was very rare) and to point us to areas where we needed to strengthen ourselves.

At the end of our senior year we faced a battery of eight three-hour written examinations over our eight seminars set by external examiners. Our papers were mailed to the examiners who soon descended on the campus. Then we sat for eight twenty-minute oral examinations. Through all of this, from beginning to end, our professors were our allies, our senior comrades, not our antagonists or judges. And they wanted us to do well, not only for our own sakes but also because those examiners were their professional peers and sometimes personal friends. Their examining finished, the visitors met for a long afternoon of evaluation and discussion, deciding who would graduate with Highest Honors, High Honors, and Honors. In unusual cases they might recommend no honors at all. Late in the afternoon a list of results was posted on a central bulletin board. Anxious students gathered around it.

A quarter-century later I had the chance to be on the other side of the Honors examining process, serving at Jim Field's invitation on three occasions as an external examiner. The experience confirmed my judgment of both the excellence and the uniqueness of Swarthmore's contribution to higher education in America.

About one-third of the juniors and seniors were members of the honors program. Among those who were not, some applied but were rejected; some did not apply, preferring the conventional graded course program for their particular academic or personal needs or sensed that they would not be accepted if they did apply. I do not recall if my anti-elitist sensibilities were aroused by this two-class system. Probably not. For one thing, I was totally absorbed in the challenge and exhilaration of my seminars. For another, I sensed little, if any, class feeling. I have no memory of honors students feeling superior to course students or course students feeling inferior to us. I may have missed such feelings. As I began writing this memoir one of my former classmates told me I had. They were there, he said. What I do remember was the collaborative effort we all made, the sharing of knowledge, the testing of ideas on each other, the swapping of papers, the sense that we were there to give and receive help from our fellow students.

Many years after I graduated, the honors program did come under sharp criticism, in part because it was not open to all students but also because some students wanted options the program did not include, such as the study-abroad adventure that became increasingly popular with American students. In the late 1970s I was invited to join a group of faculty and alumni to evaluate the program. I was a stalwart defender of maintaining it as it was but making it available to all who wanted to enter it. I was in the minority. Soon after our meeting the program changed to six seminars to be mixed with four graded courses. I feared this would lead to further compromises and the eventual gutting of the system. It did. In 1986 the new mix became four seminars, now graded, along with a bunch of graded courses. The result, I felt, effectively ended Adeylotte's dream of breaking the academic lockstep and my ideal of higher education.

Like many other former Swarthmore honors students, I wrote a long let-ter to the college president in March 1985 to protest the proposed changes. "The essence of honors," I wrote, "lies in the separation of examination and instruction, in the consequent nurturing of a collegial relationship between faculty and students, in the sustained pursuit of a reasonably coherent pro-gram of study over a two-year period, in the integration of one's knowledge and information at the end of the period, and—most important of all—in the sincerity and honesty of intellectual growth that results from the com-bination of these factors." To abandon the program, I concluded, "would be not simply to turn the College into just another center of bright American youth, lamentable though that would be; it would also be to take from the nation a vision and an example it sorely needs." President Fraser replied to say that he agreed with much of what I had said but told me that "the present program is failing to attract many of our brightest students." That, apparently, turned out to be the decisive reason for approving the proposed changes. Swarthmore retained its top ranking among liberal arts colleges but its uniquely distinguishing characteristic was fatally compromised. I sorely regretted the loss and treasured even more my Swarthmore experience.

IV

The demands of intellectual life, rewarding though they were, left little time for me to take part in extracurricular activities such as drama, which I would have enjoyed. And, as a transfer student, I was required by NCAA regulations to sit out a year before being eligible to play varsity basketball. Even without that obstacle neither time nor talent would have been on my side. The Swarthmore team was several notches up from Southwestern's. I played recreational tennis occasionally but never found out that Ed Faulkner, the tennis coach, had once captained the American Davis Cup team and had written an outstanding book on how the game should be played. In later years, when tennis became my athletic passion, I regretted having missed his mentoring.

In my insecure and sometimes lonely first semester I was befriended by members of one of the fraternities and asked to join, an invitation I happily accepted. Swarthmore fraternities had none of the spirit of exclusivity I had known at Southwestern and little of the juvenility or hazing associated with fraternities generally. Only two of the "brothers" lived in our lodge and we took no meals there, so it was mainly a gathering place for conversations, meetings, and weekend dances.

We were also progressives, tilting in Swarthmore fashion against society's windmills. Our particular fraternity—Phi Delta Theta—had a membership clause that prohibited the pledging of Negroes, as they were called then, and Jews. There were only a couple of black students in the college but there were many Jews, some of whom were already members of our fraternity. During my first year we ruminated at chapter meetings over how to confront what we called the Aryan Supremacy clause in our charter. The fraternity's national meeting was scheduled for Chicago that summer. In what I now look back on as a typical Yankee blind spot, my brothers selected me as our delegate to the convention. The reasoning was as simple as it was naïve: a Southern student with a pronounced Southern accent would be a much more effective spokesman against racial and ethnic prejudice than an accent-free Northerner would be.

I set off for the posh Edgewater Beach hotel with excitement and a reform warrior's eagerness for battle. On the first day I summoned several fellow Phis from around the country to my room for a strategy session. Room service brought us bacon, lettuce, and tomato sandwiches at a cost of $1.00 each, a stunningly high price (equivalent to $8 today) by my provincial standards. In the next day's plenary session, I marched to the podium to attack the "Aryan Supremacy" clause. I have forgotten the details of the session but I remember clearly that the last compromise we managed to get up for a vote would have allowed us to pledge converted Jews. Nothing else had a remote chance of passage. Nor did that one, as it turned out.

Before the session the delegate from Auburn University, in my home state, took me aside to assure me that he would not oppose a change in the by-laws that would allow the admission of blacks if that was what we wanted. They would not come calling at his chapter's house, so why should he be concerned. A confident pragmatist he was, not an ideologue. The South, I concluded, was not the problem. I soon learned that it was the fiery bigot from the Pittsburgh alumni delegation. There was no way, he said, that he would let Phi Delta Theta cease being a fraternity of Jew-free white men. I couldn't identify with precision the source of the applause or the votes, but I came away thinking my opponents were primarily from alumni chapters and active chapters outside the South. The light of reform, however, did not shine brightly anywhere. I would remember all of this in the years after the *Brown* decision.

After Chicago, I returned to Fairhope for my summer job as an assistant to my father, calculating land rents in one of the back rooms. Late afternoons, evenings, and weekends were once again given over to sailing and dancing at the Casino.

Back at Swarthmore in September I started my honors program career as an economics major. My plan was to take four seminars in economics and two each in history and political science. I had made no career choice, but returning to Fairhope to succeed my father as secretary of the colony was still part of my thinking. An economics major seemed to be the logical choice to prepare me for that. Once well into the program, however, I shied away from my original plan. Frank Pierson was more amused than instructed when I chose to write about Shays's rebellion to explain monetary theory and fiscal policy. Joe Conard was gentle and idealistic in his theory seminar, but for the mathematically challenged like me he had to explain everything twice. He generously let me write a paper on Henry George. Then, as my interests shifted to history, one of my professors comforted me by saying that George was no longer important enough to be reckoned with by economists but that American historians were bound to deal with his enormous importance in the late nineteenth century. As a historian I could always justify generous attention to my town's patron saint. My final program, then, was made up of four history seminars, two in economics, and two in political science.

V

During my previous year I had dated Jan Dunn, an alluring senior from Pittsburgh. We took long bicycle rides, found special places for picnics, dined occasionally in one of the two local restaurants, danced and partied at the Phi Delt lodge on the weekends. Jan graduated in 1950 so when I returned that fall I made a couple of trips to Princeton, where she was working with the Educational Testing Service. Our ardor soon faded though, a victim of time, distance, and new interests. I had occasion to write to her forty years later about her daughter's labor union work. Her reply told me she had not forgotten our student years. "My youngest was getting married," she wrote of the moment when my letter arrived, "and I was a little jealous of the heady emotions churning about. So it was nice to remember our heady days with a secret 'so there!'"

New heady days were ahead. Shaw, by this time married and a mother, was living in nearby Philadelphia. She was vigorously promoting a new interest. Had I met a Mary Wilkinson, she wanted to know. Like me, Mary was a Swarthmore junior. I had not met her and I had forgotten a letter Shaw wrote to me when I was in Korea, telling me that two of the few people in the world she hoped to keep up with for the rest of her life were me and "my Mary" in England. I did not take up her urgings, however, and made no effort to look up her Mary from England.

When finally I did meet Mary, early in the second semester of our junior year, it was not Shaw's recommendation that propelled me toward her. There was a dance at our lodge. I spied my roommate Tom Altaffer and his date, a soft, intriguing, enigmatic, quietly beautiful, and irresistibly entrancing woman. In those days, fortunately, it was *de rigueur* to "cut in," so I tapped Tom on the shoulder to dance with his date. What happened after that is disputed by Mary and me. My recollection is now deeply embedded in a hundred-times-told story. According to it I said to Tom, as we readied to turn in that night, "Tom, did you enjoy your date with Mary Wilkinson?" To which he replied, "Oh, yes, very much." I paused a moment before saying "Well, I'm glad you did, because it was your last." Which it was. (All was to work out well in the end, though: Tom married Marquita, Mary's roommate.)

Mary doubts that this well-remembered conversation ever took place and claims for herself the initiative in bringing us together. Her story is that we met in the library soon after the dance. She had never followed up on Shaw's injunction to look me up. She had seen a "Paul," whom she wrongly assumed to be me, and the sight of him sparked neither interest nor appeal. How, she wondered, could her friend be so wrong in her judgment of men. Now, after our dance, as we met in the library, the penny dropped. This was the Paul that Shaw was urging her toward. Her recollection of this encounter is that she opened a conversation by saying, "You know, we have a mutual friend in Philadelphia." That, she believes, opened the road to our first date. Lacking archival evidence to decide between these rival versions of our coming together, I settle for believing that the two stories can exist as companion truths. And that we may also give Shaw thanks for her determination that we must meet. We both agree that she was right about that.

Our first date came quickly, happily surviving gaffes and glitches. We went first to the fraternity house where Mary gently explained her disapproval of the whole Greek system, a value I shared generally but pleaded for Swarthmore as an exception to the rule. I told her of my failed reform efforts at the national convention the previous summer and of my chapter's commitment to recruiting Jewish members and to laying plans for withdrawal from the national, a step taken shortly after I graduated. To lighten the conversation I offered her a glass of Scotch—not any Scotch, but a prized single-malt I had acquired from a friend whose brother in the UN had access to the best, and at little cost. Mary pronounced the taste medicinal and left her glass unemptied. We then left to go to the basketball game. Her response made me wonder if she had ever seen one. I could detect no enthusiasm as we walked along quietly to the gymnasium. Looking for a good topic other than fraternities, whiskey, or sports, I asked if she didn't think that religion was a little ridiculous. I don't remember the words she used to tell me that her father was a priest in the Church of England. Ah, well. Fortunately, with no need for a topic of conversation, we found a common interest later in the evening. For me, our future was sealed.

We were constantly in each other's company after that first date, often at the fraternity lodge where Tom and I were the two residents. For her birthday I presented a well-shaped block of cheese with a lit match inserted in its center, recalling my nineteenth birthday celebration in Korea. There was no Scotch this time. At Tom's wise suggestion I chose a Duff Gordon Amontillado. It produced a glow then and became our good-memory drink for several years to come. Sam and Liz Hynes were new parents by this time and conveniently furnished us with their living room, where we came as grateful baby sitters. For high entertainment we attended a formal dance in a Philadelphia hotel sponsored by the Interfraternity Council, of which I was a member. Mary's seductive black velvet evening gown still shines brightly in my memory. And, from time to time, she reminds me that I did not give her the black orchid for it she requested. Philadelphia was also our destination for cultural enrichment. At Mary's suggestion we first went to see *La Bohème*. We were seated almost in reach of the opera-house ceiling. It was hot. I was tired. I fell into a sound sleep. Was I a Philistine? I thought I had lost her, but when she gave me a second chance I thrilled to *La Traviata*. Our romance was saved.

Shortly after we met I looked Mary up in the student directory to find her address: Frogmore Manor, Frogmore, South Carolina. Additional sleuthing told me that Frogmore was a small village on St. Helena, a barrier island across the Beaufort River from the town of the same name. Any visions I may have formed of her roots in the Southern Low-Country plantation aristocracy were quickly dissolved as I learned her history. Her maternal grandfather, James Ross Macdonald, from a poor immigrant family in Philadelphia, came to St. Helena early in the Reconstruction era to become a cotton merchant. A historian might have called him a carpetbagger. Until I learned the politics of his descendants I scrupulously avoided uttering that epithet.

I would have occasion a few years later to learn how explosive the term could be. Mary's Uncle Jack, a once and still then occasionally sweet man grown bitter, launched a tirade in which he portrayed carpetbaggers as the scum who had come south to pillage and stir up the blacks to insolence and worse. Their story was but another chapter in the ongoing history of Yankee meddling in the affairs of the South. I had just read a learned article on the carpetbaggers by a major historian in which their constructive work was stressed. Uncle Jack's red face told me this was not the time to share these findings.

Instead, I changed the subject, asking him to tell me about his father's experience during his early days on the island. The red, tense face softened as the son recounted with loving admiration the father's history as the man on the island loved and trusted by white and black alike. In years to come, I would tell what came to be known as the Uncle Jack story to the students in my Southern history classes, trying to help them understand the ways in which conservative white Southerners assigned unpleasant realities to a special compartment of the brain, never allowing them to come out to mingle with comforting myths. When one of my colleagues told me this was called cognitive dissonance I had two big words to give great scholarly depth to my Uncle Jack story.

VI

Frogmore Manor, which Mary's grandfather was later to acquire, was a spacious two-story frame home, impressive even without the pillars or pretense of plantation showplaces. It was larger and grander than any home ever built in Fairhope. Standing since before the Civil War, it was once occupied by William J. Grayson, author of the famous pro-slavery poem "The Hireling and the Slave." Mary's mother, her Aunt Margaret (everyone called her "Argie"), and her Uncle Jack grew up there. Their mother, Clara Macdonald ("Bamba" to everyone), died in the spring of 1951, shortly after Mary and I met. I always regretted not meeting her, the formidable matriarch about whom stories abounded. Argie and her husband, Ed Sanders, and their three children lived in the manor house; Jack and his wife Ruth lived in Atlanta; Mary's parents were in England.

I came calling in June 1951, at the end of our junior year, with courtship on my mind. I breathed in the pungent smell of marsh en route and sucked in my breath as we drove up the long tree-lined sand and shell avenue, marsh and woods on either side. The house sat in a beguiling environment of river, woods, Spanish moss, and seductive views. The whole estate occupied a hundred acres, more than a hundred times larger than any of the town homesites in Fairhope.

I was entranced by the setting, the likes of which I had never seen. It fired my imagination to conjure up romantic mysteries and scenes of Southern grace. Off to one side of the avenue entrance I saw the ruins of an abandoned tennis court, grass growing between the broken slabs of concrete that had once been its surface. I could close my eyes to imagine men in long white cotton trousers, their female partners in white tennis skirts and blouses, with colored bandannas about their necks. Wandering in another direction, past the antebellum tabby barn, I found a trail leading through another set of woods. It opened, after a hundred yards or so, onto a gray wooden dock reaching out into one of the tidal rivers. Here the family had its own private picnic and swimming space. Across from the front of the home, when the tide was out, we walked to what Mary's mother and aunt had named Friendship Island, isolated and hauntingly beautiful, an ideal hideaway for one on a courtship mission. For all its allure, however, Frogmore also spoke to me of the slave past out of which it had come and the segregation present on which it seemed now to rest comfortably. Nothing in my Fairhope experience was remotely like it.

Ed Sanders, Argie's husband, was a truck farmer whose major crop was tomatoes. He was one of the most prominent on the island. He had inherited his farm land, a few miles from the Frogmore house, from his father. Hard times had plagued his efforts during the Depression but skill, fortitude, assistance from his mother-in-law, and the generous hand of the New Deal's government aid to agriculture programs had seen him through to his present state of prosperity. My visit came during the harvesting season, so I saw little of Ed and his two sons, Mary's cousins Ross and Robin, both helping out at the farm, but I saw something of Sibet, Ed and Argie's fifteen-year old daughter. And I did see tomatoes, scores of them, at breakfast, lunch, and dinner. Good tomatoes, too, not like the thick-skinned, green-picked tasteless ones the free-market survival mechanism would later demand of the growers, including Ed's sons.

I was greeted warmly by all the Frogmore folk. And my week there with Mary was magical. Off to ourselves, we talked endlessly about our contrasting pasts and common values. We swam; explored the island; and one night following a great storm roamed the beaches of nearby Hunting Island, the ocean sparkling in the moonlight, the fallen branches taking on eerie shapes.

The week passed too swiftly and I was soon back in Fairhope, taking up my summer job working at the *Courier*. I suppose there was still some thought that I might return home after graduation, if not to succeed my father immediately as colony secretary then to follow my aunt, who might soon retire, as editor of the family newspaper. That summer I sold advertising, helped assemble the paper on Thursdays, wrote news stories and occasional editorials. Two of those opinion pieces have stuck in my mind, with the memory of my father's role in both still vivid. The first was a plea for cleanliness on our beautiful beach, too often marred by thoughtless picnickers. On the day the *Courier* appeared, my father walked into our office, next door to his, holding my editorial in his hand. "Son," he said, "your intention is good; but, you know, you should not ask the impossible of your readers." I remember bridling, protesting that nothing I asked for was impossible. "Read what you have written," Dad gently suggested, a smile barely creeping out to the edge of his mouth. I read the piece and protested again. "Well," he persisted, "try reading it aloud." I did. Slowly.

And then I saw and heard the words I had written: "remember to clean up your trash after leaving." Ah, yes.

I headed the second editorial "Whose Freedom?" And began with the famous quote from Jefferson's first inaugural: "We are all Republicans; We are all Federalists." I have kept the typescript, its paper now yellowing and brittle. I was responding to a bitter letter to the editor urging that we run out of town a group of pacifists who had recently attracted attention to themselves. I was careful to take no stand on pacifism, staking my defense of the pacifists on what I thought everyone would agree were the staples of American democracy: free speech, the right to be different, all those things embodied in the First Amendment. And, after all, this was Fairhope, the "model community." And it was E. B. Gaston's newspaper. My Uncle Spider, our linotype operator and business manager, the bon vivant of the family, walked up to me with a scowl I had never seen before. He would not print what I had written. I don't remember what else he said, only his shaking hand and the anger in his voice. But I suddenly realized the source of his deep discomfort. His son Barney, my cousin, had died a war hero's death in a flight over France. I walked next door to Dad's office, to tell him about our exchange. He read what I had written. He sat for a few moments in quiet thought. If I wished, he said, he would speak to his brother and urge him to change his mind. I had written truthfully, honestly.

Of E. B. Gaston's five children, my father, the third-born, was the one recognized by his siblings (and other Fairhopers as well) as the bearer of the founder's mantle. First-born Frances had taken over the editorship of the *Courier*, but Dad, with the title of associate editor, wrote the editorials on serious local, regional, and national matters. Second-born Jim, a charming extrovert who owned the Ford dealership and was elected to the county board of supervisors, bore the closest resemblance to their father's persuasive political skills but lacked his brother Cornie's sense of mission and immersion in Georgist and reformist literature and thought. Fourth-born Leah, living across the Bay in Spring Hill, had been devoted to Marietta Johnson and the Organic School, but was now removed from colony matters. She cared for her father at the end of his life; he died at her home. Now she was but three years away from her own, and untimely, death. Arthur

Fairhope—"Spider"—the first boy born in the colony, charmed his wide circle of friends, young and old, with his zest for life. He grew up more attached to his mother than to his father, became the most playful of the five, and seemed to carry little, if any, of the reformist zeal that had animated Fairhope's founding.

However different their personalities and the ways in which they related to their heritage, the five siblings were tightly bound to each other by their affections and loyalty. I once asked my father about the effects of the different ways in which they had absorbed, or not absorbed, their commitment to their father's vision. He looked a little surprised at my suggestion that this had somehow diminished their strong, abiding bonds. Of the five, Dad and Uncle Spider contrasted most strikingly yet I sometimes think their bond was the tightest. I probably did not realize this at the time my father offered to speak to his brother in my behalf. I thought then that Uncle Spider would, however reluctantly, do what his brother requested. It would have been a gentle request, probably citing their father's belief in free and open discussion. It would not have been put in terms of a favor to me. Special privilege, Dad had said so many times, extended least of all to members of our family.

We sat in his office a little longer, mostly in silence. Finally, I said no, don't take it to Uncle Spider. I cannot now summon up the feelings that guided me. I only remember that I was sure of my decision and that I never regretted it.

Chapter Four

DECISION MAKING

T here was a small stir of gossip about Mary and me during my week in Frogmore. Speculation by her aunt and cousins increased considerably when Mary set off a few weeks later to visit me in Fairhope. I met her in our Chevrolet sedan, now nine years old, at the Mobile train station. As we drove across the causeway, the bay opening up before us on our right, I held my breath waiting for her reaction. She showed little evidence of the thrill I had hoped for but it wasn't long before I would see it. In the days that followed we did a lot of sailing, in a Fish-class boat, a twenty-one foot keel-bottomed gaff-rigged sloop. She soon felt the magic, especially on those evenings when we returned to harbor with the sun setting behind us. Frogmore had its hundred acres and bits of tidal rivers for swimming. I had my bay, thirty miles long and ten miles across. The Gulf waters and beaches also captivated her, as did the family picnics there. Devil's Hole, however, offered a unique kind of enchantment. Upstream from Fly Creek, it was an opening with deep, clear, fresh water, a sand beach, and a surround of woods. It was destined for development and consequent desecration, but in those days it was still a seductive hideaway, stories abounding of the trysts it had accommodated, its unreachable bottom, and the awful tragedy of the Schuyler boy who died on that bottom with his homemade diving helmet still fixed to his head.

With only two bedrooms in our small home, we could not have Mary stay with us. My mother arranged for her to sleep at my cousin Joy's home, a short distance away. It seemed natural and easy to me, and Joy's screen

Fairhope beach, summer 1951.

porch provided a wonderful place for our evenings, but Mom, quite without my awareness, struggled with feelings of inadequacy. Mary would tell me the story, many years later, of how surprised she was at the very modest first-night dinner we had and how Marge (the name by which Mary and, later, our children knew her) had told her that she wept for not being able to afford something better. I think she came to feel easier soon, I hope aware of how much she did have to offer with her upbeat personality, her gift for arranging outings, and Mary's obvious affection for and admiration of her. My father, usually the reserved and correct one, gave her a bit of a shock one warm day. Sitting on the front porch after lunch, Mary remarked on how tired she was. "It must be the hot sun," she said. To which my father replied, "Not my hot son, I trust."

I

During Mary's week with me we worked together on the ill-fated editorial on the local pacifists and their critics while we also carried on with our discussions of her family history. While her grandfather Macdonald expanded his business and earned a reputation for benevolence and fair dealing among the blacks on the island, his wife, also a Philadelphian, struck off in a different direction, establishing a tradition for interracial comity that was passed on to the female descendants of the Macdonalds. Their work centered in the Penn School, established by Philadelphia Quakers in the early years of the Civil War after the exodus of most of St. Helena Island's whites. My future colleague and treasured friend, Willie Lee Rose, later described the interplay of the sea island blacks and their missionary tutors in her lyrical book *Rehearsal for Reconstruction: The Port Royal Experiment*.

Mary's mother, Elizabeth, and her sister Argie were schooled by their mother in the reformist ethic of the Penn School. By the early 1920s, when Elizabeth was working as the school's secretary, Booker T. Washington's program of industrial education was much in vogue and firmly rooted in Penn's mission. Meanwhile, in England, young Edward Francis Wilkinson was readying to sail to Nigeria to become an educational missionary. His work with the Africans would be more likely to succeed, his sponsors believed, if he were to acquaint himself with the theory and practice of industrial education. Thus, he came to the American South to visit the major centers—Hampton Institute in Virginia, Penn School in South Carolina, and Tuskegee Institute in Alabama.

On exotic St. Helena he met and fell in love with the beautiful and sensitive Penn School secretary. His early pursuit of her took him on foot over three miles of sandy roads and paths to Frogmore Manor. Much to his surprise and disappointment, he was not offered afternoon tea. He must have put the oversight down to the peculiarities of colonial culture but, whatever he thought, his ardor was not dampened. Before he set off for Tuskegee he proposed marriage. Elizabeth Macdonald would later confide to Mary that, while she liked and admired the tall, handsome Englishman, and felt a strong kinship in their religious beliefs, she did not love him. Her diary, on the other hand, speaks of blossoming love. In any case, she was strongly tempted by his offer of marriage and arrangements were made for her to sail to England to meet Ted's family. Little time passed before she wrote home to Frogmore to say that she had decided to accept his proposal.

The life ahead, as she envisioned it, would take her to Africa to be involved without reservation in fulfilling religious and educational work far from the ubiquitous racism of her native South Carolina. As early as 1913, when she was twelve years old, the news of a murder on the island of a white man by a black man led her to write in her diary that "They will probably hang him as he is a negro, and especially, as he shot a white man. It is terrible. It isn't right that negroes should be treated worse than white men. God help his wife." A month later, almost retching over the news of a lynching, she wrote of the "shame of the South." Adding to the shame was the refusal of South Carolina's governor (the notorious racist Coleman Blease) even to meet with other Southern governors to "find a cure for this terrible thing." Her later diaries, which I was eventually to read, included additional angst over lynchings and other features of her state's white supremacy culture. An extraordinarily sensitive soul, unprepared by temperament and spirit to go against those of her kith and kin who either condoned or accommodated themselves to what she could not abide, she accepted the offer of marriage in part as an escape from a world that tormented her. She would always return to it, gallantly balancing the joys of people and place against the pains of complacency and complicity.

Elizabeth and Ted divided their time between Nigeria and England, visiting Frogmore from time to time. She came home from Africa in 1926 to give birth to Clare and again in 1929 for Mary's birth, both girls to be left, for most of their early childhood, with their Frogmore family. There Mary and Clare found their second home, sharing it with their cousins, their mother's sister, Argie, her husband, Ed, and Bamba, the matriarch of the family. Two received family truths were that white children (for health reasons) should not be taken to live in Africa and that Frogmore was such an idyllic home that no one should want to live anywhere else. Elizabeth, who could not let herself live there, was nonetheless captured by the family myth, making it easier for her to accept separation from her children. Many years later Mary would write that her mother doubtless felt the experience of leaving her children "wrenching," but that "she had such faith in her mother and her sister" that she felt "we were very well off." Frogmore, to her, was a "paradise for children." It did not become one for Mary.

In 1933, Elizabeth and Ted defied the rule that barred white children from Africa, bringing Mary, age four, and Clare, age seven, to live with them in Lagos for a few months. That brief sojourn was followed by the family's return to England. For the last half of the 1930s, both girls lived with their parents, first in London and then in the small village of Eversden, near Cambridge, where their father, by then an ordained minister, had the charge of two churches. Six decades later I visited the village and the larger of the two churches. There I found my father-in-law's name, inscribed along with those of the other rectors going back to the early sixteenth century.

Mary remembers her London years with mixed feelings. School was unpleasant, requiring, among other things, uniforms she disliked. She recalls the many times she heated the thermometer to fake the fever that would let her plead illness and stay at home. On those warmly remembered days she could eat poached eggs on toast and be read to by her mother. Her Cambridgeshire years were happy ones. Always emotionally close to her mother, she now had her physical presence as well. The large rectory was without electricity but had crannies to explore, a rooftop hideaway, and a giant yew tree for sliding down. And all within the framework of a strong, devoted family, a father and mother both revered in the community, and the kind of security she had never known before. Mary later wrote of the Eversden years as her "lost utopia," much as Frogmore had been her mother's. She was never to experience that security again as a child.

In the summer of 1939 the family sailed to America to visit Frogmore. Return passage was booked for what turned out to be the very eve of the German invasion of Poland and the beginning of the Second World War. Persuaded—or perhaps persuading themselves—that it would be a short war, Ted and Elizabeth decided to leave the girls with their family in Frogmore. Elizabeth knew the pain such a decision would cause her, but she shared her husband's belief that leaving the girls behind was wise. Safety was a concern— a needless one as it turned out—and, by that time, both she and Ted were accustomed to accepting the necessity of living without their children. It would be five-and-a-half years before she saw her daughters again.

Those were difficult years for Mary. It is hard to remember now how much detail she revealed to me in that summer of 1951 and how much I was to learn later, of how she never felt truly accepted at Frogmore, never really being a Frogmore child, and how uneasy she felt in the several schools she attended—the Beaufort public school and the Ashley Hall and Hannah Moore boarding schools for girls. Her happiest time was a year and a half living with her Uncle Jack and his wife, Ruth, in Charleston. Ruth had no children and Jack's son (by his first wife), Ross Macdonald, was away at Williams College. Mary became Ruth's adored surrogate daughter. She was admired, loved, and accepted as she was. Mary would later write that "Ruth catered to my likes in food, boosted my ego, bought me clothes and asked me what I wanted for Christmas (unheard of!)."

After the war, reunited with her family in England, now in Sudbury, Mary attended a village state school for a year, then was sent away once more, this time to Leamington Spa to be prepared by a tutor for the Oxford and Cambridge entrance examinations. For two years she slogged away at Shakespeare and Chaucer and did well enough on the written exams to be invited to the two universities for interviews, an encouraging accomplishment. Among the memories of her interlocutors was the query, "Miss Wilkinson, you were 'educated' in America?" a question put to stress the improbability of such a likelihood. No offers of admission came, her parents readied to return to Nigeria, and her cousin Ross Macdonald, Jack's son, then a Rhodes scholar, told her Oxford was not all it was said to be. He suggested that she return to America to attend Swarthmore. Its honors program, he said, was modeled on the Oxford plan. And so she did, and so we met, even if three semesters intervened before our dance at the Phi Delt house and our dropping-of-the-penny meeting in the library.

Mary unfolded a little of this history to me in the spring of our junior year and added more during our time together in Frogmore and Fairhope. It would be much later before I came to realize, indeed, before she came to realize, how badly she had been damaged by her parents' abandonment of her and the insecurity of not being a Frogmore child. For both of us, however, that summer of 1951 was the time for discovery of each other and the unfolding of our love. There is no other time in life quite like it.

We did have our amusing differences. I had never dated anyone who had failed to be fascinated by my Fairhope history, the uniqueness and idealism of both the colonists and the Organic School. Mary was the first girlfriend who thought her heritage—Penn School, Africa, missionary work—was as interesting and important as mine. We even got to the point where we argued gently over whose beach was superior, her brown sand on Hunting Island or my white sand at Gulf Shores. We haven't resolved that difference of opinion but we are equally rankled by the march of free-market commercialization that eventually desecrated my white-sand beaches. Hunting Island, fortunately, became a state park. We could have used some of that government intervention at Gulf Shores.

At a more serious level, our contrasting heritages raised differences over how to go about creating a better world. We both came from cultures committed to playing some role, however small, in righting the world's wrongs. We both felt lives shaped by those commitments were the only worthwhile ones for us. But how to live them? Religious skeptic that I was, I believed that structural changes in society were the essentials. My Fairhope upbringing had taught me that a genuine democracy could not exist without an economic system that diminished poverty, narrowed the gap between rich and poor, enhanced opportunity and creativity, and simultaneously encouraged individuality and a cooperative spirit. An equally firm article of my faith was that a rigid, goal-oriented educational system that worked to socialize students, fitting them into the existing social and economic order, had to be replaced by a radically different one that diminished competitiveness and enhanced individual development, providing a lived experience of democracy and a vision of a different and better social order.

Mary's mind was and is more subtle than mine. She did not draw firm lines between presumed rival views, at least not as I did. Still, like me, she was deeply influenced by her parents, whom she loved and admired despite the sadness their abandonment of her had induced and the price she paid for it. As Christian missionaries they had the same confidence in their approach to human betterment that my grandfather and father had for theirs. Their means to that end, however, seemed to me to be fatally flawed. I had inherited, perhaps more from my mother than my father, a view of missionaries as meddlers. More to the point, Mary's heritage and mine conflicted over whether to bring about constructive social change through individual conversion, principally to Christianity, or as a result of broad changes in the social structure that would cause people to behave differently and better. We debated our differences gently during our courtship and early married years, often with an openness that actually drew our rival views, and us, closer together.

On matters of race we may have had slight differences, but we came to them out of a common wish to confront the white supremacy values and institutions that dominated our native South. In 1951, when we met, it was clear to me, and I think to Mary as well, that a formidable storm of protest for equality was brewing. School desegregation litigation was lumbering along; voting rights demands, and some increase in registration, had followed the outlawing of the white primary in 1944; and the post-war era seemed ripe with possibilities for real structural change in the South. We could not have foreseen the civil rights movement as it was to unfold in the decade after the *Brown* decision, the Emmet Till lynching, and the Montgomery bus boycott, but we were agreed that we wanted to be a part of whatever struggle was to come. That shared agreement would shape our selection of a career for me.

Before I returned to Swarthmore I persuaded my mother to let me have a beautiful opal that had been in her father's tie clasp. I remembered, from some remark Mary had dropped, that opals were her favorite stone. My mother agreed to let me have it, but only if I would promise that, should Mary and I not get married, I would manage to return it to her. I was full of confidence. She need not worry about that I assured her. And so I asked Margaret Biggar, my old silversmith teacher, to make a ring which we designed together.

I don't remember whether it was lack of that confidence I had boasted of, but as soon as we returned to college, I gave the ring to Mary, absent a discussion of marriage. It was a warm afternoon on the lawn at the home of older friends in Philadelphia. We were alone. There was no proposal. But the kiss of acceptance suggested that, when it should come, there was every chance it would be accepted. A few weeks would pass before I formally proposed. We were in the basement of the Phi Delt house. Mary was sitting on the pool table. She said yes. That week I failed to write the paper for Larry Lafore's Modern European history seminar. I told him why. His eyes twinkled as he admonished me: "Well, Paul, that's all right this time; but don't let it happen again."

II

As we began to discuss career choices, thoughts of returning to Fairhope did not disappear but they faded steadily. My father, amazing man that he was, never pressured me to succeed him. My mother had already nudged me toward a career in the larger world. Fairhope, she told me, wistfully at times, was no longer the beacon of reform my grandfather had designed and my father had worked so hard to make a reality. Better for me, she said, to find a career elsewhere. I understood her meaning—that I should find work that would allow me to take the Fairhope idea and the spirit animating it with me.

It is revealing of the times, and no small measure of embarrassment, to recall the context within which our career decisions took place. Mary's parents wished for her to postpone marriage so that she might work for a year in Africa; she herself had often thought that a good idea. In response to her letter announcing our engagement, her parents wrote asking that the wedding be postponed. We both wrote, tactfully I think, to reject that idea. The conversations that then took place all focused on what career I might have. We never discussed a career or program of post-baccalaureate study for Mary. Gareth, our incredulous youngest, once asked his mother, "Mommy, didn't *you* ever want to have a career of your own?"

Looking for some kind of career in the South, one that would give me entry into the coming Southern struggle, I applied for a fellowship in public administration that would take me to three Southern universities. Some of our older friends suggested law school for me, to be followed by a career in politics, a career for which they said I had a good combination of flair and conscience. Mary found the prospect of politics distasteful and, however fulfilling I might find it, I knew I could not hold significant public office in Alabama or, for that matter, in any Southern state. I doubt that there were then, in the early 1950s, a half-dozen white integrationists holding any significant elective Southern public office; and known atheists like me had always been forbidden to hold positions of political leadership.

So resistant to reason was this religio-racist tradition that almost twenty years would pass after our wedding before racial liberals like Linwood Holton of Virginia, Jimmy Carter of Georgia, Reuben Askew of Florida, and a few others were elected governors of Southern states. Before them, in 1966, Richmond Flowers—a white Alabamian who made me proud—campaigned for the governorship of our home state with the support of Martin King. More than once Flowers proclaimed "I do not believe that the Negro is inferior." He lost badly to George Wallace's wife, Lurleen. His political career was smashed. I have yet to hear of a single white Southerner known to possess my deadly duo of beliefs being elected to a state legislature, governorship, or the Congress of the United States. (California Congressman Pete Stark was elected more than thirty years before his atheism was revealed in 2007. He remains the only declared atheist to have served in the United States Congress.)

A more attractive prospect, one that appealed to both of us, was a career teaching Southern history in a Southern university. I could hold up a mirror to my Southern students, leading them to see the heavy material and moral costs of the culture of white supremacy. To that end, I applied to several universities for graduate study. Our principal immediate focus, however, was on a year's study abroad. Mary was eager for me to spend a season in England, to come to know the country that was her other home. Swarthmore was a prolific supplier of Rhodes scholarship winners, but applicants for that prestigious appointment could not be married or plan to be married before entering Oxford. Blocked there, I applied for a Fulbright, asking to study the welfare dimensions of the English democratic socialist state.

Sometime later I received a letter from the Institute of International Education informing me that, for the first time, Fulbright scholarships were to be awarded for study in Denmark. For the inaugural year applications were to be by invitation only. They noted that I was interested in the welfare state and, well, Denmark had one of those, too; might I be interested in studying it? Assured that I would remain in the English competition, Mary and I drafted an application for study in Denmark. I did not think, as I was later jokingly to recount this episode, that Denmark was the capital of Sweden, but I knew precious little about the country. I did learn from my father that there was a vibrant Georgist movement there with twelve members of their Justice Party in the 151-person Folketing, the lower house of Parliament. That was a special attraction. My grandfather had taken his only trip abroad in 1926 to attend an international conference of Georgists in Copenhagen; I expected we would come across several Danes who had met and admired him.

I was eliminated from the English competition before long and, in late May, I received word of my success in the Danish. As soon as the good Fulbright news arrived I set aside plans for graduate school, thanking the institutions that had offered me admission. Denmark was not England, but it was intriguing and we would at least be able to spend some time in Mary's other country. There would be time in the next year to settle on a graduate school. With our near-term future thus finally fixed we firmed up plans for a late June wedding in Beaufort, a short honeymoon on Ocracoke Island, a sea voyage to England to spend a couple of weeks on the south coast with Mary's parents, and then the journey to Copenhagen in late July.

III

We were married in a famous two hundred and twenty-year-old Episcopal church in Beaufort, the regular place of worship of the Frogmore family. Spacious and elegant, it had retained the balcony seats once reserved for the slaves, an uncomfortable reminder of a shameful past. Nor was the Christian wedding ceremony that would take place in it something I would have chosen. I was a nonbeliever and sometimes I thought of myself as a kind of anarchist as well, or at least skeptical of state power over personal decisions. I once said to Mary, after our engagement was fixed, that since neither the church nor the state had authority over our relationship perhaps we could just live together without either civil or religious sanction. That, I was firmly told, was not an option. I immediately rose above principle to agree to a church wedding.

Another test of principle confronted me the evening before the wedding. Mary's father, who would join the local minister in performing the ceremony, went over the service with me. When we got to the part where I would have to affirm marriage in the name of the father, the son, and the holy ghost my face must have betrayed my trapped feeling. "All three?" I weakly asked. "Well, son," Ted replied, "it has been in the prayer book a long time." There was no way out, I knew, so we went quietly through the rest of the service—who would say what to whom and when.

The next day we had a break in the weather. The temperature, which had been above 110 for several days, dropped to 100. The ladies of the family had been able to find almost no surviving flowers with which to decorate the church. Mary, whose feet had begun to swell, sought relief at the home of a friend, a writer, just the kind of person who would own the only air conditioner in Beaufort. Dressing there, she arrived at the church with feet comfortably ensconced in her wedding shoes and perspiration held in abeyance, at least for the moment. By the time I was on my knees, steeled to deliver my tripartite affirmation, my newly purchased white Palm Beach suit was beginning to feel clammy. As the rivulets of sweat rolled down my face, I listened to my elegant soon-to-be father-in-law say "repeat after me," and then "in the name of" and—after a bit of a pause—"God." Period. I think he saw my grateful smile. Mary thanked him later for changing the unchangeable. He smiled and explained "this was not the time to give Paul a lesson in the trinity." He, too, rose above principle. I loved him for it.

He never did give me that lesson but, as we were to learn later, both he and Elizabeth were confident that in time I would come to abandon my skeptical ways. One might have thought that a minister and his wife, facing the prospect of their daughter falling into the clutches of a nonbeliever, would have approached the union with apprehension. From all we know, they did not. Mary believes their deep confidence in their own religion did not admit of doubts coming their way. We learned later that my mother, in contrast, firm though she was in her religious skepticism, did harbor doubts, worrying that I might go over to the other side. She adored Mary from the start and perhaps thought because I was marrying such a special person I was likely to adopt all of her beliefs and views. Dad, never much given to anxiety, celebrated my good fortune, wrote enthusiastically about his own in garnering a daughter such as Mary, and relaxed in the confidence that our love was what mattered. Of course he was right.

After a small, informal reception at Frogmore, the men having shed their jackets, we set off for Charleston and the Fort Sumter hotel where we would spend our first night. Mary's sister Clare and her husband, Janos, took us there, along with the bottle of warm champagne Argie had forgotten to chill and serve at the reception. Once in our room, the four of us drank it—on ice, the first and last time I have had champagne on the rocks. The next day we traveled by bus and a hired fishing boat to Ocracoke and the Wahab Village Inn. Fleas joined us in our bed but we managed to send them elsewhere eventually. Two youngsters we met, who had never been off the island, kindly introduced us to their Uncle Pres who rented his small sailboat to us. Once out of the harbor I found the currents so strong I could not sail back in. Having previously proven my sailing prowess to Mary, I found it easier to live through the humiliation of eventually beaching the boat and pulling it back into the harbor. We remained landlubbers after this unhappy adventure, roaming the miles of unspoiled beaches and swimming in the clear Atlantic Ocean waters. Ocracoke was a jewel of beauty and simplicity, free of the rapacious march of condo builders that would later desecrate most of our country's coastline. We returned there to celebrate our twenty-fifth wedding anniversary and again twenty-five years later to scout it for a fiftieth anniversary celebration.

We left the south part of the island on a mail truck bound for the Cape Hatteras ferry and then boarded a bus to Washington. We started reading aloud George Orwell's *1984* to each other, perhaps a strange selection for a honeymoon, a book about the insidious spread and dehumanizing effects of totalitarianism. Overhearing us in his seat behind us, a man who identified himself as a State Department employee whispered something like "this is not about the future, about 1984; it's about right now in Washington, D.C." While most Americans associated totalitarianism with fascism or communism, and certainly always something foreign, our state department friend urged us to look within, especially at the frightening rise of what he called the "totalitarian" impulses of the House Un-American Activities Committee, and the rise to power of Joseph McCarthy, the communist-hunting junior senator from Wisconsin, and the movement named after him. It was a dark time in our nation's history. There had been many before; there would be others in the future.

Neither dark times nor anxious thoughts had a chance of lingering, however, not against the spirit of adventure and discovery we carried within. We stopped briefly in Washington to visit Shaw, a mother of two with a third on the way. After a couple of days in New York, where we saw Mary Martin sing her way brilliantly through *South Pacific*, we boarded the French liner *Liberté* bound for Liverpool. I had thrilled crossing the Pacific Ocean in a troop ship with my army comrades in 1947, but this voyage across the Atlantic, with a cabin to share with my bride and French chefs to prepare seven-course meals, was from another world. At the dining tables I met artichokes for the first time. It was love at first taste. Bottles of red and white wine on the table for both lunch and dinner started me on my life as an oenophile.

We had a view of the English Channel from Mary's parents' Sussex seaside home in St. Leonards and in our two weeks' residence there we took an all-afternoon walk along cliffs I found breathtaking, more beautiful than the movies of them I had seen. At some points they were more than three times the height of our Sea Cliff, which I had often told strangers was the highest point on the American coast between Maine and Texas. We picnicked in the lush countryside, under an oak tree behind an eleventh-century abbey; journeyed to London to arrange details for our travel to Denmark; and visited Cambridge where Ted reminisced as he showed us about Queens, his college. I could sense his pride in the place and understand why he wanted Mary to be a student there, or at Oxford. By this time I called Ted "Father" and Elizabeth "Mother," the form of address that had become common for some of their admiring friends as well as their daughters. To my parents, I wrote that all the people I had met—"bobbies, train conductors, shopkeepers, and people in the street"—were "friendly and cordial, thus contradicting the impression I had brought with me of English reserve."

IV

Soon we were off on our twenty-four hour journey from London to Copenhagen, via boat train to Oostend, Belgium, and rail from there to the city that would become our new, and magical, home. Gazing out the window as we passed from Germany into Denmark, we joked that all the cows we saw in the Jutland countryside were blond, like the Danes who would soon be our neighbors. Not all of them were, of course. Among the many exceptions was the dashingly handsome and charming Knud Jacobsson in whose apartment the Fulbright authorities had arranged for us to live. A once-married bachelor, Knud greeted us on the evening of our arrival with coffee freshly brewed in his glass Cona pot accompanied by small glasses of Cherry Heering, the Danish liqueur of choice. The room glowed and so did we.

Like most Danes who were to become our friends, Knud spoke fluent English, with an occasional idiomatic peculiarity that added to his charm. We had a sitting room and a bedroom to ourselves, sharing the bath and kitchen with Knud. The kitchen was down a long and dark hallway. Knud and his friend Paul Winning would later tell us how important that hallway had been to them during the war when their country was occupied by the Germans. Both men ferried Jews across the Øresund from Copenhagen to the Swedish city of Malmö. Sometimes the Nazis, suspecting that Jews were being hidden in Knud's kitchen, would come storming into the apartment. But the prospect of walking down the long, dark corridor seemed to frighten them. Jews hidden there remained safely undiscovered.

Some of our Danish friends apologized, or expressed guilt feelings, because Denmark had surrendered without resistance to the German invaders. Norway, they ruefully observed, had no more chance of defeating the Germans than they did, but Norway put up a fight. It was, they seemed to be saying, the honorable thing to do. We pointed out that the resistance was crushed the day after it started and that more than a thousand Norwegians were killed. Danish resistance would have similarly resulted in needless loss of life. Dad wrote to say what the Danes did was exactly right and that no apologies should be made. Resistance for the sake of resistance, he wrote, "could have accomplished nothing other than to have brought about a scorched earth retaliation."

Whenever the subject of resistance, and its absence, came up we countered that everyone had to admire Danish aid to the Jews along with the wondrous sense of humor that nettled the occupiers. On one occasion, during the battle of Britain, a group of Nazis was taken to view a recently discovered Viking ship. "It may interest you to know," one of the Danish guides remarked, "that we conquered England in a boat like this." On another occasion, Copenhagen's renowned bookseller, Ejnar Muksgaard, filled his store windows with English language books, accompanied by notices that read "Prepare for the future; learn English." Ordered to replace the English books with German ones, Muksgaard did. The next week the Nazis found the windows filled with German books, along with notices that read "Learn German—while there's still time."

Our first major Danish adventure was a trip to Odense, the home city of H. C. Andersen and, more importantly for us, the venue for the 1952 international conference on land value taxation and free trade. Many of the world's leading Georgists were present. I knew a few personally and had heard of others. One I did not know told me of shipboard conversations he had had with my grandfather when they were en route to the 1926 Copenhagen conference. Another recalled both Grandfather and Grandmother as guests of his parents during the conference. Several cordial invitations came our way. Still, I was hardly prepared for our reception. "From the moment we set foot on Conference grounds until we left," I wrote to my parents, "we were royally treated." Mary still sometimes teasingly recalls the remark of the delegate who announced that I was an "aristocrat of the movement," being a Gaston from Fairhope, the bearer of "a name to conjure with."

Once my presence became known to the organizers the agenda was changed so that I might speak about Fairhope. My remarks and the questions and answers that followed took up an hour and a half and made me well enough known to the leaders of the Justice Party and other Copenhagen Georgists so that our social schedule would be active. We met Viggo Starcke, leader of the party who would become premier in 1957, heading a coalition government. K .J. Kristensen, a Georgist but a member of the Radical-Venstre party and an opponent of NATO, was the government official in charge of calculating land values. He was especially friendly and would later host dinner parties for us and his large and interesting family as well as offer help with my thesis on the collection of economic rent in Denmark. Knud Tholstrup, a charmer and another member of the Parliament who would succeed Starcke as head of the Justice Party, gave us a ride back to Copenhagen in his new Ford. He regaled us with stories of Danish life, the most memorable of which was his explanation that since Denmark had a state church Danes were not obliged to pay any attention to religion.

"I quite enjoyed receiving so much adulation," I wrote to my parents about the conference. I confessed, however, that "I sympathize very strongly with your feeling, Dad, that most of the time at conferences like this is spent in patting each other on the back." I doubted that I had made much contribution to the understanding of real problems and I regretted that no "plans for action" were developed. I was no longer a literal singletaxer nor was I persuaded of Fairhope's power to change the world by its example. But the letters I wrote after the conference, and others at this time, remind me how deeply the essence of both the doctrine and the example resonated within me. I remained a Fairhoper.

For a month before my formal course work began our group of Fulbrighters, Mary included, had daily language lessons and frequent guided tours of the city and its environs. Copenhagen was stunningly beautiful in that bright summer month, its many lakes and waterways glistening, its famous Little Mermaid statue beguiling, its historic castles imposing but never forbidding, its spacious city center clean, orderly, and inviting. After our tour of the slums, flower pots in all the windows, Mary and I were tempted to ask, "but where are the real slums?" It may be that our guide could sense our puzzlement so he explained that this was the worst there was. Score one for the democratic welfare state, I thought: these streets, apartments, and homes would never qualify as slums in my home country. And our slums would have shocked Danes right down to their toes.

Tivoli Gardens, which we explored on our own and to which we would return many times over the next nine months, was in the heart of the city. It had been on the same fifteen acres since its construction in 1843. It was called an amusement park, but to an American ruefully accustomed to hot dogs, cotton candy, noisy barkers, ball throwing, rifle shooting, side shows, daring rides, and litter, Tivoli had to be seen as from a different culture altogether. Its illuminated ponds, profusion of flowers and walking paths, hanging Japanese lanterns, Chinese pagodas, twenty-one restaurants reflective of many national styles, concert pavilions, carousels, and numerous children's rides were all imaginatively constructed to please the senses and stretch the mind with wonder. Mary constantly reveled in the good taste she found in all its remarkable variety. And there was no litter.

The good taste of Tivoli was evident to us in much of Danish culture. Our favorite store, for example, was Den Permanente, The Permanent, so called because it had a permanent exhibition of Danish art and crafts for sale. To wander through it was like exploring a modern museum where you could both touch and buy. We were particularly drawn to the dozens of golden coin-like cutouts hanging from high ceilings, their light clanging noises echoing throughout the store. We took several strings home to hang them, and their many successors we made, in our living room every Christmas since. Danish craftsmanship was at a peak in the early 1950s. We could admire and lust after the furniture, but lacked the means and shipping to buy it. Silver was different. We had asked our family and friends to give us as wedding presents money so that we might buy our silver in Denmark. The search for the perfect artist and design took us to the works of the country's leading silversmiths. When we found A. Michelsen's "Ida" pattern it was love at first glance. We looked no further. The simplicity, elegance, and balance of all the pieces and the gently curved knife handles seduced us immediately. For more than forty years we never ceased to thrill when we laid the table with our silver. When we lost the entire collection to professional thieves who swept through Charlottesville we went into mourning. A treasured companion had been snatched from us.

Copenhagen for us was a cornucopia of pleasures. The Fulbrighters became good and interesting friends; our Georgist acquaintances entertained us well and brought us into contact with Danes of our own age; Knud found bicycles for us that we rode nearly everywhere; and we reveled in strolls through Strøget, the famous shopping street, and boat rides through the harbors and around the city. The Royal Danish Ballet, featuring Inge

Sand and Erik Bruhn, became a special treat. We knew Erik Bruhn was sensational, but we were too untutored to know that he was the world's premier male dancer of the 1950s. Nor did we know that he and Inge Sand were just my age. She had a head-dipping movement that reminded me of a fawn. I've never forgotten it. I had been to a ballet only once; now it was to become a serious part of our lives, and with one of the world's great troupes. We would often have a supper of smørrebrød at the Café à Porta (warming ourselves in the winter months with braziers and blankets) before walking across the square for the evening performances and back for a glass of Cherry Heering afterwards.

Work at the university began about the first of September. I continued with daily language classes so that, by Christmas, I could manage research in Danish sources. Nearly all of our friends and many of the shopkeepers we met spoke English so I had to work at finding people with whom to speak Danish. Mary had the same problem, changing green grocers three times before she found a non-English speaking clerk. Her progress went more slowly than mine, partly because she got a job teaching English in the Berlitz school. She was featured there as the teacher of Amerikansk, a lure for Danes planning to come to the States to study supermarkets. I eventually became fluent enough to carry on simple conversations. Just before Christmas I went to a youth rally where spokesmen for the three left-leaning parties were debating compulsory military service. Overcoming anxiety I managed Danish well enough to tell the Communist leader that he erred in saying compulsory military service in the United States was for three years. He seemed surprised that there was an American in the audience to challenge him and I was surprised (and pleased) that I could actually make the point I wanted to express.

Mary's job added handsomely to our income as did a couple of editing assignments she had before the Berlitz position opened. One of our Danish friends told us that Mary's Berlitz salary and my Fulbright fellowship put us in the top 10 percent of Danish income earners. I never believed that but we never felt financially pinched. And we were flush enough to go to Lillehammer, Norway, over the Christmas holidays. We stayed in a youth hostel whose Norwegian warden, as he was called, had translated Shakespeare into Swedish; been a rum runner off the Texas coast in the 1920s; played a guitar and sang folk songs in several languages; and cooked reindeer for our Christmas dinner. We rented boots, poles, and skis for four dollars for the week and somehow managed to navigate on them, neither of us having skied before. When the Winter Olympics came to Lillehammer decades later we doubted that any of the contestants or visitors could have experienced the joy we knew on those snow-covered mountains and in the sleepy village where, it seemed, all transportation was by sled or ski. We have never since experienced the same mixture of beauty and quiet.

My courses in the Danish Graduate School for Foreign Students were populated exclusively by American Fulbrighters and the lectures were in English. Demands were light and interest high. John Danstrup, our lecturer in Danish history and politics, was in his early thirties. He spoke English like an Englishman. We read his short history of Denmark and enjoyed lunches with him after the Monday lectures. In the fall semester we formed what we called a Danes for Stevenson luncheon group. We read Adlai Stevenson's speeches in the New York *Times;* they seduced us into thinking perhaps he would defeat the less literate and less liberal war hero, General Eisenhower. Professor Danstrup shared our hopes but was not surprised by the outcome. My father, who had earlier written to say of the Republicans that they were "against sin and for winning the November election" was also disappointed but not surprised. I wrote to him afterward to say that Stevenson won my heart by discussing issues, not evading them, and I was especially pleased by his forthright stand on civil rights. Joe McCarthy's slanders, I wrote, were one more ominous sign of the increasingly popular low road adopted by his followers in the Republican party.

Apart from classes and our lunches with him, we enjoyed other social occasions with Professor Danstrup, and with his wife as well on one occasion. Some of the Danish students I came to know were annoyed by the ease and frequency of our social relations with our professor. Such relations, they explained to me, did not exist between professor and student in Denmark. I suppose we were perceived as brash Americans, but from my Organic School-Swarthmore College background my reaction was to tell them they ought to ask their professors out to lunch. I doubt that they ever did. Some years after we left, Danstrup became Denmark's leading television political commentator.

Our other courses—European social problems, politics, and geography—were less interesting than Danstrup's history course, but we learned from all and, in my cynical moods, I often described our program of study as a high-class tourist's introduction to Denmark. We could go to dinner parties and other social events well-informed on the country's history and current politics, which newspapers supported which parties, and what each party stood for. The closest thing I had to a serious scholarly endeavor was the thesis I wrote under the direction of Bjarke Fog, an economist at one of the technical schools. My topic was the Georgist movement in Denmark, focusing primarily on how land value was calculated and economic rent collected and what difference it made to political and economic life in the country. I am embarrassed to report that I cannot remember what conclusions I reached. I once looked up a crucial point in the thesis, a copy of which I saved for many years, only to find that the information I was searching for appeared in a quotation—in Danish. I had to get out the dictionary to translate it.

The letters I exchanged with my father, which were frequent and long, remind me both of how faithful he remained to the single tax as the necessary fundamental reform and of how I was doubting its sufficiency. I never questioned the need to make land common property by collecting the full economic rent. But the accumulated injustices of modern industrial societies, I wrote, made it necessary to go beyond land-value taxation. The Danish welfare state, of which I wrote approvingly, seemed to help create a society in which the gap between rich and poor was narrow, the middle class was large and thriving, health care and education were both good and universally available, employment opportunities were abundant, and a culture of individualism, creativity, and good taste flourished. In addition, as I learned from Mr. Kristensen, the Georgist state official in charge of the land-value taxation program, the collection of the full economic rent would fall far short of meeting the budgetary needs of the state.

My father wrote to say he was delighted that I had decided to write on Georgism in Denmark because it was "more fundamental than the social welfare schemes that are being tried there." Indeed, the origins of the welfare state, he believed, "may be found in large part in our failure to fully apply the Georgist principle of land value collection." Never a rigid ideologue like those single taxers who scorned all public policies, including the progressive income tax, that deviated from Georgist purity, he saw the Danish public policies, in the existing circumstances, to be of "vital importance." But they were "alleviative measures" while the Georgist principles were "curative measures." Unfortunately, he wrote, "those who have elected to administer to the ills both of the social political body and the human body appear to be more attracted to the alleviative than to the curative measures."

A few years later, as I became involved in the civil rights movement and other struggles for justice in the South, that distinction between what my father called the "alleviative" and the "curative" stuck with me. More than literal Georgism it was the strongest element of my Fairhope inheritance.

V

With the coming of the new year we had decisions to make about graduate school and news to announce to our families. The news was not something we had planned, but we were thrilled to report it: Mary was pregnant. She had written earlier to my parents that we were "thinking seriously of buy-ing a motorcycle to do our traveling" about Europe. Those plans gave way to arrangements to travel by train to Hof, a U.S. army base in Germany, where Dabney was stationed, and to Salzburg, Venice, Florence, the small Swiss village of Carona, and Lausanne before an eight-week residence in the Paris suburb of Neuilly. Mary would then cross the channel to be with her parents for the accouchement (while I traveled with my mother). Soon after the birth I would sail for Chapel Hill and the beginning of my graduate work. I had applied to four universities—Tulane, UNC, Harvard, and the University of Chicago—and was accepted by all. We chose North Carolina because I thought of it as the place where Southern liberals came to study but also, as we used to joke, because we were cold in Copenhagen and Carolina would be warmer than Cambridge or Chicago.

We left Copenhagen in early May after a flurry of good-bye dinners and last visits to our favorite people and places. One sunny afternoon, sitting by a lake, we mused about staying, becoming Danes. Even as we conjured details of what our lives would be like—where we would live; what kind of creative work we would find; how many Danish children we would have—we knew we were spinning fantasies. But it was a good way to say farewell to the real-life Danish existence we were now sadly concluding.

Our pre-Paris travels, however, were full of adventure and discovery. Hof, the Bavarian city on the Saale river where we visited our old schoolmate Dabney, a corporal with a small military intelligence outfit, gave us our first sight of what Winston Churchill called the iron curtain. In this case it was the bridge across the Saale to East Germany. A red line across the middle marked the border between East and West. At the far end of the bridge, I wrote to my parents, there was "an ordinary traffic barrier, a guard post and two East German policemen. It looked so artificial but somehow you didn't feel like crossing!" The windows of many homes we saw in the East German section were boarded up so that their views of the west were blocked. Dabney told us of families split apart, only occasionally catching glimpses of each other from opposite banks of the river. I thought of the book on the shelf of my Fairhope bedroom, *Chain the War Gods*.

Mary liked to travel with a thermos of hot water so that she could make instant coffee when she wanted it. This led to her first sortie into the German language. None of the waiters at our hotel spoke English. We would not see Dabney on the morning of our departure so she asked him how to request a thermos of hot water. She practiced the phrase with him several times and, it seemed to me, a dozen times more just before she fell asleep. Rehearsing it once more in the morning—"*Würden Sie diesem Thermos mit heissem Wasser füllen, bitte?*"—she marched confidently down the stairs to the dining room. There she was greeted by a new waiter. "Good morning, madam," he said, "how may I serve you?" All that work for naught.

Our ' adventures began in the middle of the night. After we eluded aggressive hotel and pension hustlers at the train station we had a stressful trip on a canal boat to the Danish pension where I had booked a room for us. When we arrived a sleepy German told us the Danish proprietor had sold it to him. So much for my hopes of speaking to our innkeeper in his language. Venice spoke to me mostly of what once was its splendor. Its crumbling facades, slimy seaweed on once brilliant marble steps, and general lack of cleanliness contrasted joltingly with the Copenhagen we had come to love. Venice's decay was depressing but we found pleasure in the life without taxis, automobiles, and horns. We were charmed by the Piazza San Marco and drawn to the bustle and lively conversation of the locals and tourists who filled the cafes in the evenings. But we spun no fantasies of living in Venice.

Florence charmed us from the outset. We were without a lodging reservation so, relying on my phrase book, I asked an innkeeper for a *camera matrimoniale,* which I understood to be a room with a double bed. For reasons I never understood, we got a room with six beds and, fortunately, no roommates. We walked miles during our two days there. I have little memory of the many churches and museums we visited, except for the sculpture wing of the Uffizzi, and the enchanting beauty of Botticelli's Venus. A reproduction of that painting has hung in our home for nearly half a century. Most of all, I was struck by the power and grace of Michelangelo's David; it lives in my memory this half-century later.

From Florence we took the train to Lugano, Switzerland, where we were met by Arthur Carnioli, an eccentric craftsman whom we had met on the *Liberté.* He took us to Carona, a mountain village of three hundred people, where he lived and worked. We stayed in a primitive hotel with no running water, wandered the countryside, visited Arthur's workshop, and bought one of his iron sconces. It hangs in our dining room now. After Carona we stopped for an afternoon and night in Lausanne. I wrote later of the lovely lakeshore and the breathtaking views from our small hotel's balcony.

Then Paris for eight glorious weeks. We lived with Madame Pinet and her two adult daughters, Claude and Jacqueline. Mario, who spoke French with his Italian, was a sometime boarder and diner as well. A large, sunny bedroom also served as our sitting and study room. We took two meals a day with the family and spent half the day in our room where Mary tutored me. I would have to pass a French reading examination as part of my Ph.D. requirements, which was one of the reasons we decided to live in Paris. Mary had studied French as a child and minored in French literature at Swarthmore. My perfect tutor. I had begun studying the language during my second semester in Copenhagen, taking a class taught by Hr. Togeby in which I was the only non-Dane. Our textbook was called *Laerbog i Fransk* (literally, learning book in French). Trying to learn French mediated by Danish was an interesting experience but I was woefully unprepared for conversation when I arrived in Paris. I was also mightily frustrated at mealtimes as the Pinet women and Mary carried on animated conversations while I sat mute. Mary says it was the only time in our lives that I suffered in silence while she spoke freely and without interruption. As she ruefully recalls, it didn't last long. With dreadful grammar and wild guesses but a pretty good accent, I soon became an active participant in the table talk.

We quickly fell into a routine of either morning or afternoon study, rest for Mary, study for me, a half day of sightseeing and an occasional evening out. Wandering through the markets we learned of the French enthusiasm for babies and pregnant women. "*Pour le bébé, madame,*" was a common cry of hawkers of vegetables and foods of all sorts. And more than once at a restaurant, where I had asked for a table for two, the correction came immediately: "*mais vous êtes trois.*" In dramatic contrast, when Mary crossed the channel she was amused by the English reserve that kept eyes focused well above the stomach. We were hardly unique in noting the many striking differences between French and English culture but this was the one we fixed on most often. Probably it had to do with the different attitudes toward sex. There were exceptions, of course, as there always are. On the channel crossing Mary was alone, very pregnant and, owing to her swollen fingers, without a wedding band. Half way across she was approached by an Englishwoman who spoke excellent French (not, Mary told me, an English characteristic) and English with a Cockney accent. The stranger offered to look after her in London until after the birth and would have a "position" for her afterwards. With little interest in a bawdyhouse career and with her minister father waiting to meet her, Mary declined the considerate offer.

Soon after arriving in Paris, we took a train south to the nearby small town of Sivry-Courtry. It was there that my cousin Barney, a twenty-year-old P-47 fighter-bomber pilot, had been shot down and killed in August of 1944. The details of his death and exploits came to us slowly, but what I learned was that he had spied a group of German tanks, swooped down over them and knocked out seventeen before he was hit. The next day the Germans retreated from Sivry-Courtry and Barney was hailed as the liberator of the town. Charles de Pange had pulled Barney's body from the downed airplane. He later designed a monument, in the shape of the air-force insignia. I had corresponded with him from Copenhagen and gladly accepted his invitation to visit. Mary and I were surprised to be met at the train station by a dapper young man. Since we knew M. de Pange was a count (my letters were addressed to M. le comte de Pange) we had expected a gentleman with a goatee and a walking stick. In fact, he was only a few years older than we.

With M. de Pange as our host and guide we were taken to the monument in the town center. It stood ten feet high. Fresh flowers were at its base. The inscription read: "*Ici le 26 aôut 1944 le lieutenant Americain Ernest B. Gaston tomba glouriesement pour notre libération.*" (Here on the 26th of August 1944 the American lieutenant Ernest B. Gaston fell gloriously for our liberation.) Inside the school house, which we visited next, we were shown a photograph of Barney, hanging prominently from a classroom wall. We had tea with M. de Pange and his wife Chantal, a young and attractive lawyer, and their two young children.

No daydreams of living in Paris came our way, but we understood why so many American writers, artists, and intellectuals had come there to nourish their creativity. It had much of the magic for which it was famed, but I wondered if the intellectual éclat of the 1920s had not dissipated by the time we arrived. We were never in the right circles to find out. As good tourists, though, we visited Sacre Coeur, Montmartre, Notre Dame, and the Bois de Boulogne and went to the Louvre and other museums; most of all, we enjoyed lunches and occasional dinners in the Latin Quarter where we ratcheted up our wine experiences from the *vin ordinaire* of the Pinet table to what seemed to us then as extraordinary wines like Beaujolais and Mâcon. And, as I wrote to my parents, we took special pleasure in "just walking and watching fascinating people."

During the last week of our stay in Paris my mother joined us. We had worked for months planning a European trip for her. Finally it happened. She had never been outside the United States. At fifty-three, she was more excited than any youngster could have been. She would see the many places and sites she had read or heard about and she brought to her travels a wonderful sense of curiosity and spirit of adventure along with an enviable ability to be at home with almost everyone she met. This was so even when it seemed to me she stepped over the line a bit as in the time when she told the waiter in our Latin Quarter restaurant that a particular dish he brought was prepared differently from the way it was done in the French Quarter. She was an excellent cook and judge of food and New Orleans was her standard. Shouldn't the French know how things were done there? Our young waiter, who probably understood waiter's English only, was—whatever he had understood—totally charmed by my mother, as she was by him.

After Mom's intense week in Paris, she and I left for Heidelberg while Mary, nearly eight months pregnant, took the boat train to Le Havre for the crossing to England. Ed Totten, a Fairhoper and Organic School graduate, lived in Heidelberg with his German wife, Christine. We spent two days with them, then took the train to Mainz and from there a boat ride up the Rhine to Köln. I was stunned by the steep vineyards on either side of the river. I knew almost nothing then about German viticulture but when I later became charmed by the German Riesling, the memory of those steep vineyards reminded me of the hard work that went into producing such light, fragrant, enchanting wines. In Amsterdam we visited friends of other Fairhopers before taking the train to Copenhagen where we stayed in fine hotel rooms in the city center.

It would be hard to know which of us enjoyed Copenhagen more. For Mom it was a thrill to be introduced to the city she had read about so extensively in our letters to her; for me, speaking Danish fluently and knowing the city, it was a joy to be a guide. It was my hometown. I realized how much living there had meant to me and how much I would miss it. We were entertained at tea or dinner by many of our friends, including Knud who was there to show Mom our apartment and give her a glimpse of his charm. We dined at one of Tivoli's restaurants and, one memorable night, at an upscale downtown restaurant where I started up a conversation with the waiter. Mom signaled for him to come over and asked him, "Can you make an American martini?" To which he replied: "Yes, of course; I see madam does not speak so good Danish as her husband." Mom took him by the elbow, smiled broadly, and said, "Young man, your tip has just been doubled."

Among the hundreds of letters that have survived in my parents' attic there is one folder containing those they wrote to each other in that summer of '53. Dad wrote to Mom almost every day that she was gone; she wrote to him about every other day. It was their first separation of any length since the Chicago days.

Our Copenhagen days had to end; we took the train west to Esbjærg and from there a ship across the North Sea to Harwich. Mary's father took Mom on a tour of London, Oxford, and the English countryside on the way to home base in St. Leonards. I arrived to find Mary healthy, larger, and as happy to see me as I was to see her. She told me with amusement that Dr. Theo Goodwin, a shy family friend trained as a missionary doctor in China, had, with some embarrassment, said to her just before I arrived, "You know, Mary, uh, it is unwise now to, uh, have, uh, connections." Theo was the doctor, so we had a connection-less reunion. We did have a lot of sightseeing in nearby villages, picnics on the cliffs, and quiet snuggle times in our bedroom.

Mom had to leave a week before the baby came, arriving right on schedule. The birthing took place at Barchester Towers, a private nursing home in neighboring Hastings, a famous location, I thought, to have on one's birth certificate. We arrived in the middle of the August 30/31 night. I waited downstairs and was constantly tended to by a nurse offering me a cup of tea. "One more cup of tea, love?" After every cup I had to make my way to the loo where I found difficulty pulling the chain properly to effect the necessary flushing. Finally, I heard the cry of arrival and soon Theo came down the stairs to tell me I had a son. But he quickly caused my mood to shift from elation to anxiety. "Paul," he began cautiously, "do you happen to know Mary's blood type?" I did and I told him and followed with "Is there any particular reason you want to know?" She had lost a little blood, he explained, "and we need to top her up a bit." He returned to the birthing room. While waiting for the blood to arrive he felt the need to strike up a conversation with the new mother to pass the time. He began it with a question: "Have you been to church lately, Mary?" Even in her weakened and slightly feverish state, Mary knew Theo well enough to be sure he wasn't suggesting she was about to leave this world without having made adequate spiritual arrangements for the journey.

We named our son Paul Blaise, rejecting our first choice of Sven which we had decided on when we were in Copenhagen. Until the Christmas after his birth, which we spent with my parents in Fairhope, we called him Paul. With all the need to distinguish between little Paul and big Paul, Mom said, quite forcefully, "Why don't you just call him Blaise? I like that name." And so he has been ever since. Dad had frequently told us we should never consider giving our son the name of Cornelius Alonzo, after his paternal grandfather. Once, however, he was Cornelius—when he was a fetus in France. We both remember Madame Pinet tapping Mary on her tummy and inquiring, *"Et comment ça va Cornelius ce matin?"* With all this French background we were thrilled to find that one of the Barchester Towers nurses was a young French woman whose *voilà* every time she gave Mary a shot was a nice touch. She was just my age, had studied briefly as a law student, seemed widely read in French and English literature, and was working her way through Faulkner.

I had one week left to spend with Mary and Paul Blaise before sailing home. I left wonderfully relieved that my wife and son both seemed to be in high spirits and excellent health. I sailed back across the North Sea puffed up with my sense of good fortune. In Copenhagen I boarded the Swedish liner *Stockholm*. On board I found several Scandinavians about my age, including Eric Jensen, a Dane we had befriended in Copenhagen. Most were headed for university study in America. We formed a group for lively evening discussions and I found myself thinking back about what I was taking home with me from my year abroad, pondering what I had learned about Europe and what I had learned in Europe about my own country and about myself.

Of all the places we had been only Copenhagen seemed to have deepened and directed my sense of what I wanted to be about. Venice was in decay; Florence was like a museum; Lausanne was part of a Swiss retreat for rich people; and Paris, as enchanting as it was, seemed wrapped in a history far too complex for me to have unraveled or to have taken inspiration from.

Only Copenhagen seemed vital and flexible enough to address the social justice issues that I was struggling with and the conundrum of the balance between cooperation and individualism; and only Copenhagen helped to modify my thinking about my single-tax heritage. Nowhere in Europe, however, did I find guidance on the specific challenge I hoped soon to undertake, the coming struggle in the South over its history and practice of white supremacy.

My shipmates were eager to discuss American politics, especially the significance of McCarthyism. The man and the movement that bore his name, all agreed, had lowered respect for America in Europe more than any other event or person in recent history. The fierce anti-communism which they believed ran deep in my country was the source that McCarthy and his followers could tap to despoil American politics. In Europe, my friends pointed out, such irrational fears were uncommon and communist parties were both legitimate and generally insignificant. The Danish party, as I recalled, had seven members in the Folketing, five fewer than the equally uninfluential Single Tax party. In the free competition of political and economic ideas, my friends said, the communists had been roundly rejected in all of Scandinavia. Turning on me, they asked, "is America afraid she would fail in such a test of ideas?" I was on shipboard when I wrote to my father of our conversations expressing agreement with their critiques of McCarthyism and American anti-communist excesses but also saying it would be good for them to become absorbed in American intellectual life so that they could come to understand its nuances and complexities. "It would seem," I wrote, "I am in favor of a student exchange program!"

VI

Now my year abroad program was ending. It was time to become a historian. Arriving in Chapel Hill, our new home for the next four years, I hoped that I might knit together the various strands of my Swarthmore and European studies and my Fairhope values to see how they could help me to become the kind of historian of the South, the kind of Southerner, I wanted to be, one who might make a difference in the stormy future I saw on the horizon. I came expecting, or at least hoping, to find the place buzzing with intellectual and reformist ferment. The Chapel Hill of the 1930s, about which I had read, appeared to me to have been such a place. Scholars drawn to Howard Odum's Institute for Research in Social Science churned out reformist literature on all fronts; Paul Green's Carolina Playmakers performed stunning theater; and Frank Graham showed by example what a courageous liberal Southern university president could be like. Beyond these Southern liberals there was Ab's bookstore across from the campus where Marxists, radicals, and nonconformists of all stripes hung out. Sadly, as I was to find out soon enough, the things I had hoped to see were no longer there.

In my first semester I was required to attend sixteen hours a week of lectures. Except for my research seminar, my classes were populated primarily by undergraduates. I found none of the vigorous interchange of ideas I had known in my Swarthmore seminars. There was much to learn and many books to read, but I felt pretty much on my own. My fellow students were capable but uninspiring. We had almost no conversations outside the classroom that went beyond the bare elements of meeting our course requirements. I would make friends with several during my four years (making friends has always come naturally to me) but none wrote a book that excited me and none became intellectual or reform-minded soulmates.

My first-semester research seminar was emblematic of my disappointment, but also of the satisfaction I knew I could find as a historian. I worked hard on my paper, a study of North Carolina fugitive slaves in the 1840s. I wanted to examine the nature of the fugitive slave "problem" just before the passage of the 1850 Fugitive Slave Act. Mary and I would often make our way to the library in the evenings after supper, storing Blaise in a carry cot in the stacks while we copied newspaper advertisements for runaways. Occasionally his waking-up cry would reverberate through the cavernous book shelves. Mary would then find a private place to nurse him. This was my first major research project in primary sources. I found it energizing from beginning to end. Together, Mary and I discovered ways to make the runaways come alive and the sources were there for me to describe not just the harshness of slavery and the state of denial in which most slave owners lived, which was easy enough to do, but to portray the bonds among slave family members and the risks they would take to seek freedom.

There were also questions that could not be answered, mysteries that would remain forever beyond the reach of even the best historians. One that has remained to tantalize me is the story of Edward Bailey. In August 1844 an advertisement in the Salisbury, North Carolina, newspaper reported that he had been committed to the jail of Rowan County. He was described as a boy about twelve years old who was "light complected." He said he had formerly been a "race rider" for a man he named and that he was free. The last sentence of the ad read: "owner will come forward and claim." It was signed Noah Roberts, Jailer. The notice ran for a few weeks and then disappeared. I wondered what had happened to him. Did someone "come forward and claim him"? The following January a new notice appeared in the same paper. A "negro boy named Edward Bailey" had been committed to the jail of Kershaw District, South Carolina. The same description followed, ending with "said boy says he is free and that he has lately been visiting with Mr. Noah Roberts of Salisbury. Owner will come forward and claim." I would have given a lot to have heard Edward Bailey tell his South Carolina jailer that he had been "lately visiting" with Mr. Noah Roberts of Salisbury, North Carolina. But I shall never know what happened to that enterprising young man who had actually fled south to find his freedom. Many times I have wished I had the talent to write a short story about him. Or even a novel.

The presentation of our papers came toward the end of the semester. There were about six of us in the group. All of our papers were long, mine running to fifty-three pages. We read them aloud to the group. Yes, read them aloud. It must have taken two hours to read mine. Five minds had to have wandered during that time. To have mimeographed the papers would have been too much. Long as they were, preparing carbon copies, as we did at Swarthmore, might have been too onerous a task. But why we could not have filed them in the library for advanced reading was never explained. Nor did anyone ask. We did what we were told, as though it had always been that way. I felt I was in the dark ages of academia. Even worse was the lesson I learned after one of our meetings. I had raised some critical points made by the author of one of the papers. Silence, rather than discussion, followed. In the corridor afterwards two members of the seminar, second-year graduate students, told me that I should not embarrass fellow students in front of Fletcher Green, our professor. I went home to tell Mary what had happened and to wonder aloud if I had made a dreadful mistake coming to Chapel Hill.

It was about this time that I became aware of the work of C. Vann Woodward, a Carolina Ph.D. then teaching at Johns Hopkins. His masterpiece, *Origins of the New South*, was published during my senior year at Swarthmore, but Jim Field never brought it to my attention and never suggested that I study with Woodward. Only one person did, my external examiner in political theory, a professor in the Hopkins politics department. My twenty-minute oral exam was the last for both of us. As we wandered out of the examining room he asked about my plans. When I told him I intended to study Southern history he said something like, "well, sir, you must come to Johns Hopkins to study with _____" and I'm sure he said Vann Woodward, but I had too much on my mind even to hear, much less remember, that suggestion.

The more I learned about Woodward the more I wished I had chosen to work with him. I did not know then that his colleague, Charles Barker, was working on a biography of Henry George. That would have been a thrilling enterprise to join and an added temptation to move. I gave some thought to applying for a transfer to Hopkins but I held back partly because of the effort involved. Another deterrent was my reluctance to leave Fletcher Green. By mid-year I had become his research assistant (at the munificent salary of $810 a year). Dr. Green, as we all called him, had grown fond of me and I of him. He was not the most imaginative or pathbreaking of historians and his lectures—solid, informative, authoritative—lacked brilliance. But I had already come to admire his thorough professionalism, his deep commitment to history, and his interpretations of Southern history. Fugitive slaves, he would tell us in his lectures, were the real heroes of the anti-slavery movement. I liked that. He was no crusader, but there was about him a kind of rock-solid integrity that I admired. Also, as all of his students came quickly to know, Dr. Green was a fanatic about research. Before we wrote we had to know everything knowable about our subject.

No corners were to be cut, no avenues of information left untraveled. He would be horrified by the current fashion of limiting sources to what can be found on the internet. He published his own style sheet to guide us to consistency and full descriptions of our sources. For one like me, given to reaching conclusions and interpretations too quickly and easily, Dr. Green was precisely what I needed. I was lucky to know him and to be shaped by his tutelage.

And so we stayed. During the six weeks before Mary and Blaise arrived from England I lived with Bunny and Paul Smith, Shaw's parents and great friends of my parents. They became our great friends and our benefactors as well. They had recently bought the infamous Ab's business, renaming it The Intimate Bookstore, and had run into some bad publicity owing to the store's "communist" antecedents. All of that was overcome by the time we arrived. Happily for us, they decided to include a used books section in the shop and reckoned they would need a station wagon for their buying trips about the state. They let us have the station wagon when they were at home and their sedan when they were out on the road. For four years we were wonderfully supplied with excellent automobiles. And with wonderful friends. Bunny was our fairy godmother, Paul our ironic wise man. Conversations with them were always spirited and energizing.

Just as Mary and Blaise arrived I secured a small university home for us in "Victory Village," a graduate-student complex. The house was called a U.K. because it had been built during the war to be shipped to England. Someone pointed out that the walls were too thin to protect against the winter cold so it remained in the U.S. We liked our small "U.K.," with its kitchen, living room, bath, and two bedrooms. We paid $36 a month for it plus $6 a month for a complete set of university furniture. With my modest research stipend, and the fellowships I would receive in future years, we could not survive without using our savings; fortunately, we had them in adequate supply. Shortly before we were married, Elizabeth inherited a large sum from the estate of her uncle Jake. Uncomfortable with a lot of money, she immediately gave $10,000 to Clare and $10,000 to Mary and, after we were married, asked me to look after $20,000 for her to use when she and Ted and Gwyneth were in the States. We had spent some of our $10,000 to pay off my small debts and partly to underwrite our post-Copenhagen travels. The rest saw us through four years of graduate school. With our last $500 we bought a car to drive to our new home and my new job in Virginia. We would arrive broke but with the first salary check soon to be deposited.

Mary, who would not forge a career of her own for another eighteen years, would later (somewhat apologetically) describe her life then as that of a 'fifties housewife. I, with the internalized values of the day, would remark on how fortunate we were that she did not have to work. Further confessions come to mind. At the end of our second year Mary applied for a fellowship to earn a master's degree in American literature. In her statement of purpose she wrote that her husband was a doctoral candidate in American history; should she receive the M.A. in American literature she would be better able to help him with his work. I've always assumed she was denied the fellowship because of her motives in seeking it. They could hardly have had among their applicants a more brilliant candidate for work in the English department. So she remained at home—with her child (soon her children), her cooking, and her cleaning. At the end of our third year—it was May 15, 1956—our daughter Chinta was born. More happiness was brought into our lives. She was such a joyful, uncomplaining baby, regularly flashing her seductive smile, that Mary decided she wanted nothing but girls in the future.

My ambition to teach Southern history in a Southern university was realized with astonishing ease. Dr. Green (it would be several years before I came to call him Fletcher) called me into his office in October 1956 to tell me that the University of Virginia was looking to appoint two young historians to succeed T. Perkins Abernethy. One was to be a colonialist, the other a Southernist. Fletcher wanted to recommend me. I was hardly ready to leave graduate school. I would not take my doctoral exams until the spring and I had yet to begin writing the dissertation. Still, there was no way I could turn down this chance. So I thanked him and said let us try for this job; if I didn't get it I would remain in graduate school to finish the next year.

Early in November Fletcher and I drove to Durham, where the Southern Historical Association was holding its annual meeting. Oron Hale and Edward Younger of the Virginia history department were there to take my measure. As we stood in the hotel lobby, Fletcher pointed out the two Virginia professors. With determination in his voice he told me that he had a graduate student in every state university in the South except Virginia. "We need that job," he announced, and with an LBJ-like shoulder squeeze he sent me forth: "You get in there and sell yourself; I know you can do it." I thought of replying "right, coach," but prudently substituted another response, probably "yes, sir."

The conversation went well. Professor Hale and I exchanged a few letters and in the spring I received the formal offer to become a Junior Instructor at a salary of $4,500. I completed my course work, took my Ph.D. oral and written examinations and, by the end of the second semester, wrote a few pages of my dissertation. With a dream job secured and with a lamentable lack of urgency to get on with the dissertation, I sailed to England with the family to spend the summer with Mary's parents in Beer, a small fishing village on the Devonshire coast. I had a splendid study over the garage, with a panoramic view of the sea. I worked there intermittently preparing lectures but yielded regularly to temptations to sail with my father-in-law and his nautical friends and to explore the seductive countryside.

The athletic highlight of that visit was my introduction to cricket. Fourteen-year-old Gwyneth asked me to be the family representative to play in her boarding school's father-daughter cricket match. Trained scholar that I was, and plagued by total ignorance of the game, I repaired to the Encyclopedia Britannica to learn the rules, hoping that my baseball experience would see me through at least to my defense of the wicket. I can't remember if my research instructed me on the appropriate attire but, even if it had, I doubt that I would have purchased the required white trousers. I can't recall feeling embarrassed by being the only one of the gentlemen in khaki pants and when my turn came I strode to the batting crease wicket full of confidence. Once there, however, I wasn't sure of the correct way to hold the bat so I asked the wicket keeper, standing behind me. She grinned with embarrassment and left it up to me to decide. Apparently my decision was a good one. I whacked the ball furiously and watched it sail over the heads of the farthest fielders. I dropped the bat and was half way to the other end of the pitch when I recalled "batter carries bat with him." I raced back to fetch it in plenty of time to carry on. I had hit a "six," the equivalent of a home run. Bursting with self-assurance I readied myself for another towering drive. The ball, however, eluded my powerful swing to clip the wicket. My batting days were over. And so, soon, were our days in England.

We flew home in August, the first trans-Atlantic flight for all of us. As we descended toward New York's Idlewild Airport, Blaise was glued to the window, excitedly pointing out the toy cars below. When we landed they were gone. He wept in bewilderment and disappointment.

Chapter Five

The Virginia Mystique

There was a special aura about the University of Virginia. Thomas Jefferson, its founder, wrote the nation's most eloquent and enduring testament to the ideals of liberty and equality. His inspiring words were etched in stone and brick at various places around the Grounds (what elsewhere would be called the campus). A great architect, he designed the nation's most beautiful university, with its majestic Rotunda at the head of a swath of green bordered on two sides by student rooms interspersed among classical pavilions housing the faculty members—all created to form an "Academical Village" that would inspire the highest order of learning and democratic thought that would protect and expand the virtues of the Republic he had helped to create. It was to be a university with a moral and political purpose.

I

I entered this hallowed place on a hot Sunday afternoon in August 1957, carrying boxes of books to my office. Both the temperature and the humidity were in the nineties, one of those dog days of summer to which I was no stranger. The summer session had ended; the fall semester had not begun. I was alone on the Lawn, as the greensward and its surrounds were called. There was no breeze. It was quiet. I put down my box of books to try to absorb something of Mr. Jefferson's awesome creation, a creation of which I was now to become a part. I felt small. My stomach churned, a sign of both my eagerness and my sense of inadequacy.

Just as I picked up a box and started to walk toward my new office building at the south end of the Lawn I saw a short, rosy-cheeked man with thinning gray hair walking toward me. He was dressed in a seersucker suit; he was wearing white shoes. I was wearing khaki pants, a white T-shirt, and tennis shoes. He asked politely who I was and introduced himself as Professor Arthur Kyle Davis, Jr., of the English Department. He welcomed me warmly to the University and said flattering things about the History Department. He assured me I would like being a member of it.

Then, in a tone neither critical nor threatening, merely passing on to me important truths about our university, he said: "You should know, Mr. Gaston, that members of the faculty do not appear on the Lawn without coat and tie." The sweat, visible through my T-shirt, was rolling down my face when I responded with a question: "You mean even when the University is not in session and the temperature and humidity are in the nineties?" Without irony or amusement, he replied, "Precisely, Mr. Gaston; there is another entrance to your office building." He then explained to me how I could enter it from the street side, thus avoiding the indiscretion of appearing on the Lawn without coat and tie.

A. K. and I became friends in time; he was a loyal supporter when I was beaten and arrested during a civil rights demonstration, offering words of comfort and a contribution to my defense fund. After he died I determined to perpetuate his memory. I strode into class at the opening of the fall semester wearing my seersucker suit and white bucks. It was August and hot and the room was not air-conditioned. I wrote A. K.'s name on the board and announced that I would give the first annual Arthur Kyle Davis, Jr., Memorial Lecture. I told the story of our first meeting to the coatless and tie-less students in my class (how times had changed!) and then previewed the themes we would pursue in our study of Southern history. I did not remove my sweat-soaked coat.

Shortly after I joined the faculty I learned from older colleagues that some of the old-timers were distraught that important traditions were being abandoned. Had I noticed, they asked, that members of the faculty no longer wore hats? I confessed that I had not. I was never tempted to buy a hat to help restore standards of dress, but I began to think a lot about how

Two views of The Lawn: top, looking from the Rotunda; bottom, looking toward the Rotunda.

the reverence of tradition seemed to permeate the university I now felt lucky to have joined. Those old-timers would find the current students' habit of wearing baseball caps, bill to the rear, a vulgar insult to their abandoned tradition.

Some of the traditions appealed to me. In contrast to the Chapel Hill custom, no members of the faculty (except those in the medical school) were called doctor. I was told that Mr. Jefferson did not believe in titles, so we would all be called mister. Only on rare occasions would we be addressed as professor, and never as doctor. That sense of egalitarianism and scorn of bragging appealed to my Fairhoper's sensibility. I thought it a little precious that we had to say Grounds instead of campus, but I eased into that habit soon and without discomfort. Harvard had its Yard, so why couldn't we have our Grounds? Social calls could be a little intimidating, but mostly Mary and I were amused by them. We knew that we should be prepared for Sunday afternoon visits from senior members of my department. When Perkins and Rob Abernethy arrived—inquiring politely as we opened the door, "Are you at home?"—we were suitably dressed and, showing pleasure but not surprise, ushered them in. Mrs. Abernethy seemed particularly pleased when, as they were leaving, she spied a silver tray on our side table, the quite appropriate place for leaving a calling card. Mary said we had passed the good breeding test.

Perkins, whose Southern history classes were to fall to me, taught for three more years after I arrived. He and Rob lived in one of the Lawn pavilions to which we were invited for cocktails when my parents came up from Fairhope for a visit. I warned my mother that the Abernethys were impossible racists and snobs and that no good would come from leaping into any of the several openings for controversy they would provide. She promised to be on her best behavior. And she was, until the subject of the Supreme Court's school integration decision came up. Administering her supreme cut, Mrs. Abernethy announced, "Well! I understand that Hugo Black has been blackballed by every club in Birmingham." To which, after a not very long silence, my mother, unable to restrain herself any longer, deftly offered her conversation-stopping *coup de grâce:* "Well, isn't it fortunate that he doesn't live in Birmingham." Rob and Perkins were perhaps extreme in the form their loyalty to tradition took, but the reverence in which everyone held the University's fabled honor code was regarded by no one as extreme. It was, on the contrary, a central part of what the university was about. It was celebrated in every official and unofficial statement about the University and was memorialized in the oft-repeated poetic declaration, "The Honor Men," written by 1903 college graduate James Hay, Jr. It concludes:

> Remembering the purple shadows of the lawn, the majesty of the colonnades, and the dream of your youth, you may say in reverence and thankfulness: "I have worn the honors of Honor. I graduated from Virginia."

Test papers were acceptable only when the pledge of honor was appended. It read: "On my honor as a gentleman, I have neither given nor received aid on this examination." The words were inscribed on every classroom wall. If found guilty of receiving or giving aid on a test, or in any other way of lying, cheating, or stealing, the offending student was stripped of his status as a gentleman by the student Honor Committee and banished forever from the company of Virginia gentlemen. There was but one penalty for an offender against the honor code. Such a system, its champions believed, promoted a community of trust. I understood their point but I thought it also promoted a way of life in which its members could continue to think of themselves as special, above and beyond the ordinary run of human beings. They were gentleman, their reputations with other gentlemen secure and unsullied. Almost never did I see the declaration that honesty and the search for truth came not from class status but from the very nature of scholarship itself. The tribal ritual of expulsion, noted in the student newspaper within a black box, was essential to validate and perpetuate their standing.

I launched no public attacks on the honor code but I did gently twit my students. In my survey course in American History I gave one lecture on the concept of honor in the Old South. The way I structured it—emphasizing the importance of class, hierarchy, and reputation—led more than one student to come up to me afterward with a concerned look on his face. "This sounds very much like our own honor system," one troubled young man remarked.

My disingenuous reply—"Oh, really?"—did not ease his concern.

The honor code was no creation of Thomas Jefferson; I could not imagine him thinking up such a thing. In fact, it came along sixteen years after his death. I shook my head in disbelief at the thought that his university existed to protect and advance the reputation of gentlemen. Jefferson's greatest hope was that it would be a place devoted primarily to learning, to creating the educated citizenry on which the success of the Republic depended. About that he was clear and he was passionate. This was the Virginia tradition, albeit a tradition severely compromised, that drew me to the University and its possibilities. From the moment I left the Lawn that hot August afternoon, I sensed the tension between the ideals of the university's founder and the conservative mindset that had come to dominate and undermine the institution's mission. It was, I thought, a university at war with itself. That seemed a good battle to join.

II

Calls to battle were everywhere around us in those days. In 1956, the year before we arrived, the Virginia General Assembly had passed and Governor Lindsay Almond had signed a series of bills to enact what their revered senior United States Senator Harry Flood Byrd called "massive resistance." He had promised that his people would resist, and resist massively, the Supreme Court's 1954 ruling in the *Brown* case that segregated public education must end. He had an unofficial spokesman named James Jackson Kilpatrick writing editorials for Richmond's afternoon newspaper, the *News Leader*. Kilpatrick, recently arrived from his home state of Oklahoma, took up the battle for the honor of his adopted state with guts and gusto. "The Negro race," he wrote to a supporter, "has never been able to build a civilization of his own, and it has debased every society in which its blood has been heavily mixed." Kilpatrick shied away from finding out the extent to which the "blood" of black and white was already mixed in Virginia, or who was responsible for the mixing, but he warned that his new home would not be "debased" by the consequences of black and white children sitting next to each other in the public schools. The General Assembly obligingly provided that schools would be closed rather than integrated.

Jonathan Daniels, whose columns we often read in the Raleigh, North Carolina, *News and Observer* when we were in Chapel Hill, said of Virginia's massive resistance laws that they should be understood not as a proposal for secession from the union; they were a call for secession from civilization. So here we were, taking up residence in the state that was preparing to secede from civilization. Yet all around us we found claims that ours was the most civilized of American states and more than once we were told how fortunate we were to be joining a uniquely civilized university.

I did not hear leaders of the university speak in the fashion of Kilpatrick or the other agitated spokesmen of the massive resistance movement. But there had been a time when they did. At the turn of the century, for example, Dr. Paul Barringer, the chairman of the faculty (a post abolished in 1904 when the university chose its first president), wrote frequently about what he called the scientific proof of black inferiority. No longer slaves, blacks were now on the "return to barbarism" which, he wrote, "is as natural as the return of the sow that is washed to her wallowing in the mire." He believed they lacked all of the civilized characteristics valued by white people. "Comfort, health, self-respect, and gentility," he wrote, "are as a rule nothing compared with the gratification of vanity, lust, the craving for drink, tobacco, the gaming habit, etc." Supply a black man's "bodily wants, including a woman," he wrote, "and he is happy under any social conditions."

No such crude language ever came from the pen of Colgate Darden. Mr. Darden had become the University's fourth president in 1947. I did not get to know him in the two years before he was succeeded by Edgar Shannon and left Charlottesville, but I admired him from afar, appreciated his disdain for inflammatory rhetoric, and thought of him as a man of dignity and humane sensibility. He was admired by faculty and students alike for his personal qualities and for his visionary leadership. You could look on him as someone who understood the Jeffersonian tradition as Jefferson wanted it to be understood. His principal goal was to make the university the capstone of higher education in the state and to end its reputation as a party school and magnet for Ivy League rejects. He was a lawyer and former governor with democratic instincts. But he was also a friend of Harry Byrd and part of the political organization that had long controlled Virginia politics.

Mr. Darden knew the folly of the massive resistance program Harry Byrd and his friends had imposed on the state. He also knew, as he was to write, that "segregation has been used time after time as the shield for discrimination and oppression." For that, he said, "there is no justification or excuse." Knowing this and disdaining massive resistance, he still could not bring himself to speak against it publicly. I often thought of Frank Graham of North Carolina and how different, in this kind of crisis, the two men were. Part of the reason for Mr. Darden's reluctance may have stemmed from the fact that he did not favor the end of public school segregation. He had testified in the Prince Edward case that the abolition of segregation "would impede rather than improve public education in the Southern states." On the eve of the *Brown* decision he wrote a letter to George Mitchell, the director of the Southern Regional Council, the South's front-line interracial organization (of which I would one day become president), to tender his resignation. That he had been a member at all is evidence of his moderately progressive views. In 1951, however, the Council had issued a bold statement calling for the end of segregation, labeling it "a cruel penalty on the human spirit." That was a position, Mr. Darden wrote, "to which I cannot subscribe."

In the run-up to the massive resistance legislation, Kilpatrick trumpeted the resurrection of the ancient doctrine of interposition, claiming the constitutional right of Virginia to interpose its authority between its people and the decisions of the Supreme Court. Harry Ashmore of the *Arkansas Gazette* wrote that Kilpatrick believed nothing of consequence had occurred since Calhoun concluded his last debate with Webster. Such wittily cutting remarks were not part of Mr. Darden's makeup, but he knew Ashmore was right. And yet he and his Board of Visitors threw up their own legalistic defense to negate the attempts of black Virginians to enroll. In 1935 Alice Jackson, daughter of a Richmond pharmacist, became the first African American to apply for admission to the Graduate School of Arts & Sciences. The school's dean rejected her application because, he wrote, her admission would violate "the long established and fixed policy of the Commonwealth of Virginia." As if she didn't already know that. That "long established and fixed policy" would someday have to be changed. Mr. Darden, who became president in 1947, knew that. The question was when and how and by whom.

Two years before I joined the Virginia faculty I read C. Vann Woodward's new book, *The Strange Career of Jim Crow*. His earlier work, *Origins of the New South*, inspired me with its revolutionary way of looking at Southern history as well as with the elegance of his writing and the authority of his research. *The Strange Career* was a book of hope and guidance. The segregation laws, of more recent origin than most people thought, were made by men for specific reasons; they could be unmade by them for a different set of reasons. They were not a fixed part of the folkways of the South. More to the point for what had to be weighing on Mr. Darden's mind, at the very time Alice Jackson had been rebuffed by Virginia, the NAACP had launched a movement to challenge in the courts the exclusion policies of segregated universities. Forcing the Supreme Court to examine the meaning of the Fourteenth Amendment's requirement that no state be allowed to deny to any of its citizens the equal protection of the law, the NAACP led the court to dismantle, piece by piece, the fiction of equal treatment these universities maintained to protect their purity and justify their actions. By 1950, in the case of *Sweatt v. Painter*, the court virtually held that separate could not be equal. University presidents like Mr. Darden knew they could no longer bar applicants from their graduate and professional schools. That was the year Gregory Swanson applied for admission to the law school.

The debate within the administration centered on whether to force a lawsuit, which all knew Swanson would win. Swanson did sue but before his case was argued and settled the University worked out an arrangement with the NAACP to limit the application to the law school, hoping to insulate other branches of the University. Swanson then became the first African American to attend the University, enrolling in the fall of 1950. In the wake of Swanson's admission, a few other blacks were denied admission on dubious constitutional grounds, but Walter Nathaniel Ridley, already a professor at Virginia State University with advanced degrees, enrolled in January 1951. In 1953 he became the first African American to earn a doctorate at a major white Southern university, receiving an Ed.D. from the School of Education. Seventeen years would pass before Raymond Gavins became the first black scholar to earn a Ph.D. in our Graduate School of Arts & Sciences. When I arrived in 1957, seven years after Swanson, there were twenty-two African American students enrolled in the various graduate and professional schools, most studying for advanced degrees in education. They constituted less than one-half of one per cent of the student body. The College of Arts & Sciences, where I would do my teaching, remained a bastion for white men.

Vann Woodward's *Strange Career* had special appeal to me and, I thought, a special message for the university of which I had now become a part. It originated from the James W. Richard lectures the author delivered at the University in September 1954. President Darden attended all three lectures. In a letter to Edward Younger, the history department professor who had invited Woodward to give them, he wrote that he found them "most interesting and timely." A master of courtesy and diplomacy, he did not specify what it was about them that he found interesting or in what way they might be timely. When the book was published the next year it was dedicated to "Charlottesville and the hill that looks down upon her, Monticello." In his preface Woodward wrote that his lectures "were given before unsegregated audiences and they were received in that spirit of tolerance and open-mindedness that one has a right to expect at a university with such a tradition and such a founder."

Right to expect. Tolerance. Open-mindedness. Tradition. Founder. Those freighted words accompanied me as I put on my coat and tie to enter the classroom as a teacher in Mr. Jefferson's University.

III

Tolerance and open-mindedness turned out to be fragile reeds, at least as I judged from the writings and behavior of student leaders. In October of my first semester the editor of the *Cavalier Daily (CD)*, the student newspaper, wrote sneeringly of the NAACP (without whom there would then have been no black students in the University) as an organization "with leftist backgrounds and aims." The editor had no doubt that "great masses of detailed evidence" had proved the presence of communists among the members, and revealed it to be a communist-front organization perpetrating "subversive dealings" wherever it operated. An editorial the next month called for "obdurate resistance to integration, without violence," as "the only way to stay the hand that is cramming this distasteful pill down our protesting throats."

This editor was not my student but in my first years at the University I knew many like him. Some became frequent visitors to my office, eager to berate me for my liberal, integrationist leanings and betrayal. A few were thoroughly objectionable human beings who appeared to be well beyond redemption. Most, however, had a disarming charm and, wrong though I thought their views were, an engaging intellectual fervor. I welcomed them. After all, I had come hoping that my teaching of Virginian and Southern history might challenge young men of the state and region to reevaluate the beliefs that made them feel morally secure at the top of the racial-privilege pyramid.

In my first year I worked particularly closely with a tall, handsome, self-assured son of one of the First Families of Virginia, a graduate of the state's elite prep schools, St. Christopher's in Richmond and Episcopal High School in Alexandria. We had friendly, spirited exchanges in my office and agreed to read each other's favorite books. His was Kilpatrick's defense of segregation, *The Sovereign States: Notes of a Citizen of Virginia.* I've forgotten mine; it was probably James Dabbs's *The Southern Heritage,* which I valued as a beautifully written celebration of Southern virtues shackled by a culture of white supremacy. Neither of us was converted by the other's book choice. Still, we continued our occasional talks through the year. I was cheered by an essay he wrote on his final examination at the end of our second semester. In it he acknowledged humane features of the New Deal, including some of its racial policies. On the Monday after the Friday exam he strolled into my office to discuss it. I smiled and congratulated him on the New Deal essay. "Well, Mr. Gaston," he replied, "that's what I came to talk to you about." He didn't want merely to talk, he wanted to change what he had written. I was puzzled. "My father says I was wrong," he explained. "Do you mean," I asked in dismay, "that your father can wipe out in one conversation what I have been working toward for a whole year?" A pleased, almost puckish, grin accompanied his reply: "That's about it, Mr. Gaston."

This student was perhaps less than typical, but my recollection is that students with his views and self-confidence dominated the classrooms, the fraternities, the major organizations, and the student newspaper in those days of the late 1950s and on into the 1960s. For most of them, books, lectures, and discussions were weak opponents of the received wisdom handed down from generation to generation by trusted family guardians of historical truth. My notes from those days are filled with examples of tradition thwarting scholarship. One of my students who came from this tradition wrote to me years later to explain that his study of American history at elite Virginia schools "concentrated largely on a detailed recitations of the horrors of Reconstruction and a careful exegesis on the constitutional rationale for the doctrine of nullification and interposition." For so many of the young men I came to know, there was nothing in their schooling, rearing, or family values that would allow them to question the hubris of race and class they brought with them to the University.

I remember reading back then a statement of George Bernard Shaw's that helped me to understand these things. "The villainous moral conditions on which our social system is based," he wrote, "are necessarily in constant contact with our moral mucous membrane, and so we lose our sense of their omnipresent meanness and dishonor." Lose may have been the wrong verb in the Virginians' case because so few had ever had a sense of the social system's "meanness and dishonor," but that phrase about the "constant contact with our moral mucous membrane" stayed with me. What was necessary was contact of another sort, a jolting counter-experience that would expose the "moral mucous membrane" to new possibilities for the social system. That would not happen for another ten years or more.

From the beginning, though, from the time I arrived, there were students who would like to see it happen, students who saw through the patina of honor and tradition to the uglier realities beneath and the Jeffersonian promise beyond. Brilliant, caring, and dissenting students had probably always been part of the University community. An enterprising historian should one day take up the task of telling their stories. My very limited knowledge comes from my acquaintance with two radical students from the 1930s. One was Murat Williams, a Rhodes scholar, a lieutenant commander in the Navy during World War II, a foreign service officer, and an ambassador to El Salvador. He was born in Richmond, died in Charlot-

tesville, and his ashes were buried in Orange County. I met him only once
but that brief conversation lit up for me what he must have been like in the
thirties. The other was Palmer Weber, a native of Smithfield. I was inspired
by Palmer, whom I got to know and work with in later years, hearing from
him about his student days. He took three degrees, B.A., M.A., and Ph.D.,
and taught in the University for a while. Along with Murat, he headed the
Marxist club and was at the center of radical student thought. After he left
the University he was the Southern organizer for the 1948 Henry Wallace
campaign (making me wonder if Uncle Marvin ever met him), the first
Southern white man to be elected to the national board of the NAACP,
and later a wealthy Wall Streeter and philanthropist for civil rights and
liberal causes. He used to tell me that to be a successful stock broker, you
had to be able to imagine that tomorrow would be totally different from
today. That seemed a good adage for reformers and revolutionaries as well,
however un-Virginian it was.

There had, of course, been other dissenters. Staige Blackford used his
post as editor of the CD in the spring of 1952 to stir up discussion of racial
issues. Why was it, he wondered, that Swanson's admission had been followed
by a tight containment policy; why were the doors not opened widely to
black students? Were the white students ready for that? Did anyone know
the answer to that question? Announcing that "we are placing our necks
on the chopping block of student wrath with some comments on racial
segregation," Staige reported the results of a poll the paper had conducted.
Asked whether they would object to being in class with a Negro, 66 percent
of the respondents said no; 27 percent, yes; and 7 percent undecided. A
flurry of letters followed, some endorsing desegregation, some opposing,
including the one that described race mixing as "a repudiation of Southern
culture and life." Staige was nearly kicked out of his fraternity for his efforts,
but he survived. He graduated, won a Rhodes scholarship, served briefly in
the CIA, became a civil rights research director, newspaper reporter, press
secretary to Virginia's first integrationist governor, and then the long-serving
editor of The Virginia Quarterly Review where he continued to build on his
beliefs in racial justice and the free play of ideas. That, he used to say to me,
was what Mr. Jefferson's University was meant to be about.

In my own first four years at the University there was no Marxist club, no group opposing segregation, and no *CD* editor calling for change. Under the heavy cloud of conformity, however, there were brilliant, sensitive, questioning students, the kind you would be privileged to know in any university. I met a dozen straightaway. They were first- and second-year students (who elsewhere would be called freshmen and sophomores) who enrolled in a new experimental seminar-type course I helped to establish as an alternative to the large survey course in American history. I tried to fashion it somewhat in the manner of a Swarthmore seminar, with regular papers and spirited discussion. I remember nearly all of the twelve. Paul Rosenberg, whose honors thesis I would later direct, became a New Jersey lawyer with a very large wine cellar from which I received several gifts. He was my friend until his death a few years ago. His curiosity and voracious reading habits never left him. Rick Booraem is the sort of student you would never forget. One day early in the semester he walked into my office to ask if I could recommend a good biography of Millard Fillmore. I couldn't. Why, I wanted to know, did he want a biography of Fillmore. His answer was as sensible as it was stunning: he had read a biography of every president except Fillmore. Rick took a Ph.D. in history at Johns Hopkins and became a prolific author, writing, among other things, books and articles about presidents Jackson, William Henry Harrison, Garfield, Coolidge, and Hoover.

These students and a few others I came to know were moved by books and discussions to see that slavery was not benign; that segregation was instituted to protect white privilege; and that their own good fortune was rooted in the long history of exploitation of blacks by whites. A few even came to question the sainthood of General Lee. I sensed then that the University's white supremacy tradition would be ended only by students, but, given the climate of opinion that surrounded me, I felt it likely many years would pass before an effective student movement for change could be mounted. In fact, it took about ten years.

Apart from the few students I have mentioned and the sparkling twelve in my seminar, I noticed with pleasure occasional letters protesting editorial excesses, including one attacking the editor's denigration of the NAACP as "demagogic and inflammatory." That one, from a fourth-year graduate student, was matched by very few from the undergraduate students and the hostile editorial tone remained unchanged through the year. When the editor ran out of his own steam he printed a four-part series on "The Perils of Racial Mixing" by Tom Waring, the firebrand segregationist editor of the Charleston *News and Courier.* The next year, when two of the city's public schools had been closed under the massive resistance laws, the paper's new editor reached out for what he must have thought was a wise middle ground. In his "Breath of Tolerance" column he complimented two church groups that had criticized massive resistance and spoken in favor of integration. They deserved praise for the "courage of their convictions," he wrote, without endorsing the direction their courage and convictions took them. Whether they were to be tolerant or not, returning students received warnings from the Judiciary Committee, the Student Council, and the Interfraternity Council to be careful to do nothing in the midst of the school crisis that would "reflect discredit on the University." I took that to mean steer clear of getting involved.

The crisis over segregation in Charlottesville's public schools had been in the making since 1955 when the first black citizens sued the recalcitrant school board over all-white schools. Like school boards in other parts of the South, Charlottesville's was skilled in manipulating the judicial system to fend off what its attorney and some of its members must have known would be the inevitable integration order. Such an order was on its way during the summer of 1958. When it became a reality Governor Almond seized control of and closed Venable Elementary and Lane High. There we were, really seceding from civilization.

By the time the two schools were closed Mary and I had become members of the local chapter of the Virginia Council on Human Relations. In the wake of the *Brown* decision, the Southern Regional Council, with funding from the Ford Foundation, had piloted the creation of such councils in most of the Southern states. Their principal objective was to create an atmosphere and develop strategies that would encourage communities to obey the law of the land and begin to phase out racial segregation. Neither the Virginia state council nor the various local chapters had a prayer of prevailing against the will and power of the massive resistance forces. Reasoned arguments derived from mounds of evidence were routinely ignored or curtly dismissed. In Charlottesville we kept trying, with our speakers' programs, letters, broadsides, and community discussions—discussions that community leaders declined to attend. For Mary and me perhaps the major benefit was the friendships we made with black members of the community we might otherwise have not met so easily. Several became lifelong friends and comrades. A year or so later, when I joined and became a member of the executive committee of the local branch of the NAACP my friendships were extended and my understanding of the freedom struggle enlarged.

The closing of the schools threw Charlottesville into a crisis for which it had made no preparations and had neither precedent nor leadership. Neither the city council nor the school board emerged with ideas of what to do. Some perhaps thought the schools would never be closed; once they were closed they likely thought the massive resistance legislation would be declared unconstitutional. But they had no recommendations for meeting the immediate problem. Where were all those children to go to school? More than 1,700 Venable and Lane students were locked out. The city would have been burdened enough if its people were agreed that providing for the students was their only problem. They were not agreed. They were divided in ways that thrust the turbulent issue of race before them in a way it had never appeared before.

Up until school-closing time the city was split into three unequal parts. We advocates of integration were a small and uninfluential minority. Our chief organizations, the NAACP and the VCHR, had virtually no influence on public policy and precious little success in changing the thinking of the segregationists. The spokespersons for maintaining segregation, ranging from a few raging racists to a larger group of more modulated defenders of the status quo, outnumbered us by a wide margin. They were the community leaders—bankers, businessmen, some clergy and school board members, city councilors, some lawyers, and a handful of professors. Most people were in the middle; they sat on the sidelines keeping their views to themselves. They joined neither the pro- nor anti-segregation groups, wrote few if any letters to the newspaper, never publicly endorsed or criticized massive resistance. I knew several of them, and came to know many more later. Many of them had avoided wrapping their minds around the rights and wrongs of segregation. Most seemed to believe that, somehow, the schools would not be closed and they could carry on as before without having to make hard decisions. That comfortable escape route was denied them.

These moderates, as the last group came to be called, sprang into action over the summer when they saw that schools really were going to be closed. They were led by a group of Venable School mothers who changed the nature of the racial dialogue. Polling their fellow parents they stressed the imperative of maintaining public education. What they managed to do was to change the nature of the conversation by not asking whether parents favored or opposed segregation. Did they favor public education? That was the question. A substantial majority said yes; they favored the maintenance of public education, even if it meant blacks would go to school with whites. By shifting the emphasis of the discourse they managed to move a majority of school parents—and probably of the city, as well—to an acceptance of integration without ever having to say they opposed segregation or favored integration. I wondered at the time if this triumph of the moderates would have been achieved so easily if the schools had never been closed. It was the school closing—the gift of the Byrd machine—that, ironically, led to the collapse, not the success, of massive resistance, and the beginning of integration.

While we were in the midst of all this, in the early fall of 1958, "the triumph of the moderates," as I came to call it, was anything but a given. A rival group of parents, backed by some of the city's prominent segregation leaders, did its own polling and recruiting, defining the issue as racial, not educational. These opponents of integration formed the Charlottesville Education Foundation and offered to provide temporary schooling for the ousted students with the promise of creating a pair of private, segregated schools for them in the future. The Venable moderates, likewise offering temporary schooling opportunities in private homes and public buildings, promised to lead their pupils back into public schools when they opened, whatever the racial composition should be. Of course they knew that would not be all white, but they could rally support for public education by never using the word integration.

After one semester of struggle—and a workable program of instruction for the children—Virginia's massive resistance school-closing law was struck down. A federal district judge ruled that it violated the 14th Amendment to the United States Constitution. The Virginia Supreme Court of Appeals ruled that it violated the Virginia constitution's requirement that the state provide an efficient system of public education. On the day after the courts outlawed the massive resistance measures, Governor Almond made one last rhetorical assault on the integrationists, promising Virginians that what he called the "livid stench of sadism, sex immorality and juvenile pregnancy" would not infest Virginia schools. But it was bluster. Faced with the choice of going to jail or obeying the law, he prudently took the second choice. Some of the diehards called it the craven choice. Charlottesville was granted a stay until September. When public schools opened in the fall about 30 percent of the city's white students who normally would have attended Venable and Lane went to the new segregated schools, Robert E. Lee and Rock Hill Academy, their cost paid for by tuition grants authorized by the state. Public education was saved. Commentators then and since have given much of the credit for that fact to the moderates, especially the Venable mothers, who led the way.

Schools were saved, but the victory of the moderates was not accompanied by a commitment to bring whites and blacks together in the public schools. In September 1959 twelve African American students entered city schools, nine at Venable, three at Lane. The city school board, then and in years to come, successfully crafted assignment schemes to maintain tokenism and to ensure containment. Many battles lay ahead before a truly biracial school system would come into existence.

IV

In those days of the late fifties and early sixties Mary and I and our reform-minded friends spent many hours ruminating over the most likely ways of breaking down the racial status quo and replacing it with humane values and progressive public policies. Years later I was to learn about the efforts of Benjamin Muse, on assignment from the Southern Regional Council, to persuade influential Southern white moderates that it was in their best interest to support desegregation in their communities. He traveled from city to city in 1959 and 1960, testing his belief that rational argument with rational people would result in progressive change. The confidential reports he sent to Harold Fleming, the SRC executive director in Atlanta, are a revealing, albeit dispiriting, account of the evaporation of that confidence. Experience shattered his faith. In one of his reports he quoted, with apparent approval, the judgment of an Alabama Human Relations Council leader that "history will record that the lethargy and cowardice of moderates is the cause of this distress." Real change, Muse reluctantly concluded, would come only in the wake of sustained grassroots organization and protest, primarily by African Americans, leading to strengthened federal government action.

When I found and read those confidential reports many years later I was reminded of Ben's gentleness (I had gotten to know him and his wife in the sixties at meetings of the Council on Human Relations) and I could sense his deep disappointment. I also saw in what he wrote a mirror of my own inner dialogue as I thought about how the white supremacy culture and institutions of my university and community could be undone. I was committed, like Ben, to belief in the power of the mind. In my case, it was teaching history in a way that would challenge debilitating myths and open up unsuspected vistas of understanding. A university, perhaps above all other institutions, should be the place where reason and evidence and a quest for truth should shape one's views, values, and actions. But I learned very early of the shaping and staying power of a conservative tradition and the resistance of so many within the university community to the kinds of arguments Ben made and that I was trying to teach at the time.

I agreed that change would have to come from below, not above; in our case that would mean primarily from students. Starting with the Greensboro, North Carolina, sit-ins of February 1, 1960, students all over the South began to protest. Only a few white students were among them. Shortly after the first sit-ins, young black men and women met at Shaw University, in Raleigh, North Carolina, to found the Student Nonviolent Coordinating Committee (SNCC—pronounced "snick"). It became the direct-action group for the youth of the South, its star burning brightly for six or seven years. There were no black colleges in Charlottesville. Unlikely rebels though we were, we were all there was. In March 1961 our first civil rights action took place, immediately to be followed by the creation of the first University civil rights organization. It was a feeble start, but it was the beginning of a movement that would grow each year, achieving a milestone victory eight years later.

The leader of the first action was one of the twenty-five black students enrolled in the University. Virginius Thornton was the first African American admitted to the Graduate School of Arts & Sciences—and to my department. Shortly after his arrival in the fall of 1960 I arranged for Virginius to speak to the VCHR. He was joined by our friend Charlie Jones, a white maverick preacher from Chapel Hill who was an advisor to the sit-in movement there the previous spring. For Virginius, speaking was important but not enough. The subject of his talk that evening was "The Unfinished Revolution." As I recall, he spoke of having been a founding member of SNCC and of being arrested for "trespassing" in Petersburg after leading a sit-in at the city library. Once released from jail he began to organize in Petersburg and to travel to meet with leaders of the burgeoning protest movement. The September 19 issue of *Life* magazine reported on the "successful strategy" of the sit-ins and produced a photograph of Martin Luther King, Jr., and ten other leaders, Virginius among them, at an Atlanta strategy meeting. Virginius had come to UVA to earn a Ph.D. in American history. He would also get us started on the road of civil rights protest.

In those days there was a movie theater on the Corner, the area adjacent to the University where students went for shopping, dining, and entertainment. The University Theater, as it was called, was privately owned. Since it had no balcony, it had no provision for segregation and since state law would not permit blacks to sit in the same area as whites they were simply denied admission: exclusion, not segregation. Virginius, already pained by the absence of student protest against the refusal to recruit and welcome black students and by the hostile conditions at the Corner, led the protest against this. On the first day he was joined by three other black students and twenty-five white students, faculty, and spouses. The blacks asked to purchase tickets and were denied. Picketing and negotiations followed, to no avail. Organizers launched a boycott of the theater highlighted by a list of supporters' names published in the *CD*. That list appeared in the March 14 issue. A yellowing, brittle, slightly torn copy rests in my files. I see that we divided the supporters into four categories, and I count the names of 65 faculty; 114 graduate students; 135 undergraduates; and 42 "friends" (mostly wives of faculty members). Owing to lack of "advertising space" the paper noted, the names of others who had signed were not included and the petition calling for a boycott was still being circulated. We were not alone.

Among those I called asking that their names be included was Dumas Malone, the famous Jefferson scholar and, at least in my opinion, the most distinguished member of the Arts & Sciences faculty. I told him what we were about and why we needed his support. He agreed with our aim, he told me, but then wondered if he should sign on, explaining that doing so would make him feel like a hypocrite.

"A hypocrite? Why, Dumas?"

"Well, you see, Paul," he explained, "Elizabeth and I never go to the movies."

I don't recall what I said to persuade him to set aside his principles, but he agreed to be with us. Two years later, after the theater abandoned its exclusion policy, Dumas, unaware of the change, telephoned me. "Paul," he said, "Elizabeth and I want to go to the movies. Are we still boycotting that theater?" I have told this story more than once in talks given to alumni groups, citing it as a wonderful example of the real meaning of honor. Not all of my listeners recognized this as the honors of Honor James Hay, Jr., had written about.

Junius Fishburne, the *CD* editor, couldn't see it that way, either. "The main objection" to the protest, he wrote, was that it gave "an unfavorable impression of the University." A small group of people, "fighting for a personal cause," had put the University, in the eyes of many, in an "unfavorable light." Distancing the good name of the University from civil rights activities would be an ongoing theme of the guardians of tradition. In this case, a group planning to call itself "University of Virginia Committee for Desegregation of the University Theater" was told by one of the deans that the University had "no objection to the free expression of viewpoints" (how encouraging to be told, one might have thought!) but since the committee was not "an authorized activity of the University" it had "no authority to announce itself under a title including the words 'University of Virginia.'"

A flurry of letters to the editor came after the first protest, the picketing that followed, and the boycott announcement. Much of it was harshly critical of the critics, calling the editor's comments "laughable" and the University as he defended it the "barbarous village of Thomas Jefferson." Among the many criticisms of the protesters, the one I found most interesting was co-written by Jerome Rothschild, a fourth-year history major. Jerry had been my student and we had enjoyed many lively discussions. He was smart, thoughtful, and not given to what I thought of as the "honor" and "reputation" nonsense of those to whose aid he came. For Jerry and his colleagues, deft though they were with ridicule of us liberals, their main point was what they thought of as the moral rights of private property. Theater owners, they argued, had every constitutional and legal right to deny admission to anyone they wished. Given the legislation and judicial decisions up to this time, they were correct. It would take a great many more civil rights protests, and the spilling of a lot of blood, before President Kennedy would get off the dime to craft a bill that would abolish such a "right."

One of Jerry's letters that remains in my files runs to three single-spaced pages. Among other things, he wanted me to know that he thought the theater manager had done absolutely the wrong thing, denying admission because of the state segregation law. Because his theater was private property, Jerry argued, he could admit or deny "colored people" as he saw fit. He didn't need state government interference to tell him what to do. Jerry would not have favored a decision to admit, but he would have supported it reluctantly because it was the owner's private property right. Reading through his letter now, forty-five years after it was written, I can recall easily the pleasure I had in our friendship and the vigor of the sharp disagreements in our exchanges. And I understood what he meant when he told me that most of his teachers were not "the original thinkers they imagined themselves" to be but they were simply traders in the ideas of others. I'm not sure if he exempted me from that generalization, but he ended with a postscript to tell me "you're still the best teacher I ever had." In years to come two of his nephews took a class of mine—on the command of Uncle Jerry, they told me. Very recently one sent me a gracious letter of thanks and a very good bottle of Burgundy. He had long since come over to our side. Uncle Jerry, he told me, remained a vigorous spokesman for the other side.

V

Shortly after the winding down of the theater protest I met with several students who decided to form a University chapter of the Virginia Council on Human Relations. Not surprisingly, they called it the Jefferson Chapter. My colleague Tom Hammond and I served as faculty advisors. It was Tom who had directed Mary and me to the Charlottesville chapter on our arrival. Eight years my senior, Tom had grown up in Atlanta where his father was on the staff of the Atlanta *Constitution*. The father died young and Tom came under the wing of Ralph McGill, one of the South's few notable liberal journalists. Tom from Georgia and I from Alabama were the two Southern liberals who seemed to stand out in the university community in those days. Both of us were members of the Virginia Council and could arrange contacts for the students with it and with its parent organization, the Southern Regional Council, of which McGill had been a founder in 1944. Our first two meetings were held off Grounds as we met with the city chapter. We heard and got to know Sam Tucker, an African American attorney, who spoke about Virginians' hostility to integration and the ways in which the NAACP hoped to confront it. I would learn a lot from Sam and his friendship in the next years. At our second meeting we were addressed by Leslie Dunbar, the SRC's newly appointed executive director. Les was a famously slow and quiet speaker but he was appropriately dubbed by one of his colleagues as the "fastest conscience in the South." Les and I would forge a lifelong comradeship.

The students hoped to bring to the Grounds speakers like Sam and Les. Ed Lovern, our president pro tem, said we would pursue "a rational, realistic approach toward integration." In so doing, we would become the first university chapter of the Council on Human Relations, and one of the earliest civil rights organizations of any kind to appear on a Southern college campus. Whether we would be allowed to do these things, however, was up to the student council. The April 20 edition of the *CD* carried a first-page report announcing that the proposed Jefferson chapter "has not proved its worth." Acting on the recommendation of its committee on Organizations and Publications, the Council unanimously denied the Jefferson Chapter the right to become a student organization. The ostensible problem was the "uncertainty as to the means by which the group intends to pursue a moderate approach toward human relations." Withholding approval, the Council would nonetheless give "due consideration" to requests for meetings in university buildings. The University administration, however, blocked that concession. It refused such permission pending Student Council approval. With the semester nearly over, the question of Student Council recognition and the use of university rooms was put over to the next academic year.

While we waited, there was no lack of other beckoning racial issues. In June 1961, for example, the USLTA junior scholastic tennis tournament was held on the Lady Astor courts at the University. The tournament, which Virginia had hosted since 1946, brought to Charlottesville the best teen tennis players in the country. That year seventeen-year-old Arthur Ashe became the tournament's first black champion. Shortly after Ashe's victory I heard that the University had decided that it would no longer host the tournament. On June 23, Tom Hammond and I had a talk with Carl (Red) Rohmann, the university's sometime tennis coach, once its star player, and a popular sports-store owner at the Corner. Red was disappointed that the tournament would go elsewhere. He felt it was very valuable to the University and he would miss it. Why did he think we would no longer have the tournament here? The major factor, he told us, was race. A Dr. Johnson in Lynchburg, who had trained Ashe and other young black players, was "pressing too much" to get more Negro entries. This would result in more Negro spectators and their presence might cause trouble for the University. We pressed Red to tell us who had made the decision. He hedged for a moment, but, in the end, said the decision was made by Gus Tebell, the director of athletics, and Edgar Shannon, our president.

The Washington *Post* reported on June 30 that the University "asked to be excused" from its commitment to host the tournament in 1962. Asked whether race figured in the request, Gus Tebell replied: "That did not count in it at all." It was just that "interest has been dropping off lately." *Sports Illustrated* was dubious, running a story entitled "Tennis the Menace" in its July 3 issue. With no evidence but with a style not lacking in snide it claimed that the regular appearance of Negroes made people in Charlottesville "unhappy." The tournament would take place the next year at Williams College "where the sight of a Negro in white flannels does not upset white citizens as it apparently does in Charlottesville." The following September the *CD* editor took the magazine to task, writing that the decision was made because the tournament was a financial burden to the University and "it was not drawing spectators or nation-wide participation." He might have added that none of the players ever wore white flannels.

As the second semester got under way what the *CD* referred to as the "controversial" Jefferson chapter began anew to seek Student Council recognition. Several Council members were worried about a clause in the chapter's constitution that would give "honorary membership" to persons outside the University. They feared, at least as the *CD* reported, that such a possibility might lead to "radical or NAACP domination." The paper's editor joined the spreading controversy. He conceded Council's right to deny recognition but advised against using it. If, in the future, the Jefferson chapter should "conduct itself in a manner unbecoming to the University" the Student Council would then have "the power and the duty to abolish the group." That drew the reply from one of the Council members that once "unbecoming" behavior had taken place it would be too late to find a remedy. Once again University "reputation," never defined, was in the forefront.

We came to the October 31 meeting expecting recognition to be denied. Jack Jolly, the chapter president, had prepared a statement to follow the rejection vote. Tom Hammond (my department's Soviet history expert) was allowed to speak. Deftly—and with courtesy and respect—he reminded the councilors of Jeffersonian principles of free speech. He probably quoted one of the most frequently cited of Jefferson's aphorisms: "for here we are not afraid to tolerate any error, so long as reason is free to combat it." As for reputation, he wondered how the University would be regarded if it suppressed a group because of its views and values. The newspaper account of the meeting says nothing of Tom's closing remarks, but they are the ones that have stuck in my memory. The exact words have slipped away but their import has not. With a bit of irony slyly entering his tone, he drew a parallel between the proposed Council action and the repressive policies of the Soviet Union, closing with something like "you don't really want to be like that, do you?" I think some still did, but a graduate student member's motion to table the issue ended the meeting. Some of the councilors told me Tom's remarks had influenced them.

Two weeks later the chapter won recognition but only after one final concession. With rejection once again threatened, the members present retreated to the hallway to craft a hasty charter change stating that their group would not "sponsor direct action such as picketing or boycotting." The *CD* editor wrapped up the story. "A constitution now governs the Chapter's actions," he wrote. "If it is violated, the group may be ordered to desist and disband. Until such a time, the Council's positive vote appears to have been in order." Two weeks after this meeting the Student Council gave unanimous approval to the John Randolph Society of the Young Americans for Freedom, a conservative, anti-communist organization. It was not asked to include an anti-direct action clause in its charter. Tom and I rounded out our involvement in Student Council affairs a little later. After the publication of an unsigned faculty member's letter to the editor critical of the YAF, a member of the organization hinted that perhaps it had been written by someone associated with the Jefferson Chapter. Since Tom and I were the only faculty members so associated we replied that neither of us had written the letter. "Believing strongly in the principle that the University should encourage the widest range of student discussion and thought," we added, "we heartily approve the Student Council's recognition of the John Randolph Chapter."

In all the debates over recognition of the Jefferson chapter of the VCHR there were no spoken or written words about the superiority of the white race. No one critical of our integrationist leanings resurrected the crude language of faculty chairman Barringer or echoed the racist rhetoric of editor Kilpatrick. This reticence ended with a speech by Henry E. Garrett before the Jefferson Society, the University's prestigious literary and debating society. Garrett came with all sorts of academic credentials. A former professor of psychology at Columbia, where he had been chairman of the department, he had been president of the American Psychological Association. He had recently joined our Education school as a visiting professor. The announcement of his talk in the *CD* was headed "Negro Race Is Inferior To Whites." His topic was "The Equalitarian Dogma," a term he apparently coined. Since the speech was closed to the public I did not hear it. A flurry of letters to the editor followed, most from students and faculty who had not heard the speech. Some condemned the Jefferson Society for hosting Garrett, some roasted the "inequalitarian dogma" he represented, but most defended his right to speak and stressed the importance of intellectual freedom. Only one letter carried echoes of Barringer and Kilpatrick. That came from a first-year law student who wrote of how "pureblooded" Africans developed when left on their own, inviting skeptics to compare any village in the Congo with Paris or Rome, an analogy he borrowed from Carleton Putnam's *Race and Reason*, a recently published book that became the Bible of the extreme wing of the Southern segregation movement.

In his letter to the editor, the president of the Jefferson Society defended the decision to invite Garrett because he was a major scholar and the Society's policy was to bring to the University many contrasting viewpoints. Among other examples, he cited the recent sponsorship of a talk by Ralph Bunche. Then, he added, "We are planning an address by a faculty member who opposes Professor Garrett's viewpoint." Two weeks later a front-page article reported that "Gaston Will Speak For 'Other Side' of Race Differences Issue Tonight." The paper carried a report (generally accurate) of what I had said, under the heading "Arguments On 'Innate Inferiority' Irrelevant, Gaston Tells Society." Whether that report met universal agreement, boredom, or indifference I do not know, but no letters or editorials followed.

Jefferson Hall was packed the night I spoke. I came with a text, later published in shortened form in the student magazine *Plume and Sword*. As I read it over now I am struck by how earnest I was. There was much in it about the American creed and Jefferson's notions of freedom and a lot about how the black freedom struggle strengthened and affirmed American values. I admitted that I was no expert in brain measurement and intelligence testing but reported that I had consulted several experts in the University who were (my scribbled notes on these conversations run to several pages). All of our resident specialists thought Garrett was full of nonsense. In one summing up sentence I said that if any in my audience were concerned about the intelligence of their grandchildren they should make sure their child married one of Martin Luther King's offspring rather than any number of white youngsters I could think of. That was my stab at the "overlap" theory. My main point was that the whole inequalitarian argument was irrelevant anyway. In America we judge people as individuals. Constitutional protections and rights belonged to all persons without regard to their intelligence quotient.

After the talk I sent a copy of the text to Professor Garrett and suggested that we have a chat over lunch. We did. We were sitting outside the dining hall afterwards, talking politely about our differences, when Dumas Malone happened by. He and Garrett knew each other from when they had been colleagues at Columbia. "My," Dumas remarked, with a twinkle in his eye, "this is an unlikely pair." Indeed we were. Garrett was well known as an arch-segregationist. He wrote for such publications such as *The Citizen*, the journal of the Citizens' Council, the uptown Ku Klux Klan of the time; was an outspoken opponent of the *Brown* decision from the moment it was handed down; organized an international group of scholars opposed to what they called "race mixing"; and joined several ultra-right wing organizations, including the Liberty Lobby. He was far more zealous in his opposition to my concept of racial justice than any member of our faculty. I wondered who had invited him to be a visiting professor but I never bothered to inquire. A few years later he and his wife bought a house across from ours. We exchanged civil nods when we met in the street, but never broke bread together again.

Meeting Southern white segregationists like Henry Garrett was instructive, but it was a lot more pleasurable to get to know some of the leaders from the other side, my side. Sometime in the fall, while we were jousting with the Student Council over recognition of the Jefferson chapter, Mary and I drove down to Farmville, the seat of Prince Edward County, where the public schools had been shut down by the segregationists since 1959. We went to a black Baptist church to hear a rousing talk by Ralph Abernathy,

Martin King's right-hand man. He was thirty-five, I was thirty-three; young men, I thought, to be trying to make big changes in their worlds. But then I remembered my grandfather Gaston, starting up his own model community when he was thirty-three. Like me, Abernathy was born and reared in Alabama. I recall little of what he said that night but I do remember how I was rocked by the music (nothing like it ever reverberated through the chambers of Mary's monotone-constricted Episcopal churches) and how I was entranced by how Abernathy laced Old and New Testament authority into his call to struggle for justice and for civil rights. On the drive back I told Mary I might become a Christian if I heard many more sermons like that one.

We met that night in the church presided over by L. Francis Griffin, the iconic figure of the Prince Edward freedom movement and its challenge to segregated education that would become part of the *Brown* decision. I would get to hear Griffin speak later but I never got to know him as well as Gordon Moss, the gentle but steel-willed professor of American history at Longwood College, also in Farmville. A native of Lynchburg with a Yale doctorate, Gordon was a member of the VCHR and about the only white person in the county who spoke out consistently against what he called the Prince Edward County oligarchy. It was that oligarchy, he said in a Charlottesville speech I invited him to give, that closed the schools—not, he stressed, just because they were white supremacists, which they were, but because they were exploiters who wanted a cheap and uneducated labor force, white as well as black. Echoes of that kind of analysis—with their Fairhope ring—ran through much of the newer works on Southern history I read and incorporated in my own teaching.

In the spring of '62, just before my Jefferson Hall speech, I met Martin King for the first time. A small group of us drove to the Carter Glass High School in Lynchburg to attend a huge rally, filled with music and oratory. King's speech, which came late in the evening, was riveting, full of the phrases and aphorisms that were to become so familiar in the next few years. To hear them for the first time from a man who was a year my junior gave me hope for the future. After the close of the rally we drove to the home where King and his entourage were staying for the evening. One of the black members of our group knew the hosts who had invited us to come to the house. I was eager to meet King and to have a good conversation with him about the direction of the movement. As we entered the living room the group was in a circle, singing freedom songs. Greeting us, King said, "Let us widen the circle for our white friends." We joined in the singing of one or two more songs when Ralph Abernathy, much to my dismay, instructed us to hum quietly while he took Martin up the stairs. He needed his rest.

VI

Contrary to what this chapter may suggest up to now, my first five years in Charlottesville were not so filled with civil rights activities that they crowded out every other aspect of life. There was too much of my mother in me not to seek out and enjoy good friends and good times. We had both in abundance. We lived in a quite amazing junior faculty area built the year before we came on the grounds of an old plantation. It consisted of the plantation home, two apartment buildings, and a dozen or so three-bedroom bungalows. We lived in one of the bungalows. We were in the midst of mature trees with a lovely meadow at the center and deep woods and a small mountain at the rear. Children ran happily from one house to the other. We had varied interests, backgrounds, and fields of specialization that drew us together and lasting friendships were formed. We lived well and happily. We were also regulars at the faculty club formal dances. My tuxedo still fit and I enjoyed wearing it. Mary was as beautiful in her velvet evening gown as she had been when we went to our first student dance in Philadelphia, a judgment I saw frequently confirmed by my male friends.

By my neighbor across the street, the mathematician Rob Davis (son of the famous CBS correspondent Elmer Davis), I was introduced to Alexis Lichine's wine writings. With all that new knowledge (there were wines even better than Beaujolais!) I began my regular runs to Central Liquor in Washington and when my desires outran my resources I formed a three-couple wine club. We met monthly to drink good and great wine, including first-growth Bordeaux now far beyond the means of assistant professors (and, indeed, my own today). I became an obsessive wine man, educating our dinner guests with what I thought to be learned commentaries on my choices for the evening. I still recall Mary's under-the-table shin kicks those disquisitions occasioned. She didn't object when I published "In Defense of Wine" in one of the student literary magazines but I don't recall that she attended the wine tastings I shamelessly conducted for groups like the Law School Wives' Club. Probably a disproportionate ratio of talking to tasting.

THE ENTHUSIASM I HAD for wine was more than matched by the joys of being a father to Blaise and Chinta. They were four and one when we arrived, ten and seven when our six-year residence tenure was up. We rode our sleds on a winding steep trail all the way to the street during winter snowstorms; played games on the floor; read books at bedtime; and hiked the little mountain behind us. Blaise and I rode our bikes to school when he entered first grade. Chinta was the belle of Mimosa Drive, indiscreetly shedding her underwear about the neighborhood when warm weather came. She met her friend Rebecca from across the street when she was two; they have just turned fifty and have been best friends all their lives. Blaise met Philip, our next-door neighbor. They, too, have remained life-long friends. Philip, now a locally renowned photographer, makes the photographs of Blaise's art furniture for his web site; Blaise reciprocates with cabinet work for Philip. In the summers we visited Fairhope where we swam, fished, crabbed, and took trips to the Gulf. They bonded with their grandparents, knowing no other names for them than Marge and Cornie. Perhaps I would have written more and better and faster if I had spent less time with my two children, but that option never crossed my mind. Watching them live their fascinating lives, and being a part of those lives, was too important to my own growing up.

During those early years we were frequent visitors to Mr. Jefferson's home, Monticello, taking along any visiting friends. Blaise and Chinta often tagged along. On one occasion, standing by the fish pond, I explained to our guests that Mr. Jefferson always had it well stocked so that he could have fresh fish for dinner whenever he wished. With a puzzled look on his face, Blaise interjected: "Daddy, where *is* Mr. Jefferson? He's never here when we come." The man was a presence, always called Mr. Jefferson as

*Summering in Fairhope
with Blaise and Chinta*

though one had lately been visiting with him. Only those trapped in igno-rance would call him Jefferson; only philistines would call him Tom.

Much to my surprise, William Faulkner was writer-in-residence when I arrived. In future years I would often be asked if I had met the great man. I explained then (as I do now if asked) that, yes, I had. We met, I explain, at adjacent urinals in the Cabell Hall fifth-floor men's room. As Mr. Faulkner zipped up he said "Good mawnin', suh." As I zipped down, I replied, in the most authentic Alabama accent I could fashion, "Good mawnin', suh." Even though his office was just across the hall from mine we never had another conversation. I was no good at hunting, fishing, and drinking conversation, the staple of real Southern men, and Mr. Faulkner was notoriously difficult to engage in conversation about his work. He did answer questions at his required public readings, but you always had the feeling you were dueling with him to get at what he really thought. Or maybe, as I think is true, you just had to listen carefully to what he said and let it sink in.

Two occasions come to mind. At one a graduate student in the English department started in with something like "Mr. Faulkner: Malcolm Cowley says in *The Portable Faulkner* that your characters never make a conscious choice between good and evil. Do you agree with that?" I had a feeling that Faulkner's hesitation came from a feeling that the questioner should know the answer, but he gave his, in that high-pitched voice: "Well, I wrote some of them books a long time ago and I don't rightly remember. Offhand, though, I'd tend to disagree with that statement." On another occasion he was asked to discuss the use of symbolism in his novels. "Writin' a novel," he would explain, "is like buildin' a privy. You get strong boards and drive the nails true so your privy will stand against the wind and the rain—and if when you're all done the nails make an extra pretty pattern, well, that's just so much gravy." The literalists had a hard time with that answer, maybe throwing Joe Christmas at him, but others knew the truth he was speaking.

It was not until my sixth year that I taught my first graduate class in Southern history, but those first five were full of pleasure and opportunity. I taught Virginian history from the start and was often only a few steps ahead of my best students. I was behind some in knowing how to pronounce such names as Buchanan and Botetout. My bread-and-butter course was the large survey of American History; my special pleasure was the seminar version I created in my first year. In my second year Pat Hale, our chairman, gave me more-or-less free rein to modify our very modest honors program. I was early on approached by senior colleagues in the government and philosophy departments to develop a program similar to theirs. They were Oxbridge types (some were Rhodes scholars) and the main forces in a modestly populated and often criticized College Honors program. Since I was from Swarthmore they expected to find in me an ally for expanding and strengthening the program. They did. Even as I listened respectfully to some of the sneers directed toward the teas and tutorials, I shared a strong belief in ungraded tutorial and seminar instruction coupled with external examination. I would become the chairman of the College honors program the next year and I was able to expand the history program over the next few. It would eventually come crashing down under criticism from my colleagues, an indication to me of how little they trusted the fundamental ideas of the program, especially the requirement that they hand over to others the right to judge their students.

The pleasures of social and family life, the absorption in teaching, and my deepening involvement in both university and community civil rights activities took a heavy toll on my scholarship. Partly, I suppose, it was that I never learned to balance the four parts of my life; partly, of course, it was that scholarship was the most difficult of the four and the easiest to let slide. I had completed a large portion of the research for my dissertation when I arrived, but I had written very little. More than two years passed after my arrival with almost no additional pages written. Then, sometime in the middle of the 1959–60 academic year, my senior colleague Ed Younger walked into my office to tell me that some major decisions were going to be made in the history department in the next years and he wanted me to be part of the making of them. Well, sure, I told him; I'd be glad to be able to do that. I hadn't gotten the point. He had to explain it: if I didn't finish the dissertation and receive my Ph.D. I wouldn't be making any decisions in the department; the department would be making a decision about me that I wouldn't like. I sat down to write in January 1960, submitted a polished manuscript to Fletcher and his colleagues in July and drove to Chapel Hill for my successful defense in August. Everyone—Ed, Mary, my friends and neighbors, Fletcher, and I—relished the sense of relief.

Fletcher apparently felt more than relief. He thought the dissertation was pretty good, so good that when an opening in the Princeton department was advertised in the fall of 1961 he recommended me, without ever telling me. Two of his former students, Bob Lively and Arthur Link, were already on the Princeton faculty. I suppose he would have liked a third. At about the same time I heard from Mary Albertson, chair of the Swarthmore history department, asking if I would consider coming there as a visiting assistant professor during 1962–63. Mary and I found the prospect of a year at our alma mater an appealing one. I wrote to Miss Albertson to tell her so. Then I heard from Princeton asking me to come to the American Historical Association annual meeting after Christmas to talk about a position there. I had a good meeting with Bob Palmer, a European historian whose work I very much admired and whose charm was engaging. We had an enjoyable conversation and I thought I had made a good impression, probably because I wasn't in hot pursuit of the job. I had hardly returned to Charlottesville when an invitation arrived to visit Princeton.

The month or so after that January meeting forced on us difficult decisions we had never thought of having to make. I was offered the Princeton job at a salary of $7,500, $600 more than I was making at Virginia. I told Jerry Blum, the Princeton chairman, that, given the higher cost of housing and living in Princeton, I would be worse off materially there than in Charlottesville. He immediately raised the offer to $8,000. I wrote to tell Mary Albertson about that and I wrote to Jerry to tell him I'd like to come up with Mary for another visit. Miss Albertson then wrote to say Swarthmore now wanted to make me a formal tenure track appointment as an assistant professor at a salary of $9,000. She also asked me to come up to Swarthmore, which we did following the Princeton visit. Our heads were spinning.

We were lavishly entertained at Princeton, although I was suspicious when no assistant professors were invited to meet me. But I was thrilled that Eric Goldman, one of my most admired historians, liked my dissertation and offered good suggestions for turning it into a book. In fact, all five members of the departmental search committee had read the dissertation and all saw in it a major book. We were least attracted by the comment of one of the supposedly left-wing historians. He said to Mary, "You know, Mrs. Gaston, Princeton is a very civilized place." To which she replied, "Yes, that's what they tell us about Virginia."

Jim Field, in that way he had of forming a compliment wrapped in irony, greeted me at Swarthmore as "the most sought-after young scholar in the East." At a Howard Johnson's lunch, Miss Albertson asked Larry Lafore to "look over the sherries" because I was there and it was a special occasion. Larry protested, but grumpily went to look and came back with a petulant report: "They don't have any sherries!"

Now came decision time. Declining the Swarthmore offer was easier for Mary than for me. I had been told that I could teach an honors seminar on Southern history as well as on any other American history subject that appealed to me. That was very appealing. But when I saw a notice on the Parish bulletin board inviting people "to celebrate the second anniversary of the beginning of the sit-ins" I wondered what good a Southern racial liberal could do at this already liberal college, a liberal college attended by precious few Southerners. Mary felt living in Swarthmore would make her feel closed in, and her memories of the faculty life we saw sparked anxiety rather than enthusiasm. Princeton was the problem. Mary remembers that she was uneasy about moving there mainly because she preferred what she knew to what she didn't know. She would be happy to do whatever I really wanted to do, to go or to stay. What, though, did I really want to do, stay or go?

That decision was the most agonizing one I ever made. Working it out took me right down to the depths of my sense of self, what I wanted my life to be about and why. Even if I had no contemporary letters, notes, or diaries I could still recall, both in stomach and mind, the torturous route to decision-making. Reading through the six pages of typed, single-spaced, narrow-margined letters I wrote about the options and my reaction to them is reassuring in some respects, unsettling in others.

The story of myself I have told in my mature years—that I chose to teach Southern history in a Southern university as a way of helping to make a better South—resonates with my decision-making, but not as loudly as I have later represented it. "One of the reasons I got into scholarship in the first place," I wrote in my first letter, "was that I wanted my work to have relevance to problems of the South today and it seems to me that, through my courses in Southern History here, and in various roles as an officer in the local Human Relations Council, NAACP, and state Human Relations Council, I could develop a position of some importance that would make it possible for me to make contributions which I could not make in New Jersey." My conscience, I wrote, would be troubled if I accepted the Princeton offer. In a second letter I wrote of how I hoped we might make "Virginia into what Chapel Hill was in the 30's, . . . the leading center in the country for Southern liberals." Encouragement in that direction came from Pat Hale, my chairman, and Bill Duren, the Dean, both of whom, I wrote, "take the line that this is the 'challenge' I should take up instead of the personal and intellectual challenge which Princeton represents." They guaranteed a salary of $8,200 should I stay and encouraged me to think I would have a promising career with them.

On the other hand, I was mightily tempted by the Princeton offer. I had no anchor so firmly planted in my reformist mission that I could slough off the chance to move to the big leagues without hesitation or doubt. The contrary was true. I wrote glowingly to my parents about Princeton, the generous teaching options I had been given, the chance to develop Southern history there, and the thrill of joining what I called one of the "big three" of the Ivy League institutions. Intellectual stimulation was likely to be greater, the faculty and students were superior, and the Princeton connection would be a better springboard to a position of national influence. And, unlike Swarthmore, there would be many Southern students to influence. A good friend remonstrated with me for even thinking of turning down Princeton. I owed it to my family to leave the Virginia backwater for a position of national prominence. Fletcher wrote to congratulate me on the offer and to urge me to accept it. Careers in Southern universities, he wrote, would always be restricted. It saddened me to hear him say that, but I understood his meaning.

So, what decision did I make? The letter describing it is unfortunately and bafflingly absent from my files. Mary and I have similar memories, however, so I must go with them. I was feeling shaky and ill; I nervously wrote a letter to Jerry accepting his offer. I opened the front door of our home to put it in the letter box. The postman had already come and gone. I decided not to leave the letter there for the next day's dispatch. I brought it into the house and placed it on my desk. Felled by anxiety, I went to bed with what felt like a case of the flu. When I waked the next morning everything was clear. I retrieved the letter from my desk, tore it up, and sat down to write a second one. This time I declined the offer. I thanked Jerry profusely for inviting me to join the Princeton faculty and for his patience; I explained my sense of obligation to the South and the struggle there. He replied to say he understood my reasons and admired me for my decision. I have never looked back with regret. Too much of what I have treasured in my life would have been missed had I left Virginia.

Chapter Six

Movement Building

I divided the summer of '62 between our annual holiday in Fairhope and preparing lectures for my course on the history of the South, the course I came to Virginia to teach and which would now be mine. Luckily, I prepared well because shortly after the semester began Charlie Jones wrote from Chapel Hill to ask Tom Hammond and me to produce a report on school desegregation in Charlottesville. The Fellowship of Southern Churchmen and the Southern Regional Council were convening after Christmas a three-day conference in Nashville on "The South: The Ethical Demands of Integration." Martin King would give the keynote address and several of the major black and white leaders of the civil rights movement would be there. That was an invitation I could not refuse. Turning my dissertation into a book would have to wait.

I

Neither Tom nor I was up to writing the authoritative report Charlie wanted so I convened a half dozen knowledgeable local persons and asked most of them to write essays on particular aspects of the subject. We met from time to time at my home to hammer out details and to discuss strategies for speeding up the school board's very gradualist approach to a biracial school system. In the end, with all the essays in, I wrote the report, giving it a rough consistency of style. Two appendices gave a lasting value to the report. One, written by one of the leaders of the women's group that had saved the schools in 1958–59, became an invaluable primary source. The other reported on interviews (conducted by African Americans) of most of the black students in the desegregated schools. The generally favorable descriptions of their experiences gave an optimistic note to our report.

Charlie and his colleagues asked that we supply two hundred copies for the conference, so we hastily typed up and ran the forty-four-page document through a mimeograph machine. A year or so later Tom had it handsomely bound. He gave one copy to me and a few to friends. Five copies were deposited in the university library; even now, as I write in the summer of 2006, two are checked out. Amazingly, this has been the pattern for more than forty years. Librarians tell me there are frequent interlibrary loan requests and several times I have come across citations to the work in books and articles about school desegregation. We never imagined this would be the case and, as I read it over now, I regret its pedestrian style, but its accuracy still stands up to scrutiny. Its continuing usefulness is also a testament to the lack of the thoroughly researched and well-written book that should supersede it. As the only Charlottesville delegate at the Nashville conference, I summarized our findings, answered questions, and joined in a general conversation about school desegregation. The report was well-received.

Nashville was exhilarating in many ways. Meeting King was, of course, a special pleasure. This time, in contrast to our Lynchburg meeting earlier in the year, there would be opportunities to talk. I was struck by the different sides of his personality. In his opening night address he was passionate and eloquent, in the manner for which he was already known. In dealing with people he didn't know or knew only slightly he gave the impression of being keenly interested in their ideas, but kept slightly aloof. Privately, he spoke earnestly about the next steps the movement should take, but without revealing particulars. When the conversation moved to other topics he struck me as someone I would like to spend the evening with, talking about history, politics, and religion. He had a gift for humor, too. Charlayne Hunter (now Hunter-Gault) was at the conference. She had graduated the previous spring from the University of Georgia, one of the two blacks who broke the race barrier there. We were meeting just a few months after the racist outbreak and killings at Ole Miss in protest against the admission of

James Meredith. In a dead-pan style, King announced to the conferees that he had information of interest to impart: Charlayne, he said, "has decided to pursue graduate studies next year at the University of Mississippi." That brought a round of broad laughter and applause.

Three months after the Nashville conference Dr. King came to speak at the University, a guest of the Jefferson chapter of the VCHR. This was a big occasion for us and for the university. Earlier in the year some of the chapter members worried that the university might withhold permission for King to speak. Fortuitously, however, the conservative Randolph Society had invited Communist Party leader Gus Hall and American Nazi Party leader George Lincoln Rockwell to speak earlier than King. Approval of those speakers made it impossible for the University to block King's visit. Still, conferences with B. F. D. Runk, dean of the university, and Paul Saunier, President Shannon's special assistant, accompanied by long memoranda from them, made it clear they wanted to avoid trouble and prevent "embarrassment" of the University and us. Their hope was that all would go off in a "gentlemanly" manner. To that end Saunier made several specific recommendations, among them the request that we control the audience by admitting only those with tickets. His goal appeared to be to keep as many non-university people as possible away from the event. The Board of Visitors, I wrote at the time, wanted to be sure this was a student event and not "an NAACP rally!" (I don't recall having any evidence for that remark, but the board and many of the administrators lived in a world of fear and fantasy in those days.) I was sorry that the chapter agreed to the ticket requirement. "Hundreds of townspeople wanted to come, but couldn't," I wrote to my parents, possibly with some exaggeration. I estimated the audience at between 850 and 900; the *CD* put the attendance at "approximately 900."

There were conspicuous absences apart from the townspeople. President Shannon, declining an invitation to meet Dr. King, was not there. Dean Runk was present, but only as a roving observer. Dean of Admissions Marvin Perry was the only member of the administration who attended as a sympathetic observer. I wrote to Paul Saunier afterwards to thank him for his help but also to say I regretted that "such a dignitary" as Martin King could not have received "some official words of welcome from the Administration." (How much the world and our university would change was demonstrated five years later when President Shannon led a university-wide memorial service for the slain leader.) I also told him we all appreciated "the absence of the dogs and the inconspicuousness of the policemen."

Mary wrote to my parents after the speech to say that "Poor Paul & Tom have been run ragged with all the arrangements, the distrust & dismay from the university, the inefficiency & general tenseness & anxiety. Paul reminded me of me before a dinner party!" We both agreed the speech was good but we were impressed most by the standing ovation at its end and by the long line of people waiting to shake King's hand and see him up close. It was moving for me to see how the town blacks who were able to come idolized him. Students, too, including those who had kept their distance from the civil rights movement, were moved to a new awareness. More than forty years later a former undergraduate spoke to me of the sheer thrill of hearing King, whom he described as a great orator unlike any he had heard before. He jokingly recalled how he decided to move to an upper balcony to stand behind a pillar where he would not be seen, fearful that a report of his presence might cause him to be drummed out of his fraternity. When King pointed his finger at his young audience and said that the future was theirs to determine my friend could see the finger pointing directly at him. It was a scary moment. Perhaps an influential moment, too: he helped to make a better future for his community.

The editor of the *CD*, unlike this student, found nothing in the occasion to celebrate or admire. With a demeaning tone befitting a Kilpatrick wannabe, he wrote that the "abstract terms" which he believed permeated the speech might have helped "the promotional values of his way of thinking" but they were not worthy of analysis. Certainly King erred in tending "to equate the Negro cause with justice." A companion editorial took a swipe at nonviolence, warning against "coercive" nonviolent protest directed against the segregated restaurants at the Corner. Readers were urged to remain faithful to the sacred rights of private property.

After the speech the members of the Jefferson chapter and a few others moved to one of the reception rooms in the student union. We drank punch and ate black and white cupcakes. When we began singing freedom songs one of the servers was so startled that she poured drink onto the table. King explained how "We Shall Overcome" was usually sung. We formed a circle, held hands, and sang, including the verse "black and white together, we shall overcome." All of this was totally new to the punch pourers and probably to the students as well. It was certainly the first time whites and blacks had sung freedom songs together at the University of Virginia.

King was pumped with energy so we took a stroll about the Grounds— King, Mary, Wes Harris, and me. We were startled by a sharp report. I was sure it was a car backfire. Wes was not. He immediately pinned King to the wall. I was right. It was a car backfiring. Wes, an African American—he was a third-year Engineering School student and president of the Jefferson chapter—knew instinctively, from experience as a black man, that he could not afford to make the assumption I did. When I interviewed him many years later he remembered that night:

> It was without a thought, it was instinct. Out of what I would describe as the Southern experience of a black person, in that era. That we had seen so many of our leaders jailed and beaten and dragged through the streets, so a person of King's stature is priceless. So any possible threat of danger or whatever, you would need to protect him. I shall never forget that.

I never saw King again after that night. After we returned to the motel room he told us he knew he would one day be shot and killed. He hoped he would have time to complete his work. He didn't.

Other memories of King's visit stream in. Just as Wes and I were about to leave the airport after his arrival, with him in tow, Mary drove up with our two children, Chinta and Blaise. They wanted to meet the man they heard spoken of so often in our home. King was gracious and shook their hands. That evening, before we went out to dinner, we had supper ready for the children. Blaise refused to wash his hands before coming to the table. One of us asked why (not that this refusal was unprecedented!). "I shook Martin Luther King's hand," our nine-year-old son replied, holding up his right hand. "I don't want to wash it."

There was no "white" restaurant in Charlottesville where this man with such an influential hand could be entertained at dinner. A sit-in was hardly appropriate for this occasion so we drove a few miles south to Bren-Wana, a night club where our host welcomed our guest as the star he was. Our friend Ed Jackson had built it, naming it after his two daughters, Brenda and Edwana. On the weekends it was a hopping night club, the only place around where white and black folk could eat, drink, dance, and talk together. I later met the seductive vocalist at one of the city schools. She was a nurse. The trombone player had a long career as director of the high school band. I danced on occasion with Ed's sister, Teresa. One evening she stepped on my toe and followed with: "Another myth punctured, Paul: you thought we all had rhythm."

On week nights Ed let us have meetings of one of the local civil rights groups. This night was for Martin King. When we arrived we found a West German television crew setting up to film a documentary on race and religion in the United States. Surrounded by us, King did his interview. "Too bad we won't be in Germany to see it," I wrote to my parents. Ed prepared a grand shrimp dinner. I was impressed by it but even more by King's warm praise of "Brother Jackson" for his hospitality and his establishment. King was, I wrote, "friendly and talkative" as well as an "extraordinarily kind and gentle man, completely unegotistical, yet firm and humorous and human." He also told a number of stories. One was about Jim Folsom, the Alabama governor during the Montgomery bus boycott. During its first week, King told us, Folsom summoned a few of the boycott leaders to his office. At that point they were asking for seating without the moveable barrier that crowded blacks in the back, not for the end of segregation. King recalled Folsom saying, "Boys, you're going about this in the wrong way. Hell, you ought to ask for the whole thing—integration. Segregation don't make no sense anyway. But, if you quote me on this I'll call you all damn liars." The story rang true. Several years later I told it to a young scholar writing about Folsom. He said it couldn't be true and declined to include it in his book. What a pity.

King spent the night at the Gallery Court, a white-owned motel near the University. I have no memory of when or how it became integrated, or, indeed, if any blacks had previously lodged there. We were still working hard to end the exclusion policies in the local hotels and restaurants. But I wrote to my parents to say we were "happy to find that not only was the motel integrated but the management seemed honored to have such a distinguished guest. Treated King like a king!" My most vivid memory is of the black staff, with shy good manners, politely stopping by the room, some asking to shake his hand, all indicating the honor they felt in hosting him.

II

The Gallery Court's hospitality was unique in Charlottesville in those days of the early 1960s. Our city was still a closed society. The walls of segregation that cordoned off the theaters, motels, hotels, restaurants, and housing areas— as well as all of the private clubs and recreational facilities—stood firmly. Racial prejudice, combined with a fervent belief in the inalienable rights of private property, seemed to make them impregnable. Our discouraging experience with persuasion seemed to say that reason was no battering ram. That was why Floyd Johnson's words one Sunday afternoon in May 1963 were exactly what we needed to hear. We had come to the annual picnic of the city-county chapter of the Council on Human Relations to reflect on what we had accomplished in the previous year and what we needed to do in the next. Floyd gave us a challenge. Standing on a stool he asked us to gather around him. I knew him only slightly as the newly elected twenty-nine-year-old president of the local branch of the NAACP, recently arrived in Charlottesville to become the minister of one of the black churches.

He told us that he and a few other ministers had sat in at a local Holiday Inn the previous day where they negotiated an agreement for the restaurant to be desegregated in ten days. A sit-in at a delicatessen led the spunky black waitresses to say they would quit if the ministers of their race were not served. Again a desegregation agreement was reached. Other restaurants, however, needed pushing. Those of us who wanted to help with the push-ing should come to his church the next day to receive instructions and join the movement. I caught nervous glances among the whites, almost none of whom had ever been involved in direct-action protest. Most would not make their debuts on this occasion, but about a dozen of us showed up the next afternoon to receive our marching orders. Sit-ins, which had spread across the South three years earlier, were now coming to Charlottesville. History was catching up with us; or, better, we were finally catching up with history before it passed us by.

Our destination was Buddy's Restaurant, chosen because its proprietor had refused to speak to the sit-in leaders. Known to its many admirers by its motto as "just a nice place to eat," Buddy's was close by the university and was popular with many of my colleagues, especially those in the athletic department. Buddy Glover, its genial owner, was well-known and well-liked in the white community. Some who knew him thought we erred in targeting his restaurant. On occasion he had actually permitted African Americans to eat there. The editor of *The Daily Progress*, our local newspaper, took us to task for singling out a man he described as "one of the finest and most public spirited citizens of this community." That, of course, was precisely the point: If the "best" people felt entitled to deny service to African Americans as a general policy, what could one expect from the worst?

Before we left the church for our first sit-in, Floyd instructed us in the art and science of nonviolence. He read from a handbook that told how women could protect themselves from injury without provoking their attackers and how men should keep their hands at their sides. I remember saying to Mary something like, "This is Charlottesville, not Mississippi; nobody is going to attack us here." Still, some apprehension accompanied us. That first evening our group of black and white protestors packed Buddy's Restaurant. There were Christian epigraphs all about the place, none apparently to be invoked on our behalf. On the placemats were notices saying "Don't let our waitresses rush you." They didn't. Instead, one of them spat at us. No black waitresses here. We sat from a little before six until nine o'clock closing time. The atmosphere was tense but no one poured hot coffee on our heads as frequently happened in other sit-ins. We quietly felt strength in our numbers and our purpose.

The next evening a smaller contingent was dispatched to Buddy's while another group went to a second restaurant to be met by a surprise. The owner approached with menus in hand and asked, "What'll you have?" Some had come without money, never anticipating such a reception. Embarrassment was mixed with joy. The sit-in movement was beginning to have its desired effect. At Buddy's ten or so of our group got in before the door was locked, leaving the rest outside. Those who had made their way in remained until closing time. On day three the pattern changed. A bouncer was posted at the door. Acceptable customers were admitted; we were not. We formed a single-file line on the sidewalk leading to the door but did not block the entrance or try to enter ourselves or block others from entering. We were now called "stand-outs" by the local press. By now, Buddy's had become the focal point of the community's racial tensions. Hecklers driving by delivered up their insults. Buses parked strategically to spread their exhaust in our faces. Groups of protestors formed to taunt us. Some, wearing Nazi armbands, belonged to a group called Thunderbolts. The atmosphere was increasingly tense. And, at home, Mary and I were receiving an ongoing series of hate telephone calls.

On the fourth day, Memorial Day, violence erupted. I had been in the line for an hour or so in the early afternoon. Floyd, on duty since mid-morning, was hungry from no lunch. He asked me to call some of the black leaders to find a replacement for him at the head of the line while he found food. I did as he asked, but returned to tell him my mission had failed. He said I should take over as captain of the group. That would be the first time a white person had headed the line. Floyd left about a dozen of us, equally divided between white and black. Not many minutes later four distinctly unfriendly young white men drove up. They made a few more-than-unfriendly remarks on their way in. My anxiety level rose. When they emerged a short time later they greeted us as "nigger lovers" and began to shove some of us, me included, off the sidewalk. I suddenly thought: "You're the captain of the line, responsible for doing something." But what?

Police protection seemed a good idea so I made my way across the street, darting between the cars, to an outside telephone booth. I had never called the police before, so I was fishing the telephone directory out of its resting place to look up the number when a very large man lifted me out of the booth, turned me around, and informed me, "You ain't gonna call no damn police." I looked up at him, impressed by his size and obvious strength, and thought maybe I might say to him, "You're absolutely correct." But I didn't risk it. When he let go of me his wiry confederate, weighing probably no more than 130 or 140 pounds, slapped me across the face with his open hand and then hit me a couple of times hard with his fist, blood oozing from my split lip. Given my adversaries, it required no special commitment to nonviolence for me to offer no resistance. The two then led me across the street, back to the line (to my "friends," they said) and left.

By the time I was returned to the line one of my colleagues had called the police. They arrived soon, emerging from a nearby restaurant with a clear view of us. Some in our group were sure they had been watching all along. This would have been commonplace in Alabama or Mississippi, but Charlottesville? I never knew. I was nervous and reluctant to press charges, wanting the whole thing to go away, but my fellow protestors argued successfully against that. The police easily identified my assailants from the description I gave them. The large one was Thomas Henley, the smaller one, James Cowgill, each twenty-seven years old. My friend and history department colleague Everett Crosby gave me a ride to the police station where I swore out a warrant for their arrest for the misdemeanor offense of assault and battery. I asked a detective there if Henley and Cowgill were the kind of men who might go to my home to harass my family. He said they weren't, but they might go back to the line and cause trouble there. Which is precisely what they did do, with no policemen sent there to stop them. Floyd and William Johnson, also an African American, had returned. Both were beaten, Floyd badly enough to be hospitalized. Years later he told me he still had back pains from that assault.

After my lip was bandaged I drove out to the ball park. I was the assistant coach of Blaise's little league team. My bandage added an exotic touch to the event. Even more exotic was Everett's arrival a short time later to tell me that Henley had sworn out a warrant for my arrest. I left the unfinished game—the assistant coach charged with a crime—to have a friend post a property bond at the police station (there would be no release-on-recognizance for one of "us."). Blaise would later tell Chinta that I had been arrested. "My daddy's not a criminal" was my seven-year-old daughter's immediate retort. She raced to her mother hoping to be told her older brother was wrong. (Why did he always have to be right?) Mary told her, "Well, darling, sometimes the government is wrong." Thirty years later, when she was an assistant

United States attorney for the southern district of New York, Chinta told that story to a gathering of her colleagues, stressing her mother's wisdom. "Ah," one of her fellow government attorneys retorted, "but now you know the government is never wrong." Knowing laughter followed.

Meanwhile, Mary struggled through her day. With all of the stress and hostile telephone calls, she had suffered a bad case of sleep deprivation. After lunch she had taken a pill, fallen into a deep sleep, and then was awakened to be told that I had been assaulted. She was still groggy when she drove to the airport to meet her sister Clare, arriving for what had been planned as a quiet weekend of visiting with us and her parents, Elizabeth and Ted. Back at home, I reported to the family that I had been charged with "cursing and abusing" and raising my arms "in a menacing fashion." Floyd and William had been charged with similar offenses.

It was not to be the restful weekend of family visiting we had hoped for. Final exams were upon me, one on Friday afternoon, another on Saturday morning. We "stand-outs" had a meeting on Friday, deciding to have no more activity at Buddy's. I had to find a lawyer but had no idea whom to ask. Friendly advice poured in, with offers to pay my legal fees. Several previously detached people I knew called to say they wanted to spring into action. I was a "hero"; what could they do? Several of the custodial staff dropped by to see me and to say thank you. I was deeply moved. When I walked into the classroom to hand out the final exam for my Southern history class the students greeted me with long applause. I managed to say "thank you" and to hold back tears until I left the room.

As if designed to counter all these good vibes, the harassing telephone calls got worse. That Saturday night Henry and Gertrude Mitchell came to dinner. Henry was the priest-in-charge at the "black" Trinity Episcopal Church. We had bonded soon after they arrived in town, the year after us. He and Gertrude had become good friends with Ted and Elizabeth and were much admired and liked by Clare as well. This evening was to be part of our restful family visiting. Instead, we were interrupted by another harassing caller, a husky male voice, asking me: "You integratin' the niggers tonight, Mr. Gaston?" When we went to bed we buried the telephone with pillows. The next morning we discovered we had had a different kind of caller. This

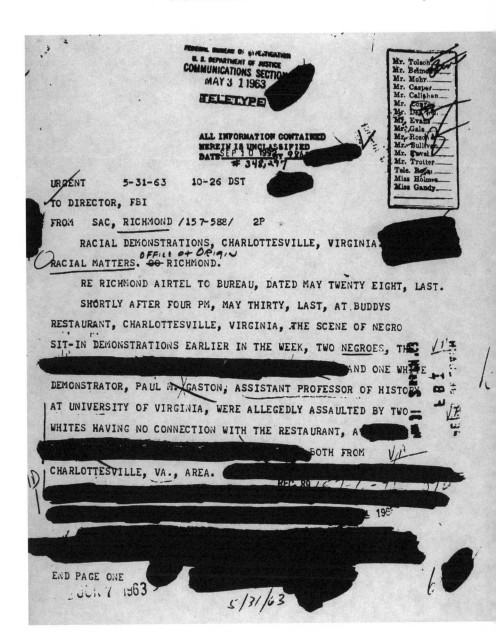

RACIAL DEMONSTRATIONS, CHARLOTTESVILLE, VIRGINIA.

RE RICHMOND AIRTEL TO BUREAU, DATED MAY TWENTY EIGHT, LAST.

SHORTLY AFTER FOUR PM, MAY THIRTY, LAST, AT BUDDYS RESTAURANT, CHARLOTTESVILLE, VIRGINIA, THE SCENE OF NEGRO SIT-IN DEMONSTRATIONS EARLIER IN THE WEEK, TWO NEGROES, THE ... AND ONE WHITE DEMONSTRATOR, PAUL M. GASTON, ASSISTANT PROFESSOR OF HISTORY AT UNIVERSITY OF VIRGINIA, WERE ALLEGEDLY ASSAULTED BY TWO WHITES HAVING NO CONNECTION WITH THE RESTAURANT, A ... BOTH FROM CHARLOTTESVILLE, VA., AREA.

END PAGE ONE

From my FBI files.

one had slashed all four of our car tires. I was not everyone's hero.

The story of the tire slasher unfolded over the summer. One of my neighbors had seen him in the act, thought he was letting air out of my tires and warned him away with a scolding, but not before getting a good look at him. Tom Hammond had an idea of who he was and produced a photograph he found in the university's files. The neighbor identified him. He was an honors student, the son of a Virginia state trooper. He had been one of our hecklers at Buddy's. When Dean Runk called him in for a discussion, he denied slashing the tires. My neighbor then entered the room for a positive identification. He was called before a university disciplinary committee, two of whose members told me that he admitted everything and then harangued them for twenty minutes about the degradation of the country and how no one would any longer stand up for principles. The youth of today, he said, must fight fearlessly for "principles."

The disciplinary committee, in the language of the time, "awarded" him a two-year "enforced withdrawal" from the university. Unfortunately for him, he had lied to Dean Runk. That was an honor offense. The honor committee dutifully ejected him permanently from the university. I often reflected on the fact that slashing a faculty member's tires would cost you two years; lying about it was an automatic life sentence. Thirty-five years later one of the slasher's classmates, now a famous poet, was in town for a party. He told me the sequel: finishing college elsewhere, the slasher had gone on to medical school and was now a practicing psychiatrist.

Somewhere in the midst of all this, the owner of the swim club to which we belonged announced that I would no longer be welcome as a member. He was an uptight, old-fashioned segregationist, determined that a white integrationist like me would not sully his establishment. Mary and the children were welcome to continue, he said, but not me. A legion of our friends, some members of the club, including some on the governing board, gave him a hard time. When the prospect of petitions, controversy, and possible mass resignations loomed, he reconsidered. He wrote to say that I could remain a member; the past would be past and forgotten. Fry's Spring Beach Club has become the premier integrated, family swimming facility of the city. Our granddaughter swims there regularly, just as her mother did.

III

The days after our beatings (studiedly called "scuffles" by the local paper) were fraught with tension as we moved toward the trial date. Cowgill joined his comrade Henley in filing charges against the Johnsons and me; I was guilty of "cursing and abusing" him as well as Henley, but also of assault and battery: hitting him with my fists. We assumed all along that the charges against us were created as bargaining chips, a view confirmed when the lawyer for Henley & Cowgill offered to drop their charges if we would drop ours. We declined the offer. They were guilty and we were not. By this time I had accepted the advice of Paul Saunier, the president's assistant, to engage a well-known local firm to represent me. Paul came to my office Monday morning for the discussions and to make the arrangements. I should not be seen coming to the president's office, he said, lest someone think I was being brought there to be reprimanded.

I was not reprimanded, or seen to be reprimanded, but the president coolly kept his distance from me for reasons he never explained. On the Monday afternoon the external honors examiners were here to conduct their oral examinations. As chairman of the college honors program, one of my responsibilities was to host a luncheon for them. The custom was for the committee chairman to escort the president to the luncheon. Sensing that President Shannon might find it awkward to be with me in private, I telephoned his office to ask if he would like me to call for him or if he would prefer to meet us at the dining room. Word came that he would get there on his own. It must have been embarrassing for him when he did arrive. My prominent bandage attracted immediate questions and a buzz of discussion of the sit-in and the assault on me. The visitors spoke as eager allies and admirers, none as critics or skeptics, all eager for details. The president sat mute through it all. He must have felt a great sense of relief when he could turn the subject to the honors program and to his appreciation of the important task the examiners had undertaken.

I wondered at the time what the president's thoughts were. A year earlier, when I had turned down the Princeton job, he telephoned me at home to say how pleased he was with my decision. He looked upon me as someone who would make many positive contributions to the university. But this time there was no telephone call, only silence. Apparently this was not the kind of positive contribution he had in mind.

The trial began on Friday morning. Jack Camblos, the Commonwealth's Attorney (elsewhere district attorney), decided to handle the case himself and to prosecute all five of us. Normally he did not get involved in misdemeanor cases but this one promised to be not only an attention-grabber but potentially explosive. When a large crowd showed up at the municipal court we moved to the large circuit court building. Two hundred viewers soon filled it up. William and Floyd had asked Sam Tucker, the NAACP attorney from Emporia, to represent them. I later regretted that I had not made the same choice. Sam was a friend and ally; my attorneys were neither. We knew the judge was unfriendly (some called him a hanging judge) but there was little we could do about that. A picture of Mr. Jefferson hung conspicuously from the wall behind his chair.

All five of us were sequestered except for when we were testifying as defendants or plaintiffs. On that first day Camblos prosecuted Henley and Cowgill vigorously, or at least so we were told. The most amusing moment for me came when Henley, asked if I had cursed and abused him, replied that I had; I had said "get away from me, you drunken fool." Perhaps that was his idea of how a professor would curse and abuse. Had I had wished to go that route I could have done a much better job. Our prosecution was left over for the following day. When Sam told Floyd and William that he would not be back then for the trial's conclusion, they were alarmed. Sam tried to ease their anxiety by assuring them that all would be well. But we did not rest easily that night.

Friends who witnessed the next day's proceedings agreed that Camblos was much lighter on violence than on civil rights demonstrations. He characterized us not as the nonviolent protestors we claimed we were. Instead, he argued that we had done everything we could to provoke an incident in order to get publicity for ourselves. Seasoned observers understood that this day was designed to convict us in the court of public opinion. It would make good copy for the Sunday paper. This was a well-trod route segregationists often took when they lacked evidence to convict in the real court. Fortunately for us, there were too many credible witnesses even for a prosecutor as disdainful as Camblos or a judge as prejudiced as ours to convict us. But the popular stereotype would play well in the press.

The trial's end came early Saturday afternoon. Camblos summed it up by saying there was not enough evidence to convict anyone. The judge wound up the proceedings with additional insults, closing with his wish that he could convict us. But he couldn't. We were acquitted. Our assailants were found guilty, fined $10, and given thirty-day suspended sentences. "That's what it costs to hit a nigger," one of them remarked as he left the court room: "ten dollars." Not surprisingly, that comment never appeared in the Charlottesville newspaper.

I found out later why Sam hadn't felt at liberty to say straight out on Friday why we should not worry. The decisions had already been reached. Early on the mayor and others had gotten together and decided that we "demonstrators" should be pilloried with words but not convicted of assault and battery; and that Henley and Cowgill should be convicted, but given the lightest possible sentences.

I believed then, as an activist, and believe now, as a historian, that the Buddy's sit-in was a major turning point in Charlottesville's history. We had been negotiating for years with local restaurants, motels, hotels, and theaters, with almost no success. Our sit-in movement accomplished what negotiation did not. About ten restaurants agreed to desegregate; so did two of the three theaters in town, including the University theater, the object of our boycott two years earlier. The sit-in also shook the city council out of its complacency and evasion. Five of us in the Human Relations Council drafted a formal request asking the mayor to appoint a biracial advisory commission. "We have been asking for this for several years," I told my parents, "and two previous mayors have promised to appoint one, but always found excuses not to do so." Now, I wrote, "as a clear result of the direct action the council has finally moved and such a commission will be appointed next week." It was appointed. Things began to get better.

President Kennedy helped. He had done little to forward the aspirations of civil rights advocates during the first two years of his administration. Now he was finally moved to take action. The Birmingham demonstrations, leading to the arrest of black children, the fire-hosing of defenseless adults, and

Bull Connor's police dogs became the staple on the evening news. Shocked Americans demanded federal action. My home state seemed to be supplying all the obscenity needed to mobilize the nation against its historic oppression. As if Birmingham and Bull Connor had not been enough, Governor George Wallace blocked the entrance of two black students who had won court approval for admission to the state university. Kennedy ordered the National Guard into Tuscaloosa to ensure the safety of the students. On June 11, 1963, he went on live television to declare himself.

We were moved by what we heard. Fresh from our own turmoil and the calumny heaped upon us, we felt he was talking about us, offering support for what we had done. It was time, he said, for every American to "examine his conscience." It ought to be possible "for American consumers of any color to receive equal service in places of public accommodation, such as hotels and restaurants and theaters and retail stores, without being forced to resort to demonstrations in the street." I remember coming near to tears when he said, "We are confronted primarily with a moral issue. It is as old as the scriptures and is as clear as the American Constitution." When he said the time had come for "the nation to fulfill its promise" because of "the events in Birmingham and elsewhere," I counted us as part of the "elsewhere." That "elsewhere" was, in fact, spread wide and deep. The Southern Regional Council would later report that in 1963 there were 900 public protest demonstrations in at least 115 cities in 11 Southern states. We in Charlottesville were part of a powerful and historic movement for justice. We were part of the reason Kennedy ended his speech with the announcement that he would submit forthwith to the Congress a civil rights bill to outlaw those things against which we had been protesting.

Sometime after the trial Alan Bruns, whom I regarded as one of the best reporters in the Commonwealth, told me that my blood was the first to have been drawn in a Virginia civil rights demonstration. In my research over the years that followed I could find no contradictory evidence. Unlikely though it seems, I apparently did earn a first in this episode, even if only by a matter of minutes. Floyd, William, and I should share the honor if, indeed, there is honor to be shared.

Buddy Glover, at the center of all this, never desegregated his restaurant.

On July 2, 1964, Lyndon Johnson signed the Civil Rights Act that made it illegal for Buddy to continue operating as a segregated establishment. That same day he put a sign in the restaurant's window. It read: "Closed to the public this 2nd day of July, 1964, at 6:57 p.m. Passage of the Civil Rights Bill forced us to take this unfortunate action." Buddy remained true to his principles. His sign was picked up by the news services to appear in newspapers both at home and abroad.

The Buddy's affair influenced our lives in many lasting ways. Perhaps the most memorable had its origins at the end of the first day of the trial. I came home that afternoon feeling the stress not only of the day but of the week that had gone before it. Anxious though I was, I knew deep down that what we had done was right and good. That was a powerful shield against the forces arrayed against us. It seemed shameful that so many human beings, especially people even given the respect of the community, should fail to understand the difference between right and wrong. At some point in the evening I said to Mary, "Let's do something to affirm life." She liked what I had in mind. Gareth was born nine months later, our civil rights son.

IV

In July we set off for our annual summer vacation in Fairhope. On the way we stopped in Greenville, South Carolina, to visit Mary's cousin Sibet and her husband Pete. At lunch Pete's brother-in-law dropped by. He refused to eat with us, said little, and seemed to stare at us. He left after a short while and I asked why he had come. Pete explained: "Oh, he just wanted to see what one of you people looked like." What one of us looked liked. Yes, I thought, one more indication—of which we had had so many in the past month—of the insular lives and the fantasies so many of our fellow white Southerners were saddled with.

Our next stop was at one of the Atlanta University colleges where a large SNCC contingent had come for a month-long retreat to study and to plan—and to take a respite from the battle fronts. I was invited to give three lectures on Southern history. I can't remember who invited me or why. Someone must have heard that I was both a historian and a white civil rights activist. In those days there wasn't a large pool to choose from. I knew some of the people by reputation but I had never met them personally. SNCC was born out of the Greensboro and Nashville sit-ins of February 1960 and the dozens of others that quickly spread across the region in their wake. They were the people about whom Frank Graham said: "in sitting down they are standing up for America." They had already taken on mythic proportions for the way they challenged the white supremacy culture and institutions of the South. Many of us were inspired not just by their bravery but also by the simplicity of their style of living, the clarity of their moral views, and the joy they seemed to find in each other, black and white together. I was particularly struck by one young man at our Atlanta conference. I asked someone who he was. "You don't know him?" my new friend said; "He's Horace Mann Bond's boy, Julian." To which I replied, "That boy's going to go places." Many years later, as his colleague at the University of Virginia, I would call up that exchange in introducing Julian at one public occasion or another.

We arrived in Fairhope in time for a swim in the Bay and supper under the shade of the trees where we watched the sunset. The tensions I had accumulated over the past month faded away as if I were having a massage by a master masseur. The martini helped, too. We soon spoke about the sit-in, the trial, and the events growing out of them. Mom told me that everyone who knew about my involvement was proud of me. Those who didn't know, and wouldn't be proud, need not be told. I protested that I thought it would be good for them to know, good for them to know that someone they already knew—and liked—was "one of those people." She said no, she had to live with them, we didn't. I acquiesced.

Soon after this conversation we all went out for the evening. Trudie, daughter of my cousin Joy and her husband Les, came to baby sit for us. The next morning Chinta said, "You know, Daddy, I don't think Trudie feels the same way about sit-ins that we do." I asked how she would know that. I suspected the answer: "Well, we told her about Buddy's and your getting beaten up and all." Ah, yes. Why wouldn't someone in our family want to know about it? Why would anyone in our family feel differently from us?

The next Sunday, at family breakfast on the beach, Les sat on the bench by me. Our voices were warm, friendly; there was no jousting, just good

Southern manners wrapping themselves around a difficult subject, reproduced here as closely as I can recall:

Les: Paul, you know that daughter of mine comes home with the strang-
est stories.

Me: Does she now, Les?

Les: Yeah, she has a way of getting things pretty mixed up sometimes.

Me: Trudie has always seemed to me to be a pretty smart girl, Les.

Les: Really? You think so?

Me: Yeah, Les, I do. I wouldn't doubt stories she told me.

Les: You wouldn't, eh? Well, okay then.

That was all. We joined the rest of the family. We spoke of other
things.

We returned to Charlottesville refreshed, the children tanned and full
of good memories to store up and good stories to pass on. Shortly after our
return I wrote to tell my parents that we had gone to a party at Bren-Wana,
given especially for us. "There were just a few of us," I added, but Ed had
asked his combo to come out to play for us and he prepared a delicious
lobster dinner." And now, after six intense years on the race-relations front,
we were ready for a change of pace and place. I had been promoted to the
rank of associate professor with tenure and I had accepted an offer of a
one-year appointment as a visiting lecturer in the Johns Hopkins University
history department. A year in Baltimore, a new city to us, with new friends,
colleagues, and sites to see beckoned. I was keen to meet Charlie Barker,
author of the Henry George biography I admired, and David Donald, a
star in Lincoln and Civil War studies. David had succeeded Vann Woodward when Vann moved to Yale. Ironically, it was David's departure from
Princeton to come to Hopkins that had opened up the Princeton position
I had declined the previous year.

We had hardly settled into our modest row house (surrounded by
rows upon rows of row houses) when we heard the news of the terrorist
dynamiting of the Sixteenth Street Baptist Church in Birmingham, leaving
four young girls buried in their white dresses under the rubble—the "massacre of the innocents," the Vatican newspaper called it. Coming just two
weeks after the euphoric charge of the March on Washington and King's

"I Have a Dream" speech, it was a grim reminder that all dreams of justice in a humane world were a long way from being fulfilled. Once again we were hit by a sense of helplessness. What could we do? We went to a black church, felt the warmth of welcome and regained strength and optimism from the feeling of solidarity and the grace of the people we touched and were touched by.

Both Hopkins and Baltimore seemed removed from the racial issues that engaged us in Charlottesville. They were no doubt there but they weren't ours and we had not come in search of them. On the other hand, I had occasional reminders of how the Buddy's sit-in had influenced my reputation. Early in the first semester, for example, I received a letter from a young Ph.D. candidate at Yale. She was writing a dissertation in the religion department on acts of courage in the civil rights movement and wanted to include me among the courageous ones she would write about. She lacked the funds to come to Baltimore to interview me so she sent me a tape and a series of questions and asked me to find a recording machine so that I could dictate my answers. I never did it. I didn't feel "courageous" and I often reflected on the fact that I would never have taken center stage that day if I had found one of the black leaders to take Floyd's place or if, when I couldn't, he had either stayed or, on leaving, had asked someone else to head the line. My "hero" status was an accident of history.

Another request, this one much more serious, brought uncomfortably to the surface the darker side of what the Buddy's involvement had revealed to me about myself. A letter arrived one day in the middle of the winter. I have forgotten who wrote it and I have long since lost it, but I vividly remember what it said. Would I agree to come to Mississippi for the summer of 1964 to be the director of the "freedom schools" that were planned to be part of what would come to be called freedom summer? (In the planning stages I believed it was called simply "the summer project.") The plan was to bring to the state young volunteers to conduct voter registration drives and to staff the freedom schools. The schools would be what I thought of as "student-centered," aiming to focus on things that properly interested the pupils. One of our aims would be to deal with both Mississippi history and contemporary Mississippi politics, subjects grossly misrepresented in

Mississippi schools. I was immediately struck by the brilliance of the idea, both as a good civil rights project and a proper calling for a devotee of organic education. But I said no, I could not come.

I had to decline the flattering offer, I wrote, because we were going to have a baby in March and I was broke and had committed myself to teach summer school on my return to Charlottesville. All true. It was also true, however, that I was frightened by the prospect. The memory of the late-night telephone calls; the slashed tires; the fists in my face; the split lip; and my constant nervous stomach had made me gun-shy, reluctant to put myself on the front lines of battle against the white supremacy thugs and terrorists. Others might think of me as a hero of our little civil rights demonstration; I saw myself as one who lacked the courage of those who regularly risked and received beatings, people like my new SNCC friends. In my future courses on the freedom struggle I would draw two related truths from my own experiences. The first was that the segregationists were right when they reckoned that threats and violence sometimes worked as efficient instruments of intimidation. The second was that the young men and women who defied the threats and the violence were a breed apart from the rest of us mortals. They showed (with apologies to Hemingway) grace under pressure.

As time passed and the visceral fear receded I wished that I had decided differently. More than thirty freedom schools were established that summer; three thousand students attended them. Missing the chance to be part of Freedom Summer became one of the few serious regrets of my life. There was plenty of danger and violence, as I had feared there would be, and not just the murders of James Chaney, Michael Schwerner, and Andrew Goodman that came to symbolize the reach of Mississippi brutality. But there was much else, much both inspiring and influential. About a thousand young "volunteers" poured in, mostly from the north; they went home with a deeper understanding of the struggle that they had become better equipped to wage. At the heart of the "summer project," though, were the SNCC workers who projected a democratic vision grounded in an understanding of economic equality that resonated with my Fairhope values. The voter registration drives and the formation of the Mississippi Freedom Democratic

Party, which would carry the voice of civil rights protest to the Democratic Party convention, marked a turning point in the freedom struggle. My friend Jim Silver, a heroic academic who taught history at Ole Miss, called it "the revolution that began to shake Mississippi." It also began to shake America. I'm sorry I missed it.

In November, before I had received the invitation to come to Mississippi, I went to Asheville, North Carolina, for the annual meeting of the Southern Historical Association. Jim Silver was the president that year and his presidential address, "Mississippi: The Closed Society," was greeted by the kind of standing ovation generally foreign to professional meetings like ours. The speech made national news; Jim received more than seven hundred letters from around the country, nearly all favorable. As I listened to his address, and especially to the concluding words in which he reminded us that what he had to say about Mississippi was fundamentally true of the other Southern states, I heard a call to arms, a forceful reminder that Southern history and Southern historians had a crucial role to play in liberating the region from its white supremacy culture and institutions.

My parents came to Asheville to attend their first SHA meeting. Mom in particular thrilled to Jim's address. Fairhope was already becoming Wallace country, she told him as she grasped his arm to thank him for his voice of sanity and plain speaking. She was also thrilled to meet Vann Woodward, whose *Strange Career of Jim Crow* she had read. She quoted or cited it as incontrovertible authority in her ever-frequent discussions of race matters in Fairhope. I had met Vann only two weeks earlier when he had come to Hopkins for a dissertation defense. Mom remembered what I had written about him: "Of all the historians in the country, he is the one I look up to most," I wrote, adding that "I was greatly relieved to discover that he is a kind and charming man . . . It is so gratifying when great men turn out to be nice men!"

Much as my mother enjoyed getting to know Jim and Vann, the principal reason she and Dad had for coming to Asheville was to see me and to hear me read a paper on interpretations of Southern history in the generation after Reconstruction, the so-called New South era. I had sweated over it for months. My dissertation was centered in this period. The paper was well-received. I was relieved. Two years later it was published in a festschrift we students of his wrote for Fletcher Green. Vann's letter to me described it as "one of the most astute and brilliant pieces of historical criticism I have seen." That was a letter to frame. His final sentence—"It makes me all the more eager to see your book"—should have made me all the more eager to finish the book. It didn't.

We returned to Charlottesville in the summer of '64 with good feelings about our time away in Baltimore. Miles Wolff, one of the undergraduates in my Southern history class, followed me to Virginia for graduate work. His master's thesis was later published as *Lunch at the 5 & 10*. It was the first good history of the Greensboro sit-ins. It is short, engagingly written, and accurate—all recommendations for its continuing usefulness. David Donald's three graduate students who served as my teaching assistants—Ibby Studley, Bill Cooper, and Mike Holt—became good friends. One of their self-assigned tasks was to counter my liberal interpretations in the discussion sections. I suppose that made the course's presentation of American history "fair and balanced." Mike would later become my Virginia colleague and companion on the tennis court. Our two dearest friends in Baltimore were Bill and Willie Rose. Both were Hopkins Ph.Ds, Willie a Woodward student. Bill came to Virginia to join the Engineering School faculty; Willie soon became one of the treasured members of my department.

Most important of all in our year away, we celebrated Gareth's March 7 birth at what we were told was the medical center of the universe, the Johns Hopkins University hospital. Both Blaise and Chinta had been quick to emerge into the world, so our Baltimore doctor decided to bring Mary to the hospital to induce labor, a recommended procedure, he remarked, "for fast girls from out of town."

V

During our nine months away we kept up with university events through the letters and visits of our friends, and occasional clips from the *CD*. The University Theater had given up its exclusion policy in the wake of the Buddy's sit-in but the private-property arguments students had used to defend it were still alive. The segregationist culture continued to hang heavily. Many Corner establishments held on to their racially exclusive ways. Most of the controversy that year centered on property rights, the absolute authority of business men to admit or exclude whom they wished. As one student put it in a letter to the *CD*: "Simply stated, capitalism is based on privately-owned means of production and distribution which are operated for profit." The question of whether segregation should stand or fall, therefore, hinged on which arrangement would more likely produce profit. In a community favoring segregation that meant businesses for profit should be segregated. Jerry Rothschild's 1961 argument was alive and flourishing. Before term opened in September, however, the Civil Rights Act of 1964 was adopted. The property-rights defense was washed away, to become another old times there that was not easily forgotten. None of which meant that the university's cautious, essentially conservative policy of holding the line against racial advances had changed.

The "sympathy for Selma" demonstration we held in March 1965, more than anything else, unmasked the university administration's ongoing determination to distance itself from the mounting pressure for racial justice that was sweeping the nation. All of America and most of the world focused on Selma that month. King's SCLC, joined by John Lewis and SNCC, had gone to that Alabama city to demonstrate the need for a voting rights act. The brutal treatment they met lit up the television screens each night. James Reeb, a white Northern supporter was murdered. Jimmie Lee Jackson, a black Alabama participant, was murdered. When someone suggested carrying him to Montgomery to place his body on the steps of George Wallace's capitol, the idea of a march from Selma to Montgomery was born. The first contingent trying to cross the Pettus bridge leading out of the city was met by Alabama state troopers and Dallas County deputies who clubbed the marchers into submission. Again the nightly news carried the terrorist acts. Soon afterwards, with the White House pressure helping to rein in Wallace and his troopers, a fifty-four-mile march down U.S. Highway 80 began, ending on the steps of the state capitol where King delivered one of his stirring orations. Many dignitaries joined the march in its final stages. But murders did not cease. Viola Liuzzo, a Northern woman ferrying civil rights people from Montgomery back to Selma, was shot and killed on one of her trips. Lyndon Johnson spoke before a joint session of Congress, announced the voting rights act he would introduce, and concluded with the words of the freedom movement's anthem, declaring of his purpose "and we shall overcome."

For us at the University of Virginia to gather to offer words of sympathy for those who had died and struggled in Selma—and to speak for the right to vote in America—seemed but a small gesture deserving at least some sympathy from our university's leaders. None came. Four decades later, as I write, I have yet to get over the shock and shame that failure aroused in me. Three personal stories help to recall that sentiment.

Tom Gardner, one of the activist undergraduates, joined a small group from Charlottesville to go to Montgomery to join the last stage of the march. Tom was a first-year student, "anxious to become a Virginia gentleman," he once wrote. He enrolled in ROTC and joined the swimming team. Soon, however, he hooked up with the Students for Social Action, one of the new student civil rights groups on Grounds. Shortly before Christmas it launched a program to collect clothes, blankets, and canned goods for Mississippi blacks who had been attacked, driven from their homes, and had their churches burned for their attempts to register to vote during Freedom Summer. The small U-Haul where the items were collected, Tom wrote, "was vandalized by some students who were probably drunk and playing Ku Klux Klan for the evening." Reflecting later on the event, he said it helped him "think more clearly about this struggle as one that didn't allow much room for fence-sitting or partial involvement. I strained against my white Southern upbringing and began to involve myself more in the activities of the new group."

My own role in Tom's decision to go to Alabama was apparently influential; I reproduce here what he wrote at the risk of unseemly flattering of myself but also, I hope, to show how young people made their decisions:

> By early spring as I leaned toward greater involvement, I looked for support wherever I could find it, especially from other and maybe older Southern whites who had broken from what Virginia Durr called the Magic Circle and took their stand with the civil rights movement. My

history teacher that year was Paul Gaston, whose eloquent lectures (the kind where you can almost see the punctuation floating in the air) were delivered in the genteel cadence of Southern Alabama's educated class. Here was a man whose every atom oozed SOUTHERN. And he was also white. . . . I was contemplating going [to Montgomery] but had a bit of fear yet to overcome. Two lectures helped me over the edge. First, Paul told our class the story of the "sit-in" at Buddy's restaurant in Charlottesville the year before, including his own role. It was just what I needed to hear. Somehow that lecture on that day gave me space I needed to finally say, "Yes, this is what I must do." It was one white Southerner speaking to another saying, "This is what WE must do." That was a powerful granting of permission for an 18-year-old looking for the right direction.

Once Tom arrived in Montgomery, where he had the thrill of walking alongside Harry Belafonte, he held aloft a poster board on which he had inscribed a Jeffersonian aphorism which he remembers as "all eyes are opened or are opening to the rights of man." Underneath the quotation he had written both Thomas Jefferson and, to let people know where he was from, UVA. It seemed simple to Tom to identify the founder of the University as one who favored the rights of man. But it didn't seem that way to one of the University's deans. An image of Tom's poster board had gone out on the wire services, to be seen by the dean. He called Tom into his office. The newspaper was lying on his desk. The reprimand swiftly followed. Tom's sign, he said, "implied the University was officially part of the march" and then added: "We can't just have anyone going out and putting the University's good name into the public debate on controversial issues." Hints of punishment followed but Tom was dismissed with urgings to pay attention to studies, not "these outside issues."

My involvement brought a different kind of reprimand. At the request of my student Bill Leary, president of the Jefferson Chapter, the group co-sponsoring the event, I wrote a letter to "Dear Colleagues." This is what it said:

At 5:45 on Wednesday, March 17, University students, staff, faculty, and wives will meet in front of old Cabell Hall, walk to the north side of the Rotunda, and there join friends from the community for a short ceremony to express sympathy for the families of James Reeb and Jimmie Lee Jackson, to extend encouragement to the Negroes of Selma, and to declare support for President Johnson's voting bill.

The University Administration has been informed of, and given its consent to, this ceremony.

I have been asked by the student committee planning the ceremony to urge your participation. Your presence will give tangible evidence of the growing national concern for Selma and all it signifies. I hope you and your family will come.

Yours sincerely,

Paul M. Gaston

Associate Professor of History

The letter had hardly been dropped in the university post boxes before Paul Saunier telephoned to express his concern. Readers had complained, he told me, that my letter implied that the University was a sponsor of the event or had expressed approval of its purposes. I told Paul, with whom I was nearly always on friendly terms (and who, in later years, would become a good friend whom I enjoyed and admired) that I couldn't be responsible for such people's reading habits. He then said, well, since you signed your rank as a university faculty member that gave the impression it was a university-sponsored event. I found that equally ridiculous and our conversation broke off. I thought Paul was simply dutifully passing on the complaint of one of the hard-core segregationists who needed pacifying and I thought no more about it.

I was wrong. Five weeks later Ed Younger, my department chairman, asked me to come by to see him. He had something to say that embarrassed him, but he was obliged to say it. The Dean of the College had passed on to him to deliver to me a message from President Shannon. President to Dean to Chairman to me. What a route! President Shannon apparently believed that my letter had, in fact, given the impression that the event was sponsored or its purposes approved by the University. His through-channels request was that, in future, I act "with more discretion." The day after my meeting I wrote to Ed to make a record of what I had been told and of my reaction. Ed was always supportive of my civil rights activities (I'm pretty sure he attended the ceremony) and I thanked him for that. I reiterated my complaint about the president's misreading of the letter, said that what I had done was right, and regretted the fact that no one in the administration had offered even an off-the-record appreciative word to anyone concerned with the event. I also resented the request that I needed to be reminded to act with discretion. "I am perfectly well aware of the Administration's desire for discretion," I wrote, "and I could submit a long list of instances in which, as advisor to the Jefferson Chapter of the VCHR, I have counseled 'discretion' in the past." I wonder what the president would have thought had I actually gone to Selma or to Montgomery for the climax of the march. I thought that perhaps I should go, but the lingering fear from 1963 and what I thought of as prudence (not discretion) kept me at home. Instead, I accepted the assignment as the Virginia organizer for the Selma project, funneling to prospective travelers information about what to expect and how to proceed.

Many years later, looking through the president's papers, my research assistant brought me more information on the episode. The Rector of the University (the position first held by Thomas Jefferson), responding to a criticism of me and my letter sent him by an offended alumnus, characterized what I had written as a "circular drumming up a crowd for the march on the Rotunda." Because of his position, he said, he could not comment further, except to say that he was not an "advocate of Government by Demonstration." President Shannon, writing to the same complainant, expressed his "regret that Mr. Gaston did not express the situation precisely and that his letter led to misunderstanding." How both the President and the Rector could have seen the letter as leading to "misunderstanding" continues to baffle me. The Rector's flippant opposition to "Government by Demonstration" puts me in mind of Frederick Douglass's truism that "those who profess to favor freedom and yet deprecate agitation are men who want crops without plowing the ground. They want rain without thunder and lightning. They want the ocean without the awful roar of its waters. Power concedes nothing without a demand. It never did, and it never will." My university could perhaps be seen as a case in point.

Our event took place on a rainy, chilly afternoon. More than three hundred people were there. Bill Leary, one of the eight speakers, said that "Alabama isn't that far away," a fact he believed was illustrated by the University's "token integration," its failure to hire black professors, recruit black athletes, and pay a living wage to its workers. Bill's speech was powerful, as were several of the others. Some, as the *CD* reported, were occasionally almost drowned out by the running commentary of a student heckler carrying a sign decrying the "asinine march for the niggers of Selma." Merrill Peterson's address, however, was both heard and accurately reported. It was the one that hit most directly at the administration's desire to distance the University from controversial public issues. Merrill had recently joined the university as the Thomas Jefferson Professor of History. He was one of the brightest stars in President Shannon's efforts to bring greater excellence to the university, all the more reason to listen to what he had to say.

"Today Selma is a vital link in the heritage of American liberty," he said. "No university—in America or in the world—has a clearer title to speak for that heritage in the present crisis than the University of Virginia. And it is high time (long past time) we were heard from! Selma is a symbol, but as President Johnson told us the other night, it has become a turning point, like Lexington and Concord and Appomattox, of America's unending search for freedom." He followed with several apt Jefferson quotes and ended by saying that "in honoring those men and women who have worked, suffered, bled, and died in Selma, we also renew our faith in the enduring values of the founder and spiritual head of this University." As I reread this speech now I am reminded of the day I first stepped on the Lawn and felt that this was a university at war with itself. Who would win was still very much in question. Merrill's words would become an important part of the struggle. We were lucky to have him on our side.

Far more dramatically than either Tom or I possibly could have, Merrill did precisely what the dean said must not be done: he put the University's good name into the public debate on controversial issues. He not only put it there; he identified the Selma struggle with the mission of our University and the fulfillment of Jeffersonian ideals. For that he was not scolded, as Tom was, nor given a through-channels mild but insulting reprimand, as I was. He was ignored. Neither President Shannon nor any member of his administration said a word to him. In a hierarchical world such as the one they lived in they could not criticize the holder of the Thomas Jefferson chair. In the cautious, defensive world that imprisoned them, they could not say, even in private, well done, be patient, we're really with you.

VI

In one of his letters to the editor, Bill Leary, who was in his first year of graduate study, wrote that the *CD* was "the most enlightened" in his five years at the University. He was quick to point out that the enlightenment bar was very low. The lead editorial on the Selma crisis illustrated the twin points Bill was trying to make. It was headed "A Time for Reason." In previous years the editor might have said that both the white racists of Alabama and their civil rights opponents were extremists who recognized no time as a time for reason. Not so in the spring of 1965. Now there clearly was "rampant discrimination" down there, the editor wrote. Lyndon Johnson's voting rights bill was a "necessary piece of legislation" that deserved "careful, considered debate." Continuation of "the demonstrations which are now sweeping across the nation and Virginia," however, could only serve to "maintain the emotional atmosphere which makes constructive action so difficult." Such a view, common among the emerging cadre of racial moderates, dismissed what we believed to be the truism that the "emotional atmosphere" was the very thing that made the constructive action possible in the first place.

For the slowly but steadily rising number of racial liberals who were coming to the University, enlarging the numbers in the Council on Human Relations and now the Students for Social Action, the creation of an "emotional atmosphere" with letters, speeches, marches, and demands was the only way the University would ever be turned into an open institution, one that would recruit and welcome black students and faculty and broaden its curriculum to include a rational study of the black experience. In the spring of 1965, as the administration's reaction to the Selma demonstration made clear, much work toward that end lay ahead. The administration's move toward racial equality was so gradualist as to be invisible.

The theater boycott, which I take to be the beginning of the student movement that would eventually secure President Shannon's support and turn the University around, was spearheaded by Virginius Thornton, joined by a small number of other blacks and a goodly number of white students and faculty. Virginius left after a year and the number of black students was so small—fewer than twenty were attending classes on Grounds in 1965—that movement-building was essentially the work of whites, virtually all of them male. Two years later, in 1967–68, there were 40 part-time and 31 full-time African American students; in 1968–69, the year the logjam broke, the numbers had increased to 35 part-time and 52 full-time.

Wes Harris entered the Engineering School in the fall of 1960 to become one of the few black students in the University that year. In a 2003 interview, I asked why he chose UVA. At Armstrong High School in Richmond, he told me, he had a physics teacher named Eloise Bose Washington who told him that was where he was to go, "not to Howard, not to Virginia Union, not to Virginia State." She was, he said, "a powerful influence." But why did she want him to go, I asked. "Number one," he answered, quoting her from memory, "you're smart enough to do well. Number two, there's no way anyone on campus could mistake you for anything other than a black person." She was right on both counts. Mrs. Washington may have sent him as a pioneer, but Wes said he never felt like one. In those days, in his community, you simply accepted the wisdom and direction of your community leaders. So he came to Charlottesville. The University would never be quite the same because of that decision.

Wes quickly found out what it was like to be black in the land of Cavalier gentlemen. In his first year he was assigned to a dormitory room for two. His designated white roommate refused to live with a black man. The housing director let Wes have the double for the price of a single. The same thing happened the next year and the year after that. "I had a full double alone," he told me, "because no white student would room with me." There were other "incidents," as Wes called them. He recalled students throwing lit cigarettes in front of him as he walked across the Grounds; in

an earlier interview with Brian Kay, author of an undergraduate thesis on
the desegregation of the University, he told of them being thrown at him
from the windows of passing cars. While he was picketing the University
Theater during the boycott a white student threw a penny on the pavement in front of him and told him to pick it up. When I asked him about
participating in the theater protest he replied simply, "Paul, to protest at
that level at that time in my life, that time in the country's history, was an
obligation. I saw no reason why I should not be there. And the very least I
could do was protest that kind of blunt, sharp racism."

I got to know Wes in those days, not just during our protests at the theater
or at the meetings of the VCHR, but also on the occasional Sundays when
he would come to our home for dinner. In his third year he was president
of the Jefferson chapter, among other things overseeing Martin King's visit
and introducing him to the huge audience that came to see, hear, and touch
him. He also thrived in the Engineering School's honors program. Two of
his professors, George Matthews and John Scott, became mentors to him in
the way Mrs. Washington had been, in their case telling him he was to go
to Princeton for graduate studies. John Longley, director of the humanities
program in the Engineering school, persuaded him to break down some
of the establishment barriers. He agreed, applied for admission to the elite
Jefferson literary and debating society, giving his probationary speech on
Kirkegaard and existentialism. That blew them away. Strange enough in the
mind of a Virginia gentleman for an engineer to know about such things,
let alone a black engineer.

In his fourth year Wes again lived alone, this time in one of the prestige
rooms on the Lawn, awarded to fourth-year student leaders. Whether by
chance or intention, however, his room was at the end of the Lawn, sepa-
rated from other student rooms by a professor's pavilion. Fortunately, he
had a congenial neighbor in Dean Robert J. Harris, an authority on civil
rights law and a friend of our efforts. I had met Bob in December 1962 at
the Nashville conference. He was then teaching at Vanderbilt. He arrived
shortly afterwards to take up the deanship. A man of good sense and good
humor, he spied me on the Lawn, robed for the 1963 graduation procession, my Buddy's bandage still on. "Well, Paul," he remarked, "it's good to

see my faculty are not in jail." He was a good neighbor to Wes.

David Nolan entered the University in 1963, Wes's third year. He was white, Northern, and already radicalized. "I remember the day Medgar Evans was shot," he told me in an interview; "it just crushed me." Then he watched the March on Washington and King's "I Have a Dream" speech on television. He arrived at UVA a fervent civil rights man, "full of fire and ready to argue with everyone on my hall." His roommate was from Danville, Virginia, scene of the civil rights protests that followed just after ours and resulted in far more violence. David had a photograph of people who had been there "with their heads beaten open." He showed it to his roommate. "Oh, they're niggers," David recalls him saying; "they get a kick out of that." They did not remain roommates. "It was one of those things I have never forgotten," he told me. "He was not a virulent racist; it was more a matter of how he had grown up, what was his 'way of life.'" In his hall David "heard every racist argument ever made, and these were from the cream of the crop." One outraged him so much he called him "poor white trash." For that he was punched in the face. "I didn't understand the class differentials of Virginia gentlemen," he recalled of that event.

Fortunately, one of the first persons David met during orientation was Wes Harris, sitting at the VCHR desk. He filled out the membership card straightaway and became an active participant. He would become vice president in his second year. In his first year he often felt lonely and isolated, but in 1964–65 "a whole new crop" of progressive students showed up; he especially remembered Tom Gardner, Roger Hickey, and Allen Ogden, all of whom would become part of our civil rights groups. Harold Marsh, another African American student in the Engineering School, became especially important to him. "Harold just took this dumb white boy under his wing, and he had a great mind and was a great part of my education at UVA." I remember Harold as an especially gentle person who became my good friend as well. His older brother Henry would rise to prominence as a civil rights lawyer and reform-minded legislator; we became good friends on the SRC executive committee (and occasionally on the tennis court). It was a great shock to all of us when Harold was killed in a drive-by shooting.

Decades after his UVA years I interviewed David in St. Augustine,

Florida. He moved there in 1977 after many years working in civil rights and social justice causes, passions that continue to guide his life. He had joined other Virginia students to work in Southside (the "black belt" area of Virginia) during the summer of 1965; he kept on with civil rights work, never returning to finish his degree. During our conversation, I suspect with a good deal of exaggeration, he said that I was a "legend" when he arrived and that "the young progressive students all wanted to study Southern history with Paul Gaston." Parker Brown, who entered the University the year following David, has a different memory of my allegedly legendary status. He writes, in his as-yet unpublished memoir of his student days, that when he enrolled "Gaston was known among undergraduates chiefly for the Buddy's incident—at the time an unflattering reference, but later to become a badge of distinction."

Roger Hickey, one of the fresh progressive voices whose 1964 arrival David remembers, came to the University from Montgomery, a graduate of Sidney Lanier High School in the year before the first blacks were allowed in. He chose UVA because his guidance counselor recommended it as the Harvard of the South. Ill-informed about the university she chose for him, he remembers that he had no idea what to expect. "I just thought it was a good school in the South. I didn't know there weren't any girls and I certainly wasn't prepared for the country club atmosphere of the town." Refusing to wear a tie, he remembers, "was a political statement." He made the statement. Roger came from the Deep South but he was an army brat who had lived in several states as well as in Spain where had gone to high school before moving to Montgomery. He remembers Spain as "a fascist dictatorship propped up by the U.S. military for the sake of global empire." His parents, he told me, raised him to do what he thought was right, but when the family moved to Alabama he was shocked to discover that his father was a friend of George Wallace who had made him an honorary Alabama colonel.

David Nolan, whom Roger remembers as "the first left-wing activist I met at Virginia" with the kind of "values and a brilliant mind" that inspired him, walked around "wearing an Americans for Democratic Action button; that's how he identified himself." Howard Romaine was just back from Freedom Summer in Mississippi to do graduate work in philosophy, bringing with him fresh news from the civil rights front. Roger joined the VCHR and helped to form the new group, Students for Social Action, of which Howard would become president. He remembers the sense of movement-building he and his new friends were structuring. They would stand in support of the civil rights struggle generally but they would also examine "what kind of university we were attending." Like his friends, Roger's experiences as a civil rights man quickly brought to light for him "what kind of university" he was attending. Soon after he arrived he put on his door a *Time Magazine* cover picture of Martin King. It was ripped and burned by an anonymous student (shades of my tire slasher) who burned the letters KKK on it. Roger remembers "things" being shoved under the door to his dorm room as he became known as the "nigger lover on the hall." A few, including his roommate, stood up for him, "but most of the other students gave us a lot of grief."

Tom Gardner, who grew up in the South, arrived in '64 from south Jersey where he had spent his last two years in high school. In our recent interview he told me of suppressing his Southern accent, for reasons of both security and shame. He was the only Southerner in the school; it was the time of Bull Connor's dogs and fire hoses; taunts regularly came his way. Except from the black students. There was an "affinity," he thought; they seemed "more Southern than the white kids." Several close friendships developed. He had planned to go to the March on Washington with one of his black friends, but his mother wouldn't allow it. She came from what Tom called the Klan side of the family.

Tom arrived in Charlottesville with the long-term ambition of having a career in the state department. He aimed to fit in and do well. He bought a blue blazer at Eljo's, the clothier of choice on the Corner, joined the swim team, and signed up for Air Force ROTC. He wasn't sure about fraternities, but he recalls that "the jock fraternities were rushing me because I was an athlete." He was ready, he said, "to be the straight Virginia gentleman—coats and ties—and the honor system seemed like a great thing too." To cap it off he "loved Jefferson." The love of Jefferson would endure, with a deeper understanding, but everything else was jettisoned. A classmate brought him to a planning meeting for what would become the Students for Social Action. He met Bill Leary and David Nolan and several others who were "outside the norm of the frat folks." He joined them in the Mississippi project. The vandalizing of their collection truck ended forever his idea of being a Virginia gentleman. Like his friend David Nolan, he would drop out of the university after the 1966 summer in Southside. He returned in 1968 after two intense years of civil rights, anti-war, and union organizing work, to resume those causes and to graduate in 1970.

These and many other students learned from bitter first-hand experience about what Wes Harris called the "blunt, sharp racism" he met at the Corner; of what David Nolan heard from his roommate's view of bludgeoned Negroes, "Oh, they're niggers; they get a kick out of that"; of Roger Hickey being the "nigger lover on the hall"; and of Tom Gardner's message from the dean: "We can't just have anyone going out and putting the University's good name into the public debate on controversial issues." To remake the "university's good name" was the task these and a growing number of other students undertook. It would not be easy.

Chapter Seven

GOVERNMENT
BY DEMONSTRATION

I visited Miles College in Birmingham during the summer of 1965. Sitting on the steps leading up to the building where I would sleep was a large and cheerful black man with a rifle across his knees. He greeted me warmly and assured me I could sleep without worries. No Anglo-Saxon terrorists would get past him. I had never gone to bed before with an armed guard outside my quarters. I slept soundly even as I reflected on the fact that, despite the passage of the great Acts of 1964 and 1965, white-supremacy terrorism remained a daily threatening reality, especially in the city known around the world as Bombingham.

Miles was one of twelve black colleges I visited that summer. Twenty-seven of them participated in the Southern Teaching Program, launched the previous summer by Yale graduate and law students to send graduate students from around the country to teach in Southern black colleges. The Carnegie Corporation asked the Southern Regional Council to evaluate the program to determine whether it should be funded for another year. Les Dunbar, then the SRC executive director, asked me to undertake that task. I could not visit all of the colleges at which 146 student instructors taught, but I received reports from those I couldn't. I sat in on classes, talked to the institutions' presidents, and had long conversations with both the students and the STP instructors. I recommended that the program be extended. It was.

In my report I noted that UVA's seven volunteer teachers placed it fifth among all participating schools and first in the South. I took on the job in the fall of 1965 to recruit and vet students from the University for the coming summer.

I

By the time I returned to the classroom in the fall the principal legislative aims of the civil rights movement had been accomplished, an achievement of the moral power and strategic genius of the movement itself. The 1964 Civil Rights Act and the 1965 Voting Rights Act authorized a slow-to-awaken national government to use its power to end segregation in public places, banish disfranchisement and move forward the 1954 *Brown* decision's long-unmet promise of school desegregation. In future years some historians would look upon these acts as the climactic triumphs of the civil rights movement. This was not the way Martin King saw it. To him the passage of the acts climaxed the reformist phase of the movement. With much of the Jim Crow debris cleared away it was easier to see the fundamental tasks yet to be accomplished. "We must recognize," he said, "that we can't solve our problem now until there is a radical redistribution of economic and political power." Among other things, this would require facing the truth that "the dominant ideology" of America was not "freedom and equality," with racism "just an occasional departure from the norm." Racism was woven into the fabric of the country, intimately linked to capitalism, excessive materialism, and militarism. They were all tied together, he wrote, "and you really can't get rid of one without getting rid of the others." What was required was "a radical restructuring of the architecture of American society." I knew what that meant. It spoke directly to my heritage, to the reason for Fairhope's creation.

I have often wondered what Grandfather Gaston would have thought of that phrase of King's. Grandfather never considered himself a revolutionary, but his doctrine of cooperative individualism, including especially the prohibition of private property in land, and his commitment to what the civil rights people would later call participatory democracy, were strong moves in that direction. Marietta Johnson's educational ideas had in general become my own and were likewise subversive of the existing "architecture" of American education. Even in matters of race, where both she and Grandfather were constrained by forces many times more powerful than any Colgate Darden and Edgar Shannon could have imagined, they were ahead of their times. They knew and declared that racial exclusion was inconsistent with their fundamental economic, social, political, and educational ideals and at odds with democracy itself. Had these Fairhope leaders ended the practice of exclusion in the colony and the school, however, both institutions would almost certainly have been destroyed, bringing to a quick end the demonstration of what each believed could be a new and better America. Had presidents Darden or Shannon taken the lead in similar steps, the University of Virginia would have gone right on (perhaps, but not assuredly, with new presidents). Their reasons for resisting the spreading movements for racial inclusion were of an altogether different order from those of my grandfather and Mrs. Johnson.

The cadre of students looking to build a different kind of university had been steadily growing since the theater boycott and the creation of the Jefferson chapter of the Virginia Coalition for Human Rights in the spring of 1961. As new members came and old ones returned, the focus remained primarily on racial integration of the student body and the faculty, and for fairly obvious reasons. Black students in the fall of 1965 constituted a miniscule fraction of the student body and students in the VCHR were the only ones trying to recruit them. There were no black faculty members, no courses in black history and culture, and no indications that the administration had plans to face head-on these and related racial problems. To many of the students (as to me) the University's white-supremacy culture came to be connected, much in the manner King described, with the larger structure and values of the institution. The fraternity system and intercollegiate athletics were more frequently targets of criticism now, the former because it seemed to be based on the will to exclude, not include; the latter because it was tainted by alumni and financial pressure to bar African Americans from participation. Tracing these and other ways in which money and tradition shaped the institution (the honor code not excluded), the dissident students strengthened the VCHR, which had been the primary center of student civil rights activity since its formation, and added new and more radical groups to their protest movement.

In the previous school year, 1964–65, newly arrived dissidents helped to found three new groups and spread their influence beyond Charlottesville. The first to make its mark on Grounds was the Students for Social Action (SSA). Howard Romaine was the driving force behind its creation and was chosen to be its first president. Fresh from his experience in the Mississippi Freedom Summer Project and before that a sit-in veteran, Howard was a Louisiana native and a graduate of Southwestern at Memphis (now Rhodes College), come to Virginia for a Ph.D. in philosophy. Full of boundless energy, fired up by his association with front-line civil rights people, Howard energized those around him with his rhetoric and his passion. He joined the VCHR but favored a more aggressive, confrontational approach to change. Roger Hickey and David Nolan, in particular, shared his views and joined with him in founding the SSA. Their first major project was the pre-Christmas collection of clothes, blankets, and canned goods for Mississippi African Americans dispossessed because of their work in Freedom Summer. In the spring SSA joined with the VCHR in sponsoring the Sympathy for Selma event. Howard was a featured speaker.

Anne Cooke also entered graduate school in the fall of 1964. She was a jewel: petite, spirited, open to the world. She came from Gastonia, North Carolina, where her lawyer father had supported mill workers against the mill owners, a sympathy Anne carried through her life as scholar, singer, song writer, and activist. With a lovely Carolina voice and a beguiling smile, she brought the best of protest music to the gatherings of the student radicals. After she left Virginia she formed the Southern Folk Cultural Revival Project, traveled throughout the region to sing, and settled in Nashville where she achieved modest fame as a country-western singer. She took me behind stage at the Grand Old Opry on one of my visits to the city. At UVA she studied with me to earn a master's degree in Southern history. Her 390-page master's thesis was unique both in length and content. She wanted to write a conventional thesis on the short history of the Mississippi Freedom Democratic Party. She had traveled to Mississippi and elsewhere to interview many of the major freedom summer leaders and planned to base her thesis on those interviews. I persuaded her to write a brief introduction to be followed by an edited version of the interviews themselves. That's what she did. The manuscript became one of the most widely circulated theses ever to go out on interlibrary loan; it remains one of the best primary sources on the history of the civil rights movement.

In the spring of 1965 Anne and Howard were married. Their home in the country became a regular gathering place for SSA members and other dissidents. Students meeting there joined others in Virginia colleges to form the Virginia Students' Civil Rights Committee, an interracial group founded in December 1964. Their first foray was into the Southside during the summer of 1965. Participants from seven colleges and universities, including UVA students Howard, Anne, David Nolan, and Richard Muller, spent the summer organizing, conducting voter-registration drives and boycotts, discussing strategies to increase job opportunities, and doing what they could to support the local blacks braving the risk of standing up for their rights. Stokely Carmichael and two other SNCC workers paid a visit. David recalls especially Stokely's discussion of organizing techniques. For all these students, the SNCC connection would be an enduring inspiration.

No one was killed that summer, but one person was shot, there was a visit from the FBI, and there was plenty of harassment and not a little violence. David and Richard were beaten by Klansmen, cars were chased or pelted with stones, and, as David remembers, "there were many attempts to run people off the road." He also recalls that some businessmen, in response to the boycott, sued "for more money than all of us had put together." A young lawyer named Doug Wilder, later to be Virginia's first (and until 2007 the nation's only) black governor, successfully defended the case. Some students stayed on past summer's end or came back for a second summer of activity in 1966. Roger Hickey and Tom Gardner joined them that year. Both Tom and David Nolan had dropped out of the University to carry on with civil rights work around the region. David took on the editorship of the Southern Student Organizing Committee's *New South Student*. After a couple of years working full time in the Southern movement, including a term as chairman of SSOC, Tom returned at mid-year 1968–69 to be one

of the leaders in the cresting movement for change in the University and
to finish his undergraduate work.

The Southern Student Organizing Committee (SSOC, pronounced
"sock") was another creation of 1964 that would play a major role in changing
the University's racial climate and policies. Up until that time SNCC was
the only regional civil rights organization for students and young people.
Most of SNCC's members were black and most of its organizational and
protest work was in the black community. SNCC field directors Sam Shirah
and Bob Zellner, both white, had begun exploring ways of mobilizing white
youth to work in the white communities, but little had been accomplished.
In April 1964, with SNCC's blessing and the addition of leadership from
Ed Hamlett of Vanderbilt, forty-five young people from ten Southern states
answered the call to meet in Nashville. None of our students attended that
first meeting, where SSOC was founded, or the follow-up the next month
in Atlanta but, once the new organization took shape, with headquarters
in Nashville, they embraced it. Howard would become the second president, Tom the third, and Steve Wise, one of my Southern history graduate
students, the fourth.

Inspired by SNCC but conceived to carry the civil rights mission into
white communities, SSOC built a region-wide membership. In the five years
of its existence it established chapters in universities and colleges in every
Southern state and mobilized young white men and women to confront
the racial practices not only of their institutions but of their surrounding
communities. Not long after its founding, members launched campus anti-
war movements and soon after that several became involved in struggles for
workers' rights as well. Unlike Students for a Democratic Society (SDS)—the
northern student movement with far-left ideological commitments—SSOC
saw itself as non-ideological. The two groups, sometimes cooperating,
sometimes competing, frequently in tension, were also set apart by SSOC's
emphasis on its Southernness. Its founding declaration—"We'll Take Our
Stand"—proclaimed "We as young Southerners hereby pledge to take our
stand now together here to work for a new order, a new South." One of
the recurring themes of these young white Southerners' struggle for change
was an affirmation of their rootedness in the South and their belief that its

history of oppression was also rich with examples of struggle against that oppression.

Both SDS and SNCC have achieved secure places in the histories of the 1960s while SSOC has seldom found its way into the narratives of the era's liberation movements. That neglect is remedied by Gregg Michel. His excellent book, *Struggle for a Better South* (Palgrave, 2004), began as a dissertation in the '90s. I remarked at my retirement party in 1997 that when one of my students began writing a dissertation about some of my previous students it must be time to retire. Gregg wrote in the preface that he brought to his study "a view of Southern history that stressed contradiction, dissent, and subversion . . . [and that] an honest reckoning with the Southern past can help to make the South of today a better place." His subjects, imbued with a similar understanding of the Southern past, drew on that understanding as they worked to persuade Southern whites to join in making their region a place "free of poverty, racism, and oppression." Will Campbell, the legendary civil rights hero and Baptist minister who preached to Klansmen and freedom fighters alike, said the young women and men of SSOC did what they did "because they want to give those from whose loins they sprang one more chance."

II

That they had been given chances before—and could have them again—became the theme of my Southern history teaching throughout the 1960s. My generation, however, was the first to recognize and then emphasize that part of Southern history that had been ignored or denied. Perkins Abernethy, whose impending retirement occasioned my appointment at UVA, represented an older school of interpretation that was gradually sent into retreat in the academy in the 1950s and '60s but still held sway in the popular mind and in most of the high school and some college textbooks. The views of U. B. Phillips on slavery and white supremacy, for example, held on tenaciously. In his *American Negro Slavery* (1918) and *Life and Labor in the Old South* (1929) slavery was portrayed as a school for civilizing blacks and the basis for a way of living that nurtured a good life for both slave and master. As the most influential historian of slavery of his generation, his famous 1928 essay, "The Central Theme of Southern History" carried special force. "Whether expressed with the frenzy of a demagogue or maintained with a patrician's quietude," the essence of Southernism was "a common resolve, indomitably maintained," that the South "shall be and remain a white man's country," he wrote. That was the "central theme" of Southern history.

Neither Phillips nor his contemporary historians of the South identified slavery and the preservation of white supremacy as underlying causes of the Civil War. To some the conflict came because of cultural or economic differences between South and North. To others a blundering generation brought on an unnecessary war. Some held tightly to the view that it was all about the South's defense of states' rights in the face of Yankee aggression, giving rise to the popular name some Southerners chose to bestow on the conflict—the War of Northern Aggression. Histories of the war itself were heavily laden with accounts of Southern gallantry, the defense of hearth and home, and the loyalty of black slaves to their white families. Well past the mid-twentieth century, Virginia schoolchildren continued to be taught to revere Robert E. Lee and to internalize his homilies about duty as life's highest command. As a schoolboy in the early 1960s, our son Blaise, an avid reader of his Virginia history textbook, knowing who won the war but puzzled about how that happened, came to me one morning to ask, "Daddy, didn't the South lose any of the battles?"

Almost from the day it ended, the era of Reconstruction took a special place in the imagination of white Americans (never white Southerners alone) and in the books the first historians wrote about it. The perfidy of Yankee oppression was detailed in the late nineteenth and early twentieth century by the Columbia historian William Dunning and his many students; it was given a dramatic and gruesome countenance in Thomas Dixon's novels and D. W. Griffith's *The Birth of a Nation,* the film based on the those novels. Margaret Mitchell's *Gone With the Wind* (1936) and the Victor Fleming-David O. Selznick movie rendition of her book (1939) swept the literary and film world, winning a Pulitzer prize for Mitchell and eight academy awards for the film. The Dunning-Dixon-Griffith portrayal of the dark and disastrous Reconstruction era, when the bottom rail was put on top and honest government disappeared, was preserved but seductively adorned with elegance, beauty, grace, and stardom by the novel and the film. (Little noticed at the time as one of Miss Mitchell's Pulitzer competitors was William Faulkner's *Absalom, Absalom!,* perhaps his best novel and probably the best history of the South ever written.) Then, in 1947, E. Merton Coulter's *The South During Reconstruction*, volume eight in the prestigious History of the South series published by the Louisiana State University Press, summed up and gave scholarly credence to the essentials of these interpretations of Reconstruction history. I met Coulter's book when I entered graduate school and soon learned, as Vernon Wharton, one of my Carolina predecessors, was later to write, that Coulter's "interpretation became the standard of general histories, college and high school textbooks, and popular fiction."

Even as scholarly works joined the 1960s civil rights movement to chip away at the racist pillars supporting the mythic view of Reconstruction as the great American horror story, old images persisted. They were commonplace in the minds of many of our students. More telling, I believe, was how even antiracists unconsciously slipped into them. I met an especially revealing example of this in 1971, listening to a speech in Atlanta by newly elected governor Jimmy Carter. Part of his theme was the need of North and South to reconcile their differences to diminish the sectionalism born of a bitter history of conflict. In a passing reference to the Reconstruction years, he said that "in those dark days all of our people here in Georgia regarded the federal government as their enemy." I spoke to him after the speech, complimented him on his theme, but offered this caveat: "You know, Governor, half of our people here in Georgia thought the federal government was their only friend." The governor's jaw dropped, his face contracted as he instantly recognized his grievous, unthinking error. Nine years later, watching President Carter debate his challenger, I saw Ronald Reagan commit the same offense. Carter pounced on him immediately. I poked Mary and remarked: "He learned." Regrettably, Reagan's alliance with the racist interpretation of Reconstruction history made little difference to the electorate—except, of course, to give comfort to white-supremacist voters.

In graduate school, the part of the Southern past I chose to make my own was the generation after Reconstruction, the so-called New South era. My first publication of any professional consequence was an essay I wrote in 1963 which appeared in 1965 in *Writing Southern History: Essays in Historiography in Honor of Fletcher M. Green*, a *festschrift* written by seventeen of Fletcher's former students. The received truths about this era of Southern history dominated both popular and professional thought until mid-century. They ran something like this: Slavery, although benign and beneficial, had outrun its usefulness; its demise paved the way for a new burst of Southern prosperity. The Civil War was fought gallantly but, with overwhelming might and resources, the North prevailed. Reconstruction was a horror story but its demise paved the way for North and South to march together down a road to reunion that left the South free to shape "good" race relations within a framework of segregation and disfranchisement and to guide the region into a new industrial age of prosperity.

With their sensibilities shaped by this kind of history it is little wonder that so many of our students came to the University with views of the past and their place in the world of the present at odds with what I would be teaching. When I arrived in Charlottesville in 1957, Virginia history seemed peculiarly immune to the winds of change beginning to sweep through the world of scholarship and to what I was setting out to accomplish. In the summer before I joined the faculty, for example, nearby Longwood College sponsored a series of lectures on the theme "Virginia in History and Tradition." Published in 1958, the essays were loaded with examples of reverence of tradition and resistance to change. Francis Butler Simkins, a charming, curmudgeonly Longwood historian with a national reputation for skeptical attitudes toward the newer interpretations, wrote approvingly of the "instinctive desire of the [school] children to retain their ancestral folkways" and equally favorably of those "inherited customs" that formed a firm base "for originality and creativeness." Simkins's friend, colleague, and critic Marvin Schlegel was in the camp of those holding the newer views—views which he said would "put our ancestors in too severe a light and would moreover be an unpleasant story." Unpleasant stories, he wrote, were "contrary to Virginia custom." School textbooks "safely disregarded" the views of African Americans because they had "no control over the preparation" of them. In the end, continuing in his mischievous mode, Schlegel concluded that "perhaps the best attitude for us all to take is that Virginia history should be approached like a Virginia tea; we go . . . simply to pay our respects." To which Lawrence Burnette would add: Virginians did not indulge in "self-criticism"; that was "regarded as a form of mental disorder." No other state, he believed, made "such a concerted effort to indoctrinate its young in its history."

And so it seemed to me. The scene we met on our arrival was one in which both Virginian and Southern history were explosive topics. The *Brown* decision and the massive resistance movement mounted to eviscerate it raised fundamental questions about the nature and future of the region. Could the South change its way of life? Could it be made to change? Everywhere Mary and I went, from cocktail parties to learned public lectures to heated public policy debates, we were struck by how one's understanding of history was the pivot on which opinions turned. Thinking back to those times I am reminded of William Faulkner's famous aphorism, "the past is never dead; it's not even past." James Baldwin said the same thing when he wrote that "history does not refer merely, or even principally, to the past. On the contrary, the great force of history comes from the fact that we carry it within us, are unconsciously controlled by it in many ways, and history is literally present in all that we do." What we had to learn, Baldwin would write in *The Fire Next Time* (1963), was that "to accept one's past, one's history, is not the same thing as drowning in it; it is learning how to use it."

III

My decision to teach Southern history in a Southern university was anchored in that desire to help prevent the drowning, to point to ways in which history could be used constructively. I hoped to build a bridge for my students—a bridge from the present to the past, to make the past live in and be a guide for the present. But in those days their idea of the past was that slavery was benign; segregation was good for everybody; and poor people were that way because they were lazy. Once those false views of the past were demolished a whole new world might be opened up to them. It was not just that they could see slavery, segregation, and inequality as the harsh consequences of a white supremacy culture. They might also see in

Southern history complexity, dissent, and the vision of a better world. They could learn of the men and women of good will who had crossed racial and class lines to change the region for the better. They could know that an honest reckoning with the Southern *past* could help to make the South of the *present* a better place. No more drowning.

Fulfilling such an ambition was made easier than it might have been by the burst of new scholarship I encountered in graduate school. My mentor played an important role as well. Fletcher had many of the appearances of an older-tradition scholar and his writings broke open no new paths of interpretation, but his teaching and his example were very much of the new order of things. I have already mentioned his conviction that the fugitive slaves were the real heroes of the abolition movement. He was similarly progressive in highlighting the positive contributions of Reconstruction, the shame of the Ku Klux Klan, and the abandonment of racial justice on the road to reunion in the last quarter of the nineteenth century. It was to that subject, in fact, that he directed me for a dissertation topic. Perhaps most important, he took me under his wing as one who might manage the kind of writing he had not. After the Swarthmore honors program I found much in graduate school boring and uninspiring. But not Fletcher. He gave me even more than I realized at the time.

The ennui of graduate school was tempered by the excitement of the books I read, especially those in Southern and American history. Every one of the accepted truths I described above had come under attack by revisionist historians of one stripe or another. Kenneth Stampp's *The Peculiar Institution* (1956) upended Phillips's portrait of slavery and opened the way for a rash of books that removed the credibility from the old stories of happy slaves and benevolent masters. A few authors began to chip away at Reconstruction historiography as early as the 1930s, but it was not until the post-war period that a phalanx of historians began to discard the Coulter synthesis. Eric Foner's *Reconstruction: America's Unfinished Revolution* (1988) completed the process. Before this, even during my graduate school days, the new era of scholarship facilitated a more appreciative view of W. E. B. Du Bois's *Black Reconstruction in America*, a powerful and provocative work of brilliance and passion. Published in 1935, the year before *Gone With the*

Wind, it attracted no interest in Hollywood and was generally ignored or patronizingly dismissed by mainline white male scholars.

Du Bois understood why his book would be shunted aside in the wake of its appearance. In his final chapter, "The Propaganda of History," he wrote of history as "lies agreed upon" and piled one example on another to illustrate the ways in which respected historians wrote disparagingly of Reconstruction because of their common belief that black people were, in one way or another, inferior to whites. Those who held such views were thus unable to see, whatever the evidence, that the admirable essence of Reconstruction was its attempt to build an interracial democracy that would acknowledge the shame of slavery and lay the groundwork for a society of justice and equality.

C. Vann Woodward did understand. More than any other white historian of his generation he built on that understanding to bring about a reconstruction of Southern history that promised not only clarity about the past, but also guidance for the present and future. A native of Arkansas, taking his undergraduate work there and in Georgia, Woodward spent his early adult years—the years of the Great Depression—immersing himself in the writings of the Southern literary renaissance; traveling through the deeply blighted areas of the poverty-stricken South; making the acquaintance of black intellectuals; coming to the defense of Angelo Herndon, an African American Communist organizer he believed to have been falsely accused of insurrection; journeying through Russia to form his own firsthand opinion of the Soviet Union; and, finally, arriving at Chapel Hill for graduate work with a book manuscript already partly written. The finished work became his dissertation and then his first book, *Tom Watson: Agrarian Rebel* (1938).

Discovering Woodward in graduate school was my greatest thrill, fortifying my belief that teaching Southern history in a Southern university might make the kind of difference I hoped for. The Watson biography told the story of a Southern Populist who reached across the color line to form an alliance grounded in common economic interests. Like Du Bois, Woodward saw in the Southern past the waste and shame of both racial and class exploitation and the possibility of an interracial democracy that would bring justice and equality to his native South. Watson's transformation into a hateful demagogue underscored the fragility, but not the absence or impossibility, of Southern stands for justice.

Woodward's masterpiece, *Origins of the New South, 1877–1913* (1951), appeared during my senior year at Swarthmore but I did not become aware of it until I came to Chapel Hill. My battered copy is full of marginalia that read to me now almost like conversations with the author. "So true!" I write on one page; "nail down your thesis" I command on another; and an excited "this is really revisionism" appears on yet another. My Fairhoper's sensibilities were aroused by what I saw as a kind of Manichean struggle unfolding before me in Woodward's pages. As he wrote later to his friend Virginia Durr, "my sympathies were obviously not with the people who ran things . . . but with the people who were run, who were managed and maneuvered and pushed around." The South of the 1890s was home to a "cult of racism" that "disguised or submerged cleavages of opinion or conflict of interest in the name of white solidarity." The one-party system "reduced political intolerance to a machine of repression." Against this repressive regime, Southern Populists leveled a frontal assault. As they did they raised "questions of land, markets, wages, money, taxes, railroads" and they "spoke openly of conflicts, of both section and class, and ridiculed the clichés of Reconstruction and White Solidarity." Some of them, the bolder ones, "challenged the cult of racism."

This was the same Populist Party that claimed my grandfather's allegiance and chose for its 1892 presidential candidate his colleague and friend, James B. Weaver, whose newspaper Grandfather edited during the presidential campaign. I was unaware of Fairhope's Populist origins when I was in graduate school, but Woodward's portrayal of the Populist positions on those questions of land, markets, wages, money, taxes, and railroads resonated with my understanding of the Fairhope mission. Henry George does not appear in the pages of *Origins* but Woodward's deft and elegant dissection of the material and class ambitions that motivated the Southern ruling class in the post-Reconstruction generation hit home for me.

In the same year that *Origins* appeared, Woodward published *Reunion and Reaction*, an original interpretation of the alliance of Southern and Northern conservatives that greased the way to Reconstruction's demise and the inauguration of a partnership across the Mason-Dixon line of the very capitalists who would become the object of the Populist revolt. Next came *The Strange Career of Jim Crow* (1955). It washed away the specious argument that segregation was an immutable folkway that could not be changed by mere law. Before long Martin King would call it the "historical Bible of the civil rights movement" while historians would soon declare it to be the most influential work ever written about American race relations. Finally, shortly after I joined the Virginia faculty, out came *The Burden of Southern History* (1960), a collection of essays on the Southern experience that gave Southern history the kind of reach and resonance Faulkner's novels had achieved for Southern fiction. What a wonderful time it was, I thought, to be a Southerner in struggle.

With these five books I felt I had an invincible army behind me as I entered the classroom in Charlottesville. Some of my students probably wished for a narrative more appreciative of Old South glory and New South progress but most seemed to find the challenges engaging. Most important of all to me was the discovery of students, especially those from the South, who found our work liberating in a way they needed but had not anticipated. Drawn for one reason or another to the civil rights movement in the region as well as in the University, many told me of the struggles they had—not just with their families but with themselves. Were they rejecting their heritage? Were they turning against their own land, the one they loved? These were tough questions with which they wrestled. It made a difference that their teacher was Southern and that Vann Woodward, the dean of Southern historians, was as well. Nor were we alone. At one of the VCHR meetings I brought a small stack of books, all by white Southerners, calling for an end to the Jim Crow system, for a South that could be home to racial justice. The Georgian Lillian Smith's *Killers of the Dream* (1949) was among these books, as was the South Carolinian James Dabbs's *The Southern Heritage* (1958). It was Dabbs who would say of Miss Smith: "She loved the South so much she tried to make it better." Robert Rosen, a South Carolinian who would become one of the leaders of the climactic student revolt of 1968–69, spoke for many of his fellow students when he wrote, in his first book, "As a student at the University of Virginia in the 1960s, I learned from Paul

Gaston, Willie Lee Rose, and the writings of C. Vann Woodward that one could be a Southerner, take pride in the South, and not feel compelled to defend the indefensible."

IV

History was important for these and other reasons; and, a generation later, the older race-based views of the Southern past would be superseded by the Woodwardian reconstruction. Racism, often in deliberately disguised forms, would continue, but people with standing in their communities, or desiring to have it, could no longer publicly defend slavery or excuse segregation. But for our times, the 1960s, the Southern history Woodward wrote and I and others taught was not in itself a force powerful enough to bring the Jim Crow system at our university, or anywhere else, to an end. Those who had the power to end it—the governor, the general assembly, the board of visitors, the president—all declined to take the needed forceful acts. Like most other Southern leaders, the racial privilege they enjoyed endowed them with both material and psychic advantages—advantages easily assumed to be part of the natural order of things. For those, President Shannon prominent among them, who did want progressive change to come, tethers of many sorts tempered their actions. Would positive actions produce a backlash? Could change come about without dramatic action? Would money, support—and even friends—be lost if one got too far ahead of popular opinion? None of these was an easy question to answer—except for the dissident students, movement leaders, and their allies. For them it was clear. In contrast to the leaders, they knew what Ben Muse and the Southern Regional Council concluded as early as 1960, that failure to lead would mean that Jim Crow's reign would of necessity be ended by grassroots direct action—the Rector's lamentable "Government by Demonstration." This became clear to a few of our students as early as 1961 when they opposed the exclusion policy of the University Theater and followed by forming a chapter of the VCHR. After five years of struggle their numbers and organizations were to the point where their belief that they could reshape the University seemed reasonable. Over the next three years that belief was fortified and finally validated.

The road to that end, however, was rocky. At the opening of the 1965 fall semester the Students for Social Action (SSA) distributed flyers to entering students, whom they mischievously called freshmen instead of first-year men, warning them against the University's conservative ways and urging them to consider joining the radical organization's efforts to end its racial and other repressive features. Race was less at the center of this broadside than University traditions, especially the reverence for the honor system (which was not itself directly attacked), the coats-and-ties "uniform" imposed by custom, and the ROTC program.

An outburst of criticism filled the columns of the *CD* and brought condemnation from its editor as well. To him the honor system and the wearing of coats and ties "were the two most revered traditions on the Grounds." The SSA, he wrote, was interested in protest for its own sake and as a means of making a name for itself. He preferred the neat dress of tradition to that of its critics, people "wrapped up in beards, sweatshirts, and tennis shoes." Letters from outraged students heaped vitriol on the "unkempt" propagandists with their "hirsute" faces; charged that the SSA "wallows in its pool of unethical stagnation"; called for action to dissolve it; and suggested that its identifying letters be reversed, changed from SSA to ASS. Such was the rhetoric of gentlemanly debate.

On the racial front neither the student body nor the administration was persuaded of the need for significant change. In November the Wesley Foundation conducted a poll of student attitudes. Of the 1,357 who responded, the *CD* reported, "63 percent stated that the University did not actually have an obligation to further integrate itself racially." The two dozen or so black students in residence were apparently enough. Never mind that they constituted less than one-half of one percent of the student body. On the sports scene at the time the number was zero. The failure to recruit black athletes became an issue in the second semester when Tom Gardner, speaking as president of the VCHR, wrote a letter to the *CD* and then appeared before the student council to report that he had "definite proof" of the University's fixed policy of refusing to recruit black athletes with offers of financial aid.

Such a charge hit home with Student Council member Frank Homer, a history graduate student, who said it struck at "the core of what this institution is all about." He successfully called for a Student Council investigation, an indication of student leaders' strengthening will to dissent. Tony Muir, a student of mine and the Student Council member who chaired the investigating committee, invited me to attend one of the group's meetings. Afterwards I wrote a letter to the chairman of the faculty committee on athletics proposing that the faculty investigate the matter as well. I had received what I thought to be credible evidence that a head coach had said privately that blacks were not recruited because he had not been given the "green light." An assistant coach told Tony's committee simply that Negroes were not recruited. The head of the Student Aid Foundation told the student committee that many donors would no longer contribute if Negroes were recruited.

President Shannon, in response to the Council's initiative, issued a boilerplate statement declaring that "the established policy of the University is not to discriminate against any person by reason of their race, color, religion or national origin." With relevance to the complaint at hand he reported that coaches had now been "instructed to make certain that no potential intercollegiate athlete who can meet the University's admission standard is overlooked in recruiting." The key word here was "overlooked." There was no call for a policy of active recruitment or for altering the conditions in the University that might discourage black students from coming. The disconnect between presidential pronouncement and the reality of recruiting was apparent. No action, in fact, was to come on those two fronts.

The VCHR's response to the president's statement was complimentary and courteous. Its satisfaction, however, was tempered because of the numerous other racial issues that had yet to be confronted. It listed several that it hoped the president and the student council would now address. Citing the miniscule number of black students, it faulted the University for its failure to recruit in African American high schools. In fact, though not mentioned on this occasion, the only recruiting of blacks that had ever taken place was done by the VCHR. Its records supply examples of students visiting the black high schools in Richmond and elsewhere, describing to the pupils there both the problems and the promises of life at the University. Other recommendations for change included a request for the hiring of black clerical workers, a generally more welcoming atmosphere for black employees, and the termination of the practice of providing to students a list of off-Grounds housing units where blacks were unwelcome. "Fully 90 per cent" of the units on the list, the VCHR claimed, "refuse to rent to Negroes."

Like the VCHR, the *CD* editor praised the Student Council for its investigation and the president for his statement. Similarities ended there. The football coach, the editor wrote, had previously made an unsuccessful attempt to recruit black players. He failed, just as future efforts would fail, because of the University's high "academic requirements" and because most blacks "with academic qualifications matching ours will prefer to go to other schools with higher percentages of Negro students." With no regret over these apparent truths or wishes for their remedy, the editor concluded with the disdain to which the dissenting students had become accustomed since the time of the theater boycott five years earlier. Perhaps now, they read, the protestors "can find something else to demonstrate about."

During the Student Council debate on Tom's charge, Tony Muir said that "the athletic department will not take a Negro athlete in a token gesture . . . because such action would be dishonorable." I remember being amused by Tony's remark. After all, in the sixteen years since Swanson's suit had broken a hole in the University's racial barrier, tokenism was the studied course it had followed in all of its admissions policies. Was that dishonorable? Janet Dewart thought it was. Janet was a student at Howard University. She had married Bob Dewart, her high school sweetheart, who was now a student in the college. Because she was black and Bob was white they could not live together in Virginia without risking arrest for violation of the Virginia Racial Integrity Act. They ran the risk, spending much time in Charlottesville, living as man and wife in violation of the state's law. Blasting the tokenism stratagem, Janet questioned whether the investigation would "look for the truth" which she said was "the traditional acceptance and adherence of ideas of one ethnic group's superiority to another," her gentle way of pointing up the University's continuing entrapment in the web spun by the white supremacy culture.

Little on the athletic front changed over the next couple of years. A year after the president's directive to the coaches the *CD,* now more liberal than it had ever been, ran an April Fool's Day spoof about the top-secret recruitment of the University's first black athlete, stolen away from a rival university. In February 1968 the local branch of the NAACP called for a boycott of a fundraiser for athletic scholarships. Citing the president's two-year-old promise to do something about athletic recruiting, the branch ruefully noted that "there are still no Negro athletes at the University." Pretty much overlooked in all the discussion about the absence of black athletes was the story of the one (and only) African American who had been a member of a varsity team—two varsity teams, in fact. George King, a Charlottesville native, entered the Engineering School in 1963. Watching the wrestlers in the gymnasium one day he decided to try out for the team. His success in what was to him a new sport led him to try another new one in the spring. He became a varsity lacrosse player. He reports that he was welcomed by both his teammates and his coaches, but that the fellowship did not carry over from the playing field or the wrestling mat to social life. George left for army duty midway through the next year, leaving the university with no black athletes.

Complaints continued about the unchanging whiteness of all the varsity teams, especially the football and basketball teams. Bob Cullen, the *CD's* sports editor (and future editor-in-chief), wrote a column criticizing what he believed to be the coaches' continuing failure to recruit black athletes. "We were getting our butts kicked by places like the University of North Carolina, with its star basketball player Charlie Scott," Bob told me in a recent interview. Citing the influence of fraternity alums as a reason for not pursuing black athletes and the racial views of fraternities on Grounds as a condition that would discourage blacks from coming should they be invited, Bob incurred the wrath of his Kappa Sigma brothers. Sitting down with them at dinner on the evening after the appearance of his column, he was stunned when the brothers rose, turned their backs on him, and walked away, leaving him alone at the dining table. He soon resigned from the fraternity to become a more vigorous advocate of active recruitment of black students and faculty.

V

My own recruiting efforts began with the fall semester of 1966. Merrill Peterson, our new department chairman, asked me to serve as director of graduate studies. We both agreed that one of my first tasks would be to find ways to attract African Americans to our graduate program. My partner in this effort was Elizabeth Stovall, a recent high school graduate, a protégé of my friend Teresa Walker, and the new departmental secretary put in charge of graduate affairs. She became my right-hand person. One of the very first black secretaries in the University, Elizabeth and I forged a bond that lasted through, and now beyond, her forty years in that position. She would become the trusted and beloved friend and counselor of hundreds of graduate students during her long tenure. In that first year we sent off scores of letters, many to instructors I had met at black colleges working with the Southern Teaching Program, announcing our interest in applications from black students. Prior to 1966 only three African Americans had applied; all were accepted and enrolled. Virginius Thornton, originator of the theater boycott, was the first; he left before finishing a degree but would later take a Ph.D. elsewhere. Raymond Gavins came from Virginia Union University in 1964. In 1970 he became the first black person to receive a Ph.D. from the University. His entire teaching career has been at Duke, where he continues as professor of history. Jim Roebuck came to us in 1966. A Philadelphia native and a graduate of Virginia Union, he had been a fellow history major there with Ray Gavins. Once well-established in our diplomatic history program, Jim ran for and was elected to the Student Council; he soon became its first black president. He left us with the Ph.D. in hand. He is now a long-serving member of the Pennsylvania legislature.

The work Elizabeth and I did in 1966–67 yielded eleven applications. We offered admission to six of the eleven. Four of those enrolled, two with financial aid. The two I remember best, Clarence (Butch) Wright and Sue Ford, earned M.A. degrees, were shining spirits in the graduate program, and went on to other careers, Sue in the foreign service and Butch in civil rights work, including a stint at the Southern Regional Council where we would spend a year working together.

Over the two academic years of 1966–68, the number of students calling for aggressive action on the integration front grew rapidly and spread beyond the VCHR, SSOC, and the SSA. Student leaders and opinion makers cast aside the defensive stances of their predecessors to put pressure on President Shannon and his administration as well as their fellow students. The *CD's* reporting became more extensive and its editorial policy came over to the camp of the reformers. The Student Council took a leadership position, calling in March 1967 for an investigation of racial and religious discrimination in fraternities, among other things. The move was led by two history students, Dan Morrow, an undergraduate, and Frank Homer, a graduate student. It did not bring about an end of the discrimination, but the revelations effectively highlighted—one might say pointedly stirred up an awareness of—one of the University's major problems. That would bear crucial positive results two years later.

No one has yet undertaken a study of the white students who entered the University in the last half of the '60s to explain why so many shared the goals, if not always the methods or the company, of the pioneer antiracist student groups. I believe that the underlying explanation must be traced back to the Southern civil rights movement itself. The students who enrolled in the late sixties had spent their high school years watching on television and reading about both the extraordinary courage, idealism, and daring of the movement leaders, most of them just a few years out of high school, and the equally extraordinary baseness, bigotry, and brutality of the defenders of segregation. The passage of the Civil Rights Act of 1964 and the Voting Rights Act of 1965 must have seemed to most the appropriate legislation to acknowledge the justice of the movement and end the bigots' resistance. Putting these two factors together, they must have been surprised, perhaps troubled, when they discovered that Mr. Jefferson's university was home to a pitifully small number of black students, had no effective policy to enlarge that number, and was in swirling controversy over how the heritage of racial exclusion could best be put to rest.

One of the students that Merrill, Elizabeth, and I recruited for the department's graduate program in my second year as director of graduate studies quickly became an important leader in the integration movement. Arthur (Bud) Ogle was someone we were keen to attract. With a B.A. from

Macalister College and a B.D. from Yale Divinity School, Bud applied for a fellowship to do a Ph.D. His credentials were outstanding but he needed persuasion so I invited him down from New Haven to look us over. We had money for such recruitment strategies in those bygone days. Bud had no doubt about the quality of our department but he told me he was concerned about racial matters. He needed to be reassured that we were not hopelessly mired in the past. The students and faculty he met persuaded him we were not, but also that this was fertile ground for the battles he wished to enter. Bud accepted our fellowship offer and soon became a member of the Student Council along with Jim Roebuck; he also soon became a leader of the radical wing of the protest movement and a Student Council member at the forefront of the revolt of 1968–69.

With the increasing number of antiracist students on Grounds and the consequent election to Student Council of more activist-minded members, the agitation for integration began to spread on all fronts. Especially during the 1967–68 academic year, the balance of opinion among student leaders and opinion makers, as well as in the student body generally, was shifting away from the die-hard segregationists. The more radical students in SSOC and SSA kept up their pressure, helped along with the appearance of a new radical publication, *The Virginia Weekly*. As black enrollment increased, albeit slowly, more black voices added power and authority to the demands for change. Accurate enrollment figures are difficult to come by because they were not officially kept. According to the best I have been able to find, there were fewer than twenty African Americans attending classes on Grounds in 1965; I have no figures for the academic year 1966–67; in the following year, 1967–68, there were thirty-one full-time and forty part-time students, a total of seventy-one out of a total enrollment of 8,332. Black student enrollment, full-time and part-time, constituted less than one per cent of the student body. For the 1968–69 year, the year when the student revolt achieved significant success, the number of African Americans reached fifty-seven full-time and thirty-five part-time, for a total of ninety-two, passing the one percent mark for the first time, eighteen years after Gregory Swanson's arrival.

In May 1967 Jim Gay, an African American law school student and

Student Council member, introduced a motion to place off-limits for all Council-recognized student groups "any facility, public or private, that pursues a non-integration policy." The motion passed 10–4. Because their existence was not subject to Council approval, fraternities were exempt from the ruling. Over the next year the regulation was debated in the *CD*, set aside temporarily while the Council studied means of implementing it, and eventually reinstated. Radical groups like SSOC and SSA, once harassed by the Council, now found support from it, receiving, for example, the green light for protests against the Vietnam war as well. Following in the Council's spirit, the *CD* editor blasted the administration for its "tolerance of prejudice" and the "furtherance of a sick heritage." Across the board, student demands for wide-ranging change had supplanted the stern resistance of the past.

VI

On Thursday April 4, 1968, as he was standing on the second-floor balcony of the Lorraine Motel in Memphis, readying to go out for a dinner of soul food, Martin King was shot to death by an assassin's bullet. The day was the forty-seventh anniversary of my parents' wedding. I thought of that as I immediately telephoned the hospital in Mobile where my mother was being treated for atrial fibrillation. I spoke to the nurse on her floor to ask that the television in her room be turned off. Her stress was great enough without adding the news of her hero's murder. Three days later—it was Palm Sunday—I met the cardiologist in the hospital corridor. He had just come from church. A sprig of palmetto leaf was pinned to his suit jacket. He greeted me warmly. I told him of my call on the evening of King's assassination. "Oh, that wasn't really necessary," he replied. "Your mother was under such heavy sedation she wouldn't have taken it in." Then he added, completely unaware of how offensive his words and manner would be—offensive in the way of so many yet-to-be sensitized white people—that he'd always considered King to be nothing but a "rabble rouser." Overwrought, something in me snapped. I grabbed the doctor by his lapels and began pushing him down the corridor. For the last several days, I blurted out, I had put my mother's life in his hands and I had accepted him as an expert whose word I would not challenge. Now I was going to tell him something about a subject on which I was an expert. I delivered an abbreviated lecture on Martin King that was no doubt very different from the one he had heard from his white minister in his whites-only church that Palm Sunday morning. I left him with a totally startled look on his face; I felt a sense of relief.

My mother, a vibrant sixty-eight, her calendar full of appointments for recent and upcoming social gatherings, did not survive. I spent a couple of weeks more in Fairhope, on two different trips, before and after her death. Shortly after my return I received a letter from her doctor expressing his sorrow for the loss of such a charming, engaging person. He appended a request to let him know when next I was in town so that we might discuss "political matters." I suppose I made some kind of impression. Back at the University, my colleagues, most of whom had known and become very fond of Mom from their time with her both in Charlottesville and at our Southern Historical Association annual parties, gave my father a long-term subscription to the *Journal of Southern History* in her memory. They correctly knew how welcome that gift would be.

Meanwhile, on the very day I shoved the startled cardiologist down the hospital corridor in Mobile, President Shannon led a memorial service at the University. Henry Mitchell gave the invocation. Reflections by President Shannon, Jim Gay, and Dean Robert Harris followed. My colleague Willie Lee Rose concluded the speaking with a eulogy. Richard Gwathmey, the *CD* editor, wrote that the program's "highlight" was Clarice Harris's rendition of "Precious Lord, Take My Hand." (Unbeknownst to Clarice, and probably to everyone else there, it was the song King had requested to be sung that evening a few minutes before he was shot.) Rabbi Raymond Krinsky gave the benediction. It was an extraordinary occasion: an African American priest, a Jewish rabbi, an African American speaker, an African American soloist; and the president of Mr. Jefferson's university endorsing as enduring truths the things Martin King had said.

There was much irony, too—at least for me. Five years earlier King had spoken in the same auditorium. There was no official greeting then; no presidential expression of pride or pleasure in his presence. Certainly no endorsement of his principles. Our friend Clarice Harris did, indeed, have a wonderful voice. We had heard it often at Bren-Wana, Ed Jackson's night club, the site also of King's only Charlottesville dinner. And it was the presence of Henry and Gertrude Mitchell at our home during the Buddy's sit-in that sparked racist phone calls we received that evening.

Times had changed in five years. No such gathering could have been imagined in 1963. But the Southern civil rights movement and the Virginia students it inspired had opened the way to a new era. Now President Shannon could come out of the shadows to speak eloquently and movingly of King's legacy. In a stunning conclusion, reminiscent of Merrill Peterson's eloquence he could not acknowledge only three years previous, Edgar Shannon quoted the slain leader's own words:

> To end poverty, to extricate prejudice, to free a tormented conscience, to make a tomorrow of justice, fair play, and creativity—all these are worthy of the American ideal. We have an opportunity to avoid a national disaster and create a new spirit of class and racial harmony. We can write another luminous moral chapter in American history. All of us are on trial in this troubled hour but time still permits us to meet the future with a clear conscience.

The president then finished with his own inspiring challenge: "Ladies and gentlemen: may you and I be worthy of this future."

There would come a time, and soon, when I knew for sure that Edgar Shannon was "worthy of this future." The acts of a leader that would warrant this conclusion, however, still lay in the future. *CD* editor Gwathmey found the service "a fitting tribute to Dr. King, and an even better tribute to the University which held it." But he worried. Were the high ideals of which President Shannon and the dean spoke "anything more than 'words wasted on the desert air'?" He remained unconvinced "that the University, in its hiring practices and its admission of students and recruiting of athletes, subscribes to those principles" of which its leaders had spoken. He urged them to address these specific issues soon, and within the framework of the lauded King's principles.

Richard was hardly alone in his skepticism. The VCHR, newly renamed the Martin Luther King, Jr., chapter, met with the administration in mid-

April to urge it to deal with what it saw as the real problems facing black students and employees. Chapter president Robert Yuhnke was reported by the *CD* to be "shocked and appalled" by conditions at the University. He promised demonstrations if the University failed to act to eliminate discriminatory practices and promised that marches would come "until the legitimate demands of Negroes have been met." A seventy-person march on the Lawn followed in May accompanied by criticism of the University's "traditional" approach to the admission of black students and the hiring of black faculty. A series of proposals given to the president included the appointment of a black administrator to oversee the recruitment of black students; the appointment of black faculty; and the inclusion of black studies in the curriculum. A three-thousand word exchange of letters between the VCHR and President Shannon was made public in mid-May. The president responded sympathetically and announced some positive changes that had been made.

Prominent among the changes was a memorandum from Vincent Shea, the University's comptroller and a power figure in the administration, that reiterated what he said was the institution's long-standing opposition to discrimination of any sort. He added, to avoid "misunderstanding," that "the University's policy requires that all official University groups refrain from using facilities which practice discrimination." Once enforced, as it came to be, this ruling hit hard at the several segregated private clubs, most notably the elite Farmington Country Club, where numerous University events took place. Recruitment lunches, among other events of common occurrence, would become a thing of the past; the ban on Farmington would last a quarter-century.

Another sign of progress the administration announced was that University-underwritten mortgages must in future require re-sale agreements void of racial restrictions. Since racial covenants had been outlawed by the Supreme Court in 1944, I wondered at the time how this announcement could fall into the category of progress. Still, the director of Development and Public Affairs explained the need for such a regulation "if the University is to succeed in its efforts to attract qualified Negroes to the faculty and staff." With only one African American on the faculty, a professor in the School of Education, one had to wonder about the hiring efforts over the previous decade and more. We all knew there was no vigor. Students calling for active recruitment of black faculty and students and significant improvement in the conditions they would find at the University ended the semester with confidence that it would be up to them to make those changes happen. They were right, and, in the next academic year, their success was considerable. The story of what happened in that dramatic year is one I cannot tell from first-hand experience. We were in Chapel Hill where I was a resident fellow in a joint Duke-UNC research center. I kept up with UVA affairs through letters, telephone calls, and occasionally copies of the *CD.* I would later return to the archives.

VII

The 1968–69 academic year began, as other recent ones had, with flyers circulated by one of the left-leaning groups, this time SSOC, striking out at the University's leadership, structure, and values. Editorial response, in contrast to previous years, found virtues along with excesses in the critique. From this point on, in fact, both news reporting and editorial comment hit hard and frequently on the University's racial shortcomings. The VCHR, now in its eighth year, reported that there were eleven black students in the entering class, an improvement over past years, but the previous year's call for the appointment of a black student recruiter had gone unanswered and President Shannon's assurance that the athletic department would recruit black athletes remained unmet.

Wes Harris, just shy of his twenty-seventh birthday, with his Princeton Ph.D. in hand, had joined the Engineering School faculty to become the second black appointed to the faculty. A protégé of George Mathews, himself a Princeton Ph.D., Wes had followed George's recommendation that he take his Ph.D. there, which he did in a record four years. I'm sure George was behind the move to bring Wes back to Charlottesville and that he was warmly supported by his fellow engineering professor John Scott. Wes's Charlottesville home would become a principal gathering place for African Americans as the student revolt unfolded in the months ahead and he would be one of the key persons in shaping the events.

The first signs of widespread protest turned not on University policies but on continuing problems at the Corner. When a medical school professor reported having seen a barber rudely turn away a young Negro boy waiting for a haircut, the *CD* editor termed the incident a "disgrace." A series of irate letters condemning "Barber Bigots" followed; the Student Council endorsed a plan for a boycott of all offending barber shops to help "break the structures of racism in this town." Surveys, interviews, and one-on-one conversations followed. The VCHR released a plan for picketing to be added to the boycott but withdrew it when, after two weeks of pressure, three Corner shops agreed to change their policies. Negroes who were "neat, clean, well-behaved" would be welcome customers. (No similar requirement was announced for whites.) "One more brick has been removed from the wall between the races in Charlottesville," the *CD* editor wrote, adding that "it's hardly more than a drop in the bucket, considering the size of the wall." Bud Ogle wanted Student Council to boycott downtown barbers who had not yet capitulated, but his motion was defeated 8–13.

Soon the students turned their energy and imagination to their own bailiwick. The Interfraternity Council adopted a new rule at the end of October that would deny its recognition to all fraternities "with discriminatory clauses in their constitutions." When I heard of this I was reminded of my fraternity's war on its racial and religious exclusionary clauses, the fight we had taken up almost two decades earlier; when we did not win we soon withdrew from the national organization. UVA was hardly in the forefront of the march toward freedom from racial and religious prejudice, but it had taken a difficult step in the right direction. Fraternities, especially those alumni chapters, were tough opponents, as I had learned during my failed mission to Chicago.

In November, with Bud Ogle and Jim Roebuck leading the charge, the Student Council called on the president and his administration to adopt a plan for active recruitment of black students and faculty. Among other things, the Council asked for "full support to the recruiting drive of the Black Student Union." The Black Students for Freedom, the newly formed activist organization of black students, had begun its own trips to African American high schools, just as the students in the VCHR had done in earlier years, but now with the greater advantage of having black people as the recruiters. Still, as the Council made clear, this was hardly enough. The University, with a miniscule black enrollment, remained what it had always been, a place for "well-to-do white men." That had to change. And change would not occur without vigorous recruiting action on the University's part, including the long-overdue appointment of a black officer to oversee the effort.

As I now read through the accounts of the Student Council's actions that November, I find a part of the report that stirs up a forgotten memory. "In accordance with commitments made last year by Professor Gaston, then Director of Graduate Studies in the Department of History," the Student Council announced that it had established a committee, chaired by Jim Roebuck, "to work toward the establishment of progress in African American History and the Afro-American experience." I have no doubt that I worked with Bud and Jim, and perhaps others, to frame such a proposal, but the details have slipped away. As the 1968–69 year unfolded, however, the creation of such a program became, along with recruitment of black faculty and the appointment of a black recruiter, a central demand of the Council and of the spreading student movement for positive action on the racial front. In its November action, the Council set as "minimal acceptable action" for the current year the hiring of "one black professor in Afro-American & African history."

The Council kept up its pressure for the rest of the semester. Its president, Martin Evans, characterized President Shannon's policy of "non-discrimination" as one that "offends few and accomplishes little." Shannon, he said, was "sympathetic" to the goal of enrolling more black students, but he refused to assume the leadership and take the actions that would make that a reality. Given what he called Shannon's policy of "non-accomplishment" and "lack of commitment to aggressive recruiting," more pressure would have to be brought on the administration. He suggested contacting state officials, circulating petitions, and creating publicity to make responding to demands for change "more desirable than the bad publicity of continued student unrest." The consequence of continued administrative inactivity, he promised, much as Martin King or Frederick Douglass might have, "would be escalation of student pressure."

The *CD* editor agreed. In the same December 10 issue in which Evans's interview was recorded, Gwathmey added a bit of sarcasm. The administration, he wrote, has "a perfect record . . . of formally and politely opposing discrimination; consequently it has a perfect record of doing nothing of any significance to work away from tokenism of the most odious sort." The administration had "regularly failed to take an active role against discrimination anywhere, much less on Grounds." Two days after this double blast at the president the Student Council declared the appointment of a black admission officer to be a "top priority." Bud Ogle suggested the creation of a committee, to be headed by Wes Harris, to provide a list of suitable persons to the president. He added a call for Shannon to meet "in open forum" to discuss the need for such an admissions officer.

That call was not answered. Instead, the day after the Council's meeting the *CD's* front-page headline read "University Hires Negro for Admissions Office." Fred T. Stokes, a thirty-four-year-old master's degree candidate in the School of Education, was appointed part-time assistant to the Dean of Admissions. He would work twenty hours a week, not as an assistant dean, but as an assistant to the dean. His charge would be to help recruit "disadvantaged high school juniors and seniors interested in higher education." The language was characteristic of the time and place. The appointment came in response to the student demands for a black recruiter to bring black students, not disadvantaged students, to the University. And no one had urged going after high school pupils who were not interested in higher education. The phrasing of the administration's announcement seemed to me to be but another example of its hidden assumptions about the pressure on it to recruit black students. In all of its statements about practicing non-discrimination it invariably placed the adjective "qualified" before the noun "Negro." That in itself was a form of discrimination. It never advertised the University as being open to "qualified" whites "interested in higher education." Some things went without saying; some were said to make a point, a not very subtle one, that the student protestors favored admitting unqualified black students. Genuine discussion of the meaning of "qualified" never took place.

VIII

Shortly after the Christmas break, various elements of the student movement coalesced to form what came to be called the Student Coalition. It was endorsed by the presidents of the Interfraternity Council, the Student Council, the University Union, the VCHR, and the editor of the *CD*. At the outset it tended to steer clear of SSOC and the small SDS chapter, looking to present a solid front of establishment organizations and to send the president requests and suggestions rather than nonnegotiable demands. Soon, however, SSOC and SDS folk became important members as well. The newly formed Black Students for Freedom, with George Taylor as its principal spokesman and Wes Harris as its faculty advisor, became an ally and prod. In mid-February, the Coalition launched its first unified protest march. The *New York Times* reported that "some 1,500 students, and some faculty members," gathered at the Rotunda for speeches and the enumeration of eleven proposals whose adoption, as the CD reported, was declared to be necessary "for ending the University's racist atmosphere." The attire of most those present caused the event to be labeled a "coat and tie demonstration," giving it a unique standing in the history of 1960s activism.

Coalition head Robert Rosen declared that the peaceful and respectful manner of the demonstration merited a prompt response from President Shannon. Bud Ogle, the principal speaker, and Jim Roebuck, now vice president of the Student Council, both stressed the urgency of long-overdue action on every front, including aggressive recruitment of black faculty and students and the incorporation of black studies in the curriculum. Faculty member Bill Elwood described the "deplorable" working conditions at the University and stressed the importance of the Coalition's call for decent wages. Howard Gordon, a young Presbyterian minister (from the church attended by President Shannon), called the University's wage policies "inhuman and inadequate."

The wide array of students in the Coalition was both a guarantee of its influence and a source of disagreement among its constituent parts. Some, most from SSOC or SDS, peppered the "Coat and Tie" demonstration with chants calling for the dismissal of C. Stuart Wheatley, the only member of the Board of Visitors who had played a prominent role in crafting the Massive

Resistance program. A sixty-three-year-old Danville resident, Wheatley had been appointed to the BOV the previous spring by Governor Mills Godwin, a notorious Massive Resistance architect. The more radical students in the Coalition found it unacceptable to have an advocate of school closing to avoid integration among the University's ruling elite. They failed to get Wheatley removed, but put the issue of his presence and values before the student body and into the letters pages of the *CD*. Ron Hickman, president of the Student Council, publicly apologized for the anti-Wheatley outbursts. In opposition to their president, Jim Roebuck, Bud Ogle, Jackson Lears, and other members of the Council asked for Wheatley's resignation, but their motion failed to pass. Who, they wanted to know, would apologize to the black students for the man's presence? The issue soon lost traction as the Coalition moved forward with its principal recommendations.

In his reply to the Coalition proposals, President Shannon expressed his "deep concern for the economic welfare of the employees of the University" but said it was up to the legislature, not him, to raise wages, a move he favored (but apparently had not recommended to the General Assembly). This was followed with boilerplate disavowals of racial discrimination, the listing of recruitment efforts of which he was aware and reaffirmation of the University's commitment to seek black athletes. But he could not favor the appointment of a full-time black assistant dean of admissions. That, as he had said before, would violate the University's non-discrimination policy. A black studies program was a matter for faculty action, action on which he reported there was some movement. In what must have come across as a rebuff to the Coalition leaders, who thought they had carefully crafted for the president's consideration a long list of essential steps that had to be taken, Shannon concluded by promising to appoint a faculty-student-administration committee "to receive and consider proposals for furthering equal opportunity and racial harmony at the University."

He did appoint such a committee, naming twenty-four persons to serve on it, including as chairman my neighbor Bill Rotch, a professor in the business school. Tom Gardner, Kevin Mannix, and Judy Wellman were the three left-leaning white student members; Professor Nathan Johnson, in his second year as a professor in the Education School, and Paul Garrett, a law school student, were the only African Americans. Neither Wes Harris nor any of the leaders of the Black Students for Freedom were included. The promise of a presidentially appointed group "to receive and consider proposals for furthering equal opportunity and racial harmony at the University" did little to satisfy the BSF and the Coalition. Their protests and dissatisfaction with the administration only increased. No report from the committee would appear until the end of the summer.

Dissatisfied with the president's actions, the students issued a critical response. A Bud Ogle letter, formally endorsed by the VCHR and the Coalition, conceded Shannon's good intentions but dismissed them as beside the point. What was at issue was his "understanding of the University's problems and his methods of dealing with them." Disappointed by what he called the president's "wavering response" to the Coalition proposals, Bud wrote that

> we continue to belabor the obvious: despite non-discriminatory official policy Black people are not presently attracted to the University. The problem is not one of blatant discrimination but of subtle discrimination which, compounded in a racist state and a racist society, becomes a more sinister form of discrimination. In other words, rather than constantly reiterating non-discrimination pledges, the University must provide creative leadership to encourage Black people to participate fully in University life.

In essence, the students asked once again for an aggressive policy to recruit black students and faculty, more attention to the need for a black studies program, and genuine support of better wages and working conditions. Bud's letter was followed by a formal Coalition press release declaring that "the proposals of the Coalition are virtually refused rather than considered conscientiously." President Shannon's "tone" was "defensive and patronizing," not "conciliatory." The critical failure of his response was "substance, not tone." Following hard on the Ogle letter and the Coalition press release, *CD* editor Gwathmey added his own severe criticism of the president's "misunderstanding" of the real nature of the problem growing out of "150 years of unequal opportunity."

By the end of February the Coalition, with full support across the spectrum of student opinion, was at loggerheads with the president, the board of visitors, and the governor. A rally on March 4 featured five speakers, beginning with Coalition leader Robert Rosen who playfully opened the occasion with a welcome to the "FBI man in the blue coat with the green hat." Mathematics professor Jim England excoriated his Arts & Sciences colleagues for failing to give "unified support" to the students. He was dead right, I thought, when he claimed that "the students are educating the faculty and administration on how to be responsible citizens in this society." Former Student Council president Rick Evans highlighted the importance of public opinion and promised more action to shape it, including a trip to Richmond to confront Governor Godwin. Sociology major George Taylor, leader of the Black Students for Freedom, presented a detailed black studies program; and Tom Gardner, the SSOC leader and veteran spokesman for the more confrontational wing of the Coalition, spoke once more about the need for better working conditions and decent wages. He closed by promising a motorcade to Richmond "to present demands," hoping in this way to bring more pressure for change on President Shannon.

As I read back through the speeches and proposals coming out of the Coalition in the spring semester of 1969 I am struck both by the uniqueness of the Virginia movement and the vision and prescience of its proposals.

From the outset, Coalition head Robert Rosen was determined that his university could be turned around by reasoned argument, grounded in appeals to the principles of Thomas Jefferson, the founder. In an institution putatively devoted to reason, evidence, and the pursuit of knowledge, Robert believed, storming the gates, occupying administrative buildings, or hurling objects stronger that words should not be necessary to win important arguments. His movement, he argued passionately, should avoid those confrontational strategies that had marked the demands for racial justice and world peace in other universities. The "campus guerilla warfare" that brought "disruption and coercion," he wrote on one occasion, should not be the Virginian way. On the other hand, the "coat and tie" label, adopted by many journalists and others, distorted the essence of the movement. The

Virginia protestors might be well dressed and they might avoid trampling on the sacred Lawn, but those were trivial realities when set alongside the courtesy, appeal to reason, respect for evidence, and intellectual and moral power that marked the debate they fostered.

Robert became a prolific writer, sometimes as editor of his own alternative publication, *Rapier*, more frequently in the pages of the *CD,* and on occasion in regional newspapers. His speeches, often embellished with classical allusions and regularly fortified with appeals to Jeffersonian idealism and Enlightenment rationalism, gained attention beyond the Grounds, once as far away as his home town of Charleston where the notorious segregationist Tom Waring blasted the Coalition on the editorial pages of his newspaper, *The News and Courier.* Noting that "one of the planners" of the Coalition rallies was Robert Rosen of Charleston, South Carolina, he likened the protestors to "university wreckers . . . interested in propaganda instead of scholarship." Their effect was like "cancer cells" that "spread and cause widespread havoc." For the leaders of such activities, "prompt expulsion is in order." Should the administration fail to remove them, "the state has an obligation to act." In a letter as long as Waring's editorial, Robert's father, Morris, blasted Waring, long the nemesis of progressive South Carolinians. "We are very proud of our son," the elder Rosen wrote. "He is a compassionate, honorable man, and needs no lesson in ethics from *The News and Courier.*" At a lunch in Charleston recently with both Robert and Morris, I enjoyed listening to the father recall with admiration the son's leadership at Virginia and his own pleasure in dressing down the irascible Tom Waring.

Mills Godwin was one of those state officials Waring believed had "an obligation to act." Robert and the Coalition he headed agreed. But the action they sought was of a different order from that which Waring and Godwin favored. The governor, imprisoned by his heritage and shaped by his racist record, was beyond being able to see the world as they did. He dismissed the students and their proposals, sending them back to Charlottesville where he said they should be concerned with education, not social protest. The *CD* editorial response—"Massive Resistance 1969"—found Godwin's behavior toward the students "flabbergasting" and "callous."

Robert understood Virginia politics and politicians well; he was not surprised by the governor's rebuff. Turning it to his advantage, he arranged for an assembly on the steps of the capitol the day after Godwin sent the students home to gather their books and put away their placards. Robert's speech, widely reported in the press and printed in full in the *CD*, called up memories of Patrick Henry, Thomas Jefferson, and Martin Luther King, Jr., and excoriated the leadership of both the University and the Commonwealth and pointed the way to change that must come. "We assemble here today," he said "to petition, to remonstrate, to supplicate. . . . We have come seeking liberty and justice for all. . . . We have come to seek 'liberty' and the 'pursuit of happiness' for our brothers long deprived of the reality of those noble ideals." Turning to Martin King, he recalled the civil rights leader's warning to his putative friends who wrongly believed they could "set the time table for another man's freedom." He closed by warning that the time for change was running out: "Our time of inaction is gone. If the University of Virginia is ever to welcome the black man, it must be now. For if it is not, protest upon protest will burden its Grounds." The protest would continue throughout the semester.

The black students generally supported the Coalition's goals and one of their leaders, usually George Taylor, was customarily included as a speaker at the rallies. They also met privately, away from their white supporters, at Wes Harris's home. My student Ray Gavins, working furiously to complete his doctoral dissertation and become the first African American to receive a Ph.D. from the University, spoke to me of these meetings in our recent interview. Three BSF leaders—George Taylor, Roland Lynch, and John Charles Thomas—recalled them vividly in a 2006 appearance at the University. Those meetings, they said, were of critical importance to African Americans not just for the openness they provided for discussing strategies to change the University. They were also important as occasions when black students might come out from under the demands and pressures of the white world. None knew more about this than Wes, who had endured them for four years as an undergraduate. Now as their young mentor, he helped them draft their program for Afro-American studies that the Coalition adopted and the Student Council endorsed.

I had begun tentatively to design a black studies program with Jim Roebuck and others before I left for Chapel Hill, so I knew something about the work of the BSF, but not much. And some that I had once known I had forgotten. As I was recently studying a brief summary of the BSF proposal in the March 1969 files of the *CD*, and wishing for more detail, I decided to launch an internet search for George Taylor, with whom I had not been in touch for thirty-six years. Almost immediately I found him, a faculty member at the University of Michigan. In his first email to me George told me that, in his mother's garage in Hampton, Virginia, he had recently come across the extensive archives of the BSF. He had turned them over to Roland Lynch, his classmate and comrade from BSF days, to photocopy. Before long Roland sent a packet of some two hundred pages, including a few exchanges between Wes and me. I tipped my hat once again to Mr. Google and the world wide web he roamed.

The BSF proposal, endorsed by the Coalition, boldly challenged the conventional thinking of the president, the dean of the faculty, and much of the faculty itself. George, as BSF chairman, and Wes, as its faculty advisor, sent copies of their plan to President Shannon and several chairmen of Arts & Sciences departments on March 14. The twelve-page document begins with a long preface linking black studies to black liberation. Much more than an addition to the curriculum, it was critical "to meet a debt to the black community," to break out of the "tokenism" that afflicted most technically desegregating universities, and to bring integrity and accuracy to the academic enterprise. It was not, as the dean and the president seemed to look on it, a proposal for just another program to fit into the interdisciplinary major's studies structure already in place. Far beyond that, it was part of a national movement, present in scores of universities. To the famous radical historian Eugene Genovese, writing in the *Atlantic Monthly*, "the black student movement [for black studies] represents an authentic effort by young people to take a leading role in the liberation of an oppressed people." But it was important not for blacks alone, he added, because it could "help immeasurably to combat the racism of white students." Bill Abbot, acting that year as chairman of our history department, with his characteristic wisdom and sensitivity, saw its importance to both races. In a letter to George and Wes he welcomed their proposal because it would make the University "a more attractive and rewarding place for black students and more broadening for white students."

A month after the BSF submitted its plan I traveled to Philadelphia for the annual meeting of the Organization of American Historians, where Vann Woodward was to give the presidential address. His title was "Clio with Soul." I cringed when I heard the eminent historian who introduced him announce his topic as "Clio with a soul." I wrote a note to myself about this additional evidence of how distant even some of the best white historians were from an understanding of the black experience. Vann moved right into his speech without bothering to correct his colleague. I asked him later why he didn't. He shrugged and replied, "Why bother?" But in his speech he told us that throughout academia universities were reacting to the demand for black studies programs "clumsily, belatedly, heartily, or half-heartedly." Such programs emerged, Vann told us, as "the overdue ends of justice sought." Even the most famous of American historians—he singled out especially Frederick Jackson Turner and Charles A. Beard—had written with "a certain moral obtuseness and irresponsibility regarding Negro people." Turner predicted that, in time, slavery would be seen as just an "incident" in American history. Beard wrote that black struggles during Reconstruction "would have been ludicrous if they had not been pitiable." Even among antiracist white historians, the emphasis was generally on the "moral, social, political, and economic problems of white men and their past." In their telling, "the Negro is a passive element, the man to whom things happen. He is the object rather than the subject of this kind of history." In these circumstances, he concluded, "American history, the white man's version, could profit from an infusion of 'soul.'"

The BSF proposal looked to a large infusion of soul into Mr. Jefferson's Academical Village. Unsatisfied with just another interdisciplinary major or introductory course (both of which it recommended), the authors of the proposal outlined a plan for many new courses, a research dimension that would give authenticity to their program, and the recruitment over the next few years of black professors in the several relevant departments to teach the courses and run the program. The budget, laid out in dazzling detail, came to slightly more than three-quarters of a million dollars.

Student protests of various sorts continued right up to the end of the semester; President Shannon met more than once with Coalition and other student leaders; the dean and the faculty made progress on tentative plans for a black studies program, but decided to leave its completion and approval to the next session. With the continued pressure of the students on all racial fronts, the administration and the faculty moved as well, though not nearly as rapidly nor as far as the protestors wished. The will to recruit, not just accept, black students and faculty seemed to have become a reality, though few results were yet evident. No progress toward paying the workers a living wage could be reported.

President Shannon, in a post-retirement interview for the University's oral history program, recalled that "I guess we weren't actively recruiting [black] faculty and students as much [before the protests of 1968–69] as we've done since then." Still, he was positive about the achievements early in his administration, believing that "we quietly became fully integrated . . .on our own," without federal pressure, by 1963 or 1964. We would have said that token desegregation had been achieved by then. Full integration, the object of the student protestors, was still a long way off. Only mounting student demonstrations in 1968–69 and beyond would accomplish that. "Perhaps we weren't as alert in the early days as we should have been," he confessed, sure that "black people felt that we didn't go far enough at times, and I'm sure some of them are even questioning whether there was good faith or not, but certainly there was." Good faith, as the BSF and the Coalition saw it, was not enough. As Bud Ogle put it after the president's response to their proposals, Mr. Shannon's "good intentions" were beside the point. What was at issue was his "understanding of the University's problems and his methods of dealing with them." In the years ahead, from 1969–70 until his retirement in 1974, Edgar Shannon's "dealing with them" would change. He would become a leader. The black and white student protestors could take some, but not all, of the credit for helping him along the way.

Chapter Eight

WIDENING VISTAS

On a hot August day in 1969 we packed up our belongings for the drive from Chapel Hill to Charlottesville, traveling the same route we had followed twelve years earlier. Our world had changed dramatically since that first journey. Marge had died, leaving a great gap in our sense of family. The memory of her, and the stories we told about her, kept her firmly in our consciousness. Dad visited us in Chapel Hill, continued on as secretary of the colony, and seemed to be coping well, structuring a sustaining daily routine. He and I exchanged frequent letters that nurtured both of us. Blaise had become so unhappy with the rigidity of the public schools, both in Charlottesville and Chapel Hill, that we spent part of our year on leave looking for alternatives. I was sure that, somewhere, there must be a school with something of the "Organic" approach to life and learning. He and I set off on a northern journey to visit likely possibilities. We settled on the Barlow School, near Amenia, New York. It was a good choice. It was there that Blaise came to know he wanted to make beautiful things with wood as his life work. Gareth, Chinta, Mary, and I settled in our old home, readying for the adventures of a new year.

My university, and my role in it, had also changed dramatically since my 1957 arrival. This time, instead of being greeted by a senior professor instructing me in the niceties of university traditions, I was called into the office of David Shannon, the new Dean of the Faculty, for orders to break university traditions. Dave was a historian, both a biographer and an admirer of Eugene Debs. Since his arrival in July he had studied the proposals for a black studies program drawn up by the Black Students for Freedom and the record of discussions and tentative plans of the faculty and his predecessor, Fredson Bowers. He was ready for action—action which I assumed would have the full support of the president. He gave me three charges.

First, I was to design an introductory course on black studies that I would teach in the second semester. I was eager to do that but only if I were furnished with adequate financial resources to invite black scholars and public figures to give some of the lectures. I wasn't about to be the white boy who inaugurated, all by himself, the University's maiden venture. Dave agreed. It was good to be with a dean whose values and vision connected with my own, and to have such easy rapport. Next, he asked me to chair a committee to design an interdisciplinary major in black studies. He knew we lacked sufficient courses and faculty to do much more in the first year than make a commitment and lay a foundation, but we had to do what we could. We talked about whom he should appoint to my committee. I suggested both my graduate student Ray Gavins and George Taylor, former president of the BSF. He appointed them. Wes Harris was an Engineering School faculty member, so Dave lacked authority to appoint him. Instead, he asked him to consult with me and the committee. Wes agreed. Finally, I was to chair a search committee to identify and recruit an eminent black scholar to become the director of our program and the architect of its expansion.

I met all three goals. I designed both the course and, with my committee's help, the interdisciplinary majors' program early in the first semester. They were approved with ease by the faculty. No more wrangling. The events of the previous year, most importantly the student protests, had cleared away all effective opposition. We were finally on our way, supported by both the faculty and the administration. The president made an especially vivid demonstration of his commitment early in the second semester at one of the meetings of my black studies course. There were 175 students in the class, a very large number for those days and a striking illustration of the widespread interest in the subject. Edgar Shannon and his wife Eleanor sat prominently in the front of the auditorium, giving visible evidence of their approval of this new venture. I found it exhilarating and rewarding to have my president in the room as cheerleader rather than critic.

The search for a prominent black scholar to teach the course in the future and to take over the directorship of the black studies program also succeeded. Joseph R. Washington, Jr., a distinguished religious studies scholar, accepted our offer. Gone, overnight as it were, was President Shannon's refusal to sanction searches that focused exclusively on black persons. After his retirement from the presidency, he recalled in an interview for the University's oral history program that I taught the first black studies course "and did a very good job"; but, he added, for it to be "completely acceptable," we had to hire a black scholar.

At the same time the president's backing of our new ventures came to the fore our personal relationship changed as well. In the fall of 1969, shortly after my return from Chapel Hill, we discovered that one of the Shannon girls was attending the same kindergarten as our son Gareth. (There were no public kindergartens in Charlottesville then.) I frequently drove up to Carr's Hill, the president's mansion, to fetch her. Eleanor became an enthusiastic admirer of Gareth. A couple of years later, Edgar turned to me at a garden party to ask, "Paul, when is the history department going to get off the dime and hire some black professors?" The new level of comfort and accord that marked my relationship with both Edgar and Eleanor, like our agreement on the future course of race relations in the University, had been a long time in coming. Its arrival was a special gift for me. I hope it was for them, too. We never discussed the past.

I

For our university, as well as for most around the country, the spring of 1970 was filled with turmoil that far exceeded the previous years' protests against racial inequality. There was a modest national outcry in May against the midnight police killing of two and the wounding of twelve other black students during a protest at Jackson State College. The Southern Regional Council's special report on the incident detailed the long way both Mississippi and the country had to go in their journey toward justice and civility. Shocking though the Jackson State event was, the nationwide student protest against the war in Vietnam captured most of the country's attention and produced unprecedented crises in academia. Institutions around the country were shut down by student strikes; administrative offices were stormed and occupied; demands for the elimination of ROTC programs flourished; and riotous receptions awaited recruiting agents of the federal government and manufacturers of chemicals used to kill Vietnamese. At Kent State University, in Ohio, the student protest against the invasion of Cambodia ordered by President Nixon led to what came to be called the Kent State Massacre—the killing by the Ohio National Guard of four students and the wounding of nine others, one of whom was paralyzed for life.

Our protesting students, including among their leaders veteran critics Tom Gardner and Bud Ogle, saw themselves as patriots with a responsibility to help end a cruel and unjust war. Their idealism seemed to me to shine brightly. Anti-war editorials in the *Cavalier Daily*, protest marches, speeches, and demonstrations had been part of my university's scene through the last half of the 1960s, usually led by members of SSOC and SSA, but they took second place on Grounds to the demands for upending the University's heritage of white supremacy. SSOC leaders did travel through the South on peace missions, changing some minds and confronting a measure of verbal and physical abuse. Here at the University the emphasis moved from race to peace in 1970, partly because of the student victories already achieved on the racial front and partly because the Vietnam war took on shocking new dimensions, most importantly the invasion of Vietnam's neighbor, Cambodia, at the end of April. I did not play a major role in the protests, either as participant or adviser, but I watched sympathetically and joined hundreds of my colleagues in a condemnation of the Kent State massacre. The full story of the spring events awaits its historian.

That story would include a student strike; the seizure of a university building; the aborted fire-bombing of another building; the importation of two famous radical speakers (William Kunstler and Jerry Rubin) who led a march of more than fifteen hundred students on the president's house (where they "shouted and chanted in frightening fashion," the president later wrote); a police sweep through the Lawn coupled with arrests; and constant negotiations. Still, in contrast to many universities, ours was not shut down. Students were given options for completing course requirements: they could take their class average as the final grade, sit for the final examination, or opt for a special examination to be completed over the summer. Emotions were at fever pitch. President Shannon kept his cool, worked with the striking students, kept a lid on violence from all quarters and, on May 10, standing on the steps of the Rotunda, addressed the university community.

Mary and I, guests of one of the professors living on the Lawn, viewed the event from his pavilion's balcony. It was a warm day. The Lawn was packed with students from one end almost to the other. Shortly after President Shannon began to speak, a shirtless student at the far end of the Lawn, responding to Edgar's account of what had taken place, cupped his mouth and shouted for all to hear: "Bullshit." I couldn't help thinking about how much had changed since my first appearance on the Lawn. Little time passed before Edgar captured both the attention and the warm enthusiasm of the mass of students before him. He was on his way to becoming a hero.

Elegantly and persuasively, he discussed his intention to keep the University open. To the aroused students, whose right to protest he supported, he said that "the University must continue to teach, and to discover, and therefore to remain open. We must continue to educate and train for the future, while we meet the emergency of the present." His following sentences set off a roar of applause: "I know your anguish over the military involvement in Southeast Asia. I want promptly to end the war. I feel furthermore it is urgent that the national administration demonstrate renewed determination to end the war and the unprecedented alienation of American youth caused by that conflict. I have conveyed that intention in a letter to our senators."

He concluded by urging students to make their views known to national leaders. To help in that cause he announced that he had arranged for a delegation of students to meet the next day with the state's two United States senators, Harry Flood Byrd, Jr. and William Spong. The group would be led by history graduate student Jim Roebuck, longtime advocate of progressive causes, the first African American president of the Student Council, and a leader destined to be a legislator himself. Jim would carry a message of support from President Shannon. Almost five thousand students and faculty members signed a petition that afternoon and evening calling for the war's end. Jim would carry it with him to put in the hands of the senators.

The mass of students on the Lawn that day began to look on their president as a hero. When word spread soon afterwards that the Board of Visitors was considering responding to calls from disgruntled alumni and others across the state for his dismissal the students drew up petitions supporting him. He was not relieved of the presidency. At the June graduation ceremony on the Lawn, faculty, students and their relatives gave him a long, standing ovation. That day I felt a pride in my university I had not known before.

The day after the speech Mary sent Edgar a dozen roses. Two days after that I wrote a long letter to my friend Staige Blackford, press secretary to Governor Linwood Holton. The student strike, I wrote, had become "increasingly imaginative, constructive, and—in my judgment—inspiring." What made the difference, I wrote, was President Shannon's speech:

> On the one hand he forcefully stated his concept of the functioning university as one devoted to reason and the free play of competing ideas. On the other hand, he recognized the extraordinary malaise that has permeated our society, and especially the young people, and he paid the highest compliment possible to the integrity and wisdom and moral courage of the young men whose intellectual guidance is our responsibility: he gave them the encouragement and the maneuvering room to carry on their protest against our foreign policy in southeast Asia. He did this, as you know, without "closing down" the university—an act which would have detracted from the integrity of the student movement.

I sent a copy of my letter to Edgar. He replied with his "heartfelt thanks . . . for the understanding concern which it expresses as well as your encouragement and support." We had, indeed, reached a new era in our relationship.

II

The spring of 1970 also marked the appearance of my first book, *The New South Creed: A Study in Southern Mythmaking*. It had been in the making since my dissertation defense in 1960. I thought I had completed the last revision at the end of the summer of 1968 when we set off for Chapel

Hill to take up my fellowship at the joint Duke-UNC research institute. Knopf editor Angus Cameron had been patiently awaiting its arrival. Before putting it in his hands, however, I sent the manuscript off to a few friends in early September, asking for their critiques.

Vann Woodward was one of those friends. He wrote to say that both he and his students liked it. We would discuss it when we met in November at the annual meeting of the Southern Historical Association. Which we did. He was generous with his praise but then, looking out a window, away from me, asked if perhaps I would consider adding another chapter, taking the story from its ending point in the 1890s up to the present, providing a commentary on the enduring (and pernicious) influence of the New South creed. I heaved a huge sigh. "Yes, I understand," I remember Vann saying. "You've worked long enough on it; I'll urge Angus to publish it." I returned to Chapel Hill and straightaway posted the manuscript to New York. Within a fortnight, Angus wrote to say how much he liked what I had written. But, he asked, could I add a chapter or two "connecting it up, as the lawyers say, with the present." I knew I had no option. I replied that I could write an epilogue to do that. Would that be satisfactory? Almost by return mail I had a contract offer with the promise of a generous advance on royalties. Several years passed before I said to Vann something like, "You didn't, by any chance, make any suggestions to Angus about adding something to my manuscript, did you?" I remember one of those enigmatic Woodwardian smiles, a kind of "Who, me?" expression.

In the long run, I was glad Vann intervened. The epilogue turned out to be one of the most satisfying parts of the book, giving it a modest cachet in the discussion of contemporary affairs it otherwise would have lacked. In the short run, however, it torpedoed the research plans that had brought me to Chapel Hill. I spent four stressful months writing and rewriting what became a thirty-page epilogue. The year was not lost, but I returned to Charlottesville without enough material for a new book. I learned a lot, however, working through the archives in Chapel Hill and the papers of the Commission on Interracial Cooperation at Atlanta University. One of these days, I thought, I would write a book on Southern racial liberals.

Meanwhile, *The New South Creed* attracted some glowing reviews in newspapers, magazines, and professional journals. Major figures in the profession found it "first rate" (Kenneth Stampp, Berkeley); "enormously relevant . . . in our present-day confusion and perplexity (Arthur Link, Princeton); "beautifully written" with "a subtlety which cannot be reflected in a brief review (Dumas Malone, History Book Club); and "a major achievement which has few counterparts in the historical literature of the postbellum South" (George Tindall, UNC). Newspaper men in my home state were likewise welcoming, seeing it as an "exhortation . . . to continue asking the tough questions" (Brandt Ayers, Anniston), and a book that should be "on the shelf of every Southerner" (Duard LeGrand, Birmingham).

I was flattered by the near-universal approval, but some of the more extravagant reviewers seemed to think more highly of my book than I did. I was acutely aware of how much better it could have been and I never internalized the sense that it was one of the major works in my field. Still, it remained in print—first by Knopf, then Vintage, then LSU—for just shy of thirty years. A new edition, for which my former student Jeff Norrell wrote an introduction and I wrote an afterword, was published in 2002 by NewSouth Books and remains in print. The blurbs for this edition proclaimed it to be "brilliantly prescient"; "thirty years ahead of its time"; "a powerful blend of grace and passion"; and "one of the few books in our profession that can truly be called a classic." My son Blaise, glancing at these encomia, remarked of their authors: "These are all your buddies aren't they, Daddy?" He was no innocent.

One of the negative reviews of the original edition I particularly liked characterized the book as a tract for the civil rights movement. The reviewer erred, but his point probably made me more aware of my growing desire to play a wider role in that movement, beyond my university and my city. That chance came quickly when Paul Anthony, Les Dunbar's successor as executive director of the Southern Regional Council (SRC), invited me to join the Council staff. Hoping my move might be a long-term one, he offered me a good salary, a generous allowance for moving expenses, and a title as historian in residence, an apparent opportunity for me to define my own role. Merrill Peterson, then my department chairman, granted me a leave of absence so that I might have adequate time to explore the possibility of changing professions while also, we both hoped, forwarding my study of Southern liberalism. We left for Atlanta early in the summer of 1970.

The organization I was now to join had deep roots in the struggle for a decent South. It was founded in 1944 as the successor to the Commission on Interracial Cooperation (CIC) which was launched in the immediate aftermath of World War One. Will Alexander, the CIC's first executive director, wrote in 1921 that it would take between twenty-five and fifty years to make a substantial dent in the racist structure of the South. "It is essential for us to keep our feet on the ground," he added, "and never forget how much there is yet to be done." Beginning with a membership of white men only, the CIC soon added white women and African Americans, female and male. Genuinely distraught by racial injustices, its members nonetheless believed that they must do their work without challenging the region's segregation laws. Instead, they established programs to supply legal aid to blacks in need; agitated for an end to police brutality; vigorously condemned lynching and the rise of the Ku Klux Klan; advocated equal pay for equal work; and tried to encourage greater and more accurate reporting of African American accomplishments. With headquarters in Atlanta, the CIC established state and local branches throughout the region. The spread of interracial meetings and discussions, often at the risk of physical and financial danger to those who participated, along with the extensive research centered in the home office, distinguished the organization and schooled a generation of Southern racial liberals. Mary's grandmother—Bamba—was one of them.

The SRC, a quarter-century old by the time I joined the staff, had been through tumultuous times, divided at its outset over whether to issue a forthright condemnation of segregation. In the 1950s and '60s, it became the region's most reliable and extensive source of information about the ongoing civil rights struggle and a major force for change itself. By the time I joined the staff, following the formal demise of Jim Crow, a third era of its history had begun.

In its first seven years (1944–51) the Council brought together leading white and black Southern racial liberals from around the South to pursue a more vigorous assault on racial inequities than its predecessor had. Its founding charter pledged it "to attain, through research and action, the

ideals and practices of equal opportunity for all the peoples of the South."
Almost immediately, however, the absence of an anti-segregation declaration
led to tough criticism. J. Saunders Redding, a young professor at Hampton
Institute, and the author Lillian Smith, already the region's most eloquent
white antiracist, protested. Pursuing equality while maintaining segregation was impossible, both critics argued in much-publicized essays in the
magazine *Common Ground*. Both black and white SRC leaders defended
the Council's policy. Guy Johnson, the executive director, wrote in *Common Ground* that his new group's democratic objective was to "improve the
social, civic, and economic life of our region in spite of a deep-seated and
undemocratic pattern of segregation." African American Council leaders
like Carter Wesley ("We must be realistic") and Gordon Blaine Hancock
("I'm more interested in getting something done than something said")
joined the response to Redding and Smith.

The debate over whether to denounce segregation endured for almost
eight years. Most of the board members calling for a direct renunciation—
college and university presidents like Benjamin Mays (Morehouse College),
Albert Dent (Dillard University), and Rufus Clement (Atlanta University)—
were African Americans. Most of those in opposition were white. Some,
like Richmond *Times Dispatch* editor Virginius Dabney and University of
Virginia president Colgate Darden, their values in conflict with racial integration, would resign their memberships after the December 1951 annual
meeting when the Council broke with its cautious past.

I was in my senior year at Swarthmore at the time. I had barely heard
of the SRC and I doubt that I read about the statement of principle written by Harold Fleming, a Georgia-born Council staff member. I would
later get to know and admire Clement, Dent, and Mays. Fleming would
become a friend and valued counselor. His 1951 statement stands as one
of the Council's major declarations of principle:

> The South of the future, toward which our efforts are directed, is a
> South freed of stultifying inheritances from the past. It is a South where
> the measure of a man will be his ability, not his race, where a common
> citizenship will work in democratic understanding for the common good;

where all who labor will be rewarded in proportion to their achievement; where all can feel confident of personal safety and equality before the law; where there will exist no double standard in housing, health, education, or other public services; where segregation will be recognized as a cruel and needless penalty on the human spirit, and will no longer be imposed; where, above all, every individual will enjoy a full share of dignity and self-respect, in recognition of his creation in the image of God.

Those who steadfastly remained with the Council knew they would pay a high price for their principles and their boldness. The SRC had little money and more than a few of its members would join Dabney and Darden in the white retreat. Vicious attacks also followed the anti-segregation resolution. James Jackson Kilpatrick, from his post at the *Richmond News Leader*, was in the form that would distinguish him throughout the 1950s and '60s and prepare him for his role as the theoretician of massive resistance. The SRC was a "Communist-front" organization, he wrote, a home for "fellow-travelers." Georgia journalists and politicians churned out similarly abusive attacks. Governor Herman Talmadge declared that SRC activities were "subversive." He was right, of course: its activities were, indeed, meant to be subversive—subversive of the white supremacy values and institutions of their region. To the Talmadges and Kilpatricks of the time, however, if you were an integrationist you must also be a communist (or at least what they called a "fellow traveler").

Under the directorships of George Mitchell (1947–57), Harold Fleming (1957–61), and Leslie Dunbar (1961–65) the SRC survived the desertions and defamations to become a major national voice for Jim Crow's dismantlement. With an enlarged staff of writers and researchers, made possible by increased foundation grants, the Council seemed to be everywhere, reporting in authoritative detail on racial matters throughout the region. John Popham, the Virginian who covered the South for the *New York Times*, used to tell the story of being greeted by foundation heads in New York who had just read one of his pieces based on SRC research. "Pop," as his friends called him, used to regale me and others years later with tales of how such incidents helped bail the Council out of its financial difficulties. Popham's successors at the *Times*, Claude Sitton (Georgia) and Roy Reed (Arkansas), were also Southern liberals. Much of what the nation learned about the civil rights movement came through the *Times* from them and much of what they reported had major assists from the SRC. The Council's Atlanta office was a regular port of call for all serious journalists writing about what was happening in the South, and why.

As soon as the *Brown* decision was handed down in May 1954 the Council, with the financial backing of the Ford Foundation's Fund for the Republic, set about creating statewide councils on human relations whose principal purpose would be to create an atmosphere favorable to school desegregation. Mary and I joined the Charlottesville-Albemarle branch of the Virginia council shortly after our arrival in 1957; I would soon serve on both the local and state boards. We had little success in rallying support. The same was true of the other state councils. The SRC's hope that fact-based rational argument and appeals to law and order would turn the tide against segregation was sadly unfulfilled. As I noted in chapter five, the SRC's Ben Muse's attempts in 1959–60 to enlist Southern leaders in the cause of desegregation got nowhere. Out of his experience and that of the several state councils, the SRC concluded that research, accurate information, and appeals to reason and the American creed of fairness and equality were not enough to overturn the deep-seated commitment to white supremacy. The region-wide resistance to racial integration would have to be overcome with a different set of tools. What was needed, Muse concluded and the SRC leadership adopted as policy, was sustained grassroots organization and protest, primarily by African Americans, that would cause the federal government to abandon its chariness to create strong, effective antiracist leadership and legislation.

The African American-led grassroots protests, beginning with the 1955 Montgomery bus boycott, spread through the South and dominated the civil rights scene for ten years, culminating with the 1965 Selma demonstrations and the march across the Pettus bridge and along U.S. Highway 80 to Montgomery. The violence, murders, tortured logic, vulgarity, and everyday meanness that shaped the white South's resistance eventually aroused the conscience of the nation, making possible the introduction and passage of the Civil Rights Act of 1964 and the Voting Rights Act of 1965. Neither would have emerged from presidential or Congressional leadership absent the awareness of the reality brought to the surface by the civil rights movement.

The role of the Southern Regional Council in these events, and in bringing to a formal end to the Jim Crow structure of segregation and disfranchisement, was secondary to the work of the major black activist groups (SCLC; SNCC; CORE; NAACP; and the NAACP Legal Defense and Educational Fund). Their leaders and the troops they mobilized made the difference. Still, the SRC played a pivotal role as ally and fellow warrior. For one thing, bonds of comradeship were formed so that, at crucial moments, Les Dunbar and his colleagues could offer helpful strategic advice. Publications, too, played a more important role than ever before as virtually every major black-white confrontation was astutely analyzed and widely publicized to become part of the national record.

Perhaps the SRC's most important civil rights contribution began in April 1962 with the creation of the Voter Education Project (VEP). Plans for establishing it had begun the previous year, led by Harold Fleming (in his last year as executive director), philanthropist Stephen Currier and his wife Audrey, and members of the Kennedy administration. Their common objective was to create a tax-exempt agency, funded generously by sympathetic foundations, to act as an umbrella group overseeing the financing of voter registration work to be undertaken by several of the major civil rights groups. Les Dunbar oversaw its establishment and was accompanied by Kennedy officials on his successful visit to the IRS to seek tax-exempt status. Five years later Pat Watters and Reese Cleghorn, two of Atlanta's best journalists (later to join the SRC staff), published *Climbing Jacob's Ladder*, a riveting, authoritative history of the VEP.

With headquarters in the SRC's Atlanta offices, the VEP was headed by African American men already known as major civil rights leaders and, as time passed, as prominent national figures. Wylie Branton, famous as the attorney for the Little Rock Nine, came first, followed by Vernon Jordan and John Lewis. Under their stewardship the VEP funneled funds, counsel, and support to civil rights organizations, mostly in the Deep South. President

Kennedy and his brother Bobby, by now solid advocates of expanding the franchise, had supported the VEP in part because they hoped concentration on voter registration would produce fewer of the violent reactions than had accompanied the sit-ins and freedom rides. It didn't happen that way. Sustained efforts by VEP field workers to register black voters was no more palatable to white resisters than integrated lunch counters or buses. Both carried the same risks to life, limb, and livelihood as had the sit-ins of 1960 and the freedom rides of 1961. The Selma demonstrations of 1965, focused on voter registration, led to the infamous beatings on the Pettus Bridge, the march to Montgomery, and the public outcry that encouraged Lyndon Johnson to introduce what became the Voting Rights Act of 1965. In the wake of its passage black Southerners would finally obtain the democratic right to vote and hold office. The SRC could lay claim to a significant part of the responsibility for that achievement. I had good reason to admire and be a part of it. Its history and mission spoke to my values and to what I had tried to be about over the previous thirteen years, its history and institutional ambience far more congenial than that of my university (or, indeed, any university).

III

By the summer of 1970, when I took leave from Virginia to join its staff, the SRC was well into the third phase of its history. Les Dunbar had left for New York to direct the Field Foundation and funnel grants to progressive Southern groups. Vernon Jordan, still on the staff as VEP director when I accepted the offer from Les's successor, Paul Anthony, had also left, to head the United Negro College Fund and soon after that the National Urban League. The VEP, for several years the brightest star in the SRC's civil rights firmament, had been spun off to become an independent agency, its headquarters still in Atlanta, with John Lewis as its director. Sadly for me, neither Vernon nor John would be a colleague that year, but I would be fortunate to count both of them as friends in the years to come. As I came on board, the SRC staff numbered upwards of thirty people, headed by the executive director. He, in turn, was appointed by an executive committee numbering about a dozen people. The Council itself now consisted of 120 elected members from the eleven states of the former Confederacy.

The great legislative victories of 1964 and 1965 were not followed by an era of tranquility and equality. Far from it. Violent racial confrontations had spread through a dozen non-Southern cities before August 1965. In that month the Watts district of Los Angeles exploded with six days of violence that led to thirty-four deaths, more than a thousand injuries, and four thousand arrests. The explosion, coming so soon after President Johnson had signed the Voting Rights Act, cast a new light on American racism. Soon demands for a deeper respect for black people and a more radical agenda for achieving economic and political equity emerged, especially in the Black Power movement. Prominent in Alabama's black belt and other parts of the Deep South, it was national in its scope.

By the time I joined the SRC staff there was a general awareness that racism was an American phenomenon, not a Southern monopoly. Partly for this reason the SRC expanded its research and information activities, with frequent special reports and two regular publications, the quarterly *New South* and the monthly *South Today*. Its outstanding group of writers and editors—Pat Watters, Reese Cleghorn, and Bob Anderson—turned those publications into the place to look if you wanted to know the real story of what was happening not only in the so-called post-Jim Crow South but in the nation as well. The emerging "Southern strategy" fashioned by Republicans to capture Southern white Democrats discomfited by the political and social gains of African Americans came in for incisive analysis, its racist assumptions and partisan objectives brought into bright light. It seemed to me, as I came on board in that summer of 1970, that the SRC had the potential to be a more national research and information agency than it had ever been.

Shortly after I arrived I took over the school desegregation desk and saw this possibility more clearly. I met frequently with my counterparts in other civil rights groups (the American Friends Service Committee and the NAACP prominent among them) both to monitor the slow and uneven abandonment of school segregation, now sixteen years after the *Brown* decision, and to frame recommendations for its acceleration. Early in the new year we published a handsomely bound special report for which I wrote the fifteen-page introductory essay on "The Region in Perspective." The tone was guardedly optimistic, in part owing to Supreme Court decisions in cases from Mississippi and Virginia, outlawing the strategies of tokenism and declaring positive steps to achieve integration to be a constitutional requirement. I reported the significant statistical advance desegregation had taken in 1970–71 but emphasized the partisan manipulation of those figures by the Nixon administration and scored the false claims of presidential adviser Daniel Patrick Moynihan that "the dual school system in the South . . . has quietly and finally been dismantled." It was, sadly, a long way from being dismantled. Achievement of that goal was made more difficult, I wrote, by President Nixon's opposition to busing, coupled with his sloganeering for "neighborhood schools." One civil rights veteran remarked at one of our strategy sessions that "You used to be able to telephone Washington; at least somebody would listen sympathetically. Now, there's nobody to talk to."

I had come to Atlanta with the option a two-year leave of absence from the University, but before the first year was out we made a family decision to return to Charlottesville in the summer of 1971. I knew I did not want to become a permanent member of the SRC staff and Chinta was eager to return to her school and her friends. Mary had won a Coretta Scott King fellowship from the American Association of University Women for a year's study at Atlanta University where she would take a master's degree in early childhood education. She finished her residency in the late spring and then, taking Gareth with her, went to England for field work studying British infant schools. After that she was ready to begin a teaching career in Charlottesville.

For me, the year at SRC was both exhilarating and instructive as it widened my understanding of Southern struggles for justice and brought me into a new circle of friends who shared my values, understood without explanation what we should be about, and had rich histories of experience. In addition to my staff colleagues and the members of the policy-making executive committee, I got to know the major journalists covering the South and civil rights leaders from every state in the region. From this large group of men and women I would form enduring friendships and develop the kind of invaluable contacts no university could furnish—an extended family of black and white comrades such as I had never had.

The work of the Council I witnessed and shared in was both influential and inspiring. Staff member Reese Cleghorn, for example, did extensive research on the segregation academies, those new private schools set up to provide instruction for whites only. He took his findings to Congress. His testimony was decisive in the government's removal of their tax-exempt status. The range of the Council's work was impressive and instructive. On one occasion, at the invitation of students and faculty at the University of Florida, three of us flew to Gainesville to hold day-long hearings on their complaints about wages and working conditions. The university president fired off a telegram before we left Atlanta telling us he would not allow us to meet on the campus or permit any of his faculty to testify. We met off campus and did hear the riveting testimony of a few of the brave souls who risked the ire of their president. Our report and recommendations were published but rejected by the university administration. Still, it was useful for me to experience yet another kind of work the Council could undertake.

One of my greatest pleasures—and surprises—came during the November annual meeting of the Council. I was given the Lillian Smith prize for *The New South Creed*. The award had been established two years previous to honor writers of books that reflected Miss Smith's values and the stands she had taken. I was near tears when I read the plaque I was handed, its last sentence stating that the award was made "to honor her memory and to recognize the achievement of one who, like her, contributed to the life of the South." It felt good, too, to acknowledge in my acceptance remarks that receiving an award in Miss Smith's name—she once a vigorous critic of the SRC—spoke well for the organization for which I now worked. She had, as I knew, become a strong supporter after the Council's 1951 denunciation of segregation.

Another act of generosity came in April after I gave a series of three lectures on race and education at Miami University in Ohio. Paul Anthony, knowing that I had to be in New Orleans for a meeting of historians a week after the conclusion of the lecture series, suggested that I explore Mississippi, especially the Delta, in the interval. I rented a car in Memphis and spent six days driving to New Orleans.

I have in my files a "tentative itinerary" that Paul arranged to acquaint me with the problems, promises, and key leaders of civil rights work in Mississippi. Memory, however, does not serve as well as I should like. I do recall Mound Bayou, the all-black town founded after the Civil War, and chatting with town mayor Earl Lucas. I also met two black brothers, both political candidates, in Marks. I spent two nights at Rainbow Plantation with Bill and Betty Pearson, two of the rare white liberal cotton planters in the Delta. I learned a lot from them about their civil rights struggles and the infamous Parchman Penitentiary but perhaps my most memorable experience was driving a tractor to lay out rows for planting cotton seeds. Bill and Betty wrote in August to tell me my admirably straight furrows were producing handsomely. It was a good experience for a Southern historian who regularly lectured about the cotton kingdom.

In Greenville I spent the evening with Hodding Carter, celebrating his thirty-sixth birthday. His mother Betty, whom I had met in Fairhope, was charming and fascinating, but her husband, stilled by a stroke, had lost the power that once made him a courageous newspaper editor. Other visits included most of a morning with the Delta Ministry, an afternoon with the Federation of Southern Co-ops, and a night spent in Jackson with Patt Derian (like Hodding a member of the SRC executive committee) and her husband, a doctor readying to perform the next day Mississippi's first hip replacement.

These were all heady meetings but my Mississippi sojourn left me most deeply moved by the rows upon rows of shacks in which so many of the black farm workers lived and the mixture of courage and optimism I encountered in so many of them and their white allies. They put me in mind of my grandfather's writings about the evils of sharecropping, the damage it did to white and black alike.

I arrived in New Orleans in time for dinner with Cliff and Virginia Durr, special friends and great civil rights heroes from Alabama, Vann Woodward and his wife, Glenn, and the Durrs' son-in-law, Sheldon Hackney. The next day, at the Organization of American Historians meeting, I chaired the session at which Sheldon read a paper on Vann's *Origins of the New South*, then twenty years after its publication. Sheldon found little to fault and much to praise in his mentor's classic work. The only critical question from the audience was posed by another of Vann's students (also his close friend and great admirer), my colleague Willie Lee Rose. With a puckish grin, she asked why women were hardly to be found in the great book. I've forgotten Vann's reply.

After the session I flew to Mobile to spend the weekend with Dad and, on the Monday following, gave a lecture at the University of South Alabama, a condensed version of my three Ohio lectures. Back in Atlanta, I met Sheldon who had come to spend ten days working in the SRC archives. He boarded with us his last week, during which we had spirited evening conversations and forged an enduring friendship.

The archives that attracted Sheldon's research interests were (and are) one of the great sources for the study of the origins and course of the civil rights movement and of Southern history generally. One of the tasks I took on during my year as a staff member was to organize and provide an index of the materials. Fortunately for me and for the project, a brilliant young Columbia University Ph.D. candidate, Jacquelyn Hall, was living in Atlanta then and came to manage this task. In time the papers were lodged in the Atlanta University library (joining the papers of the Commission on Interracial Cooperation) and subsequently made widely available on 225 reels of microfilm. In time, too, Jacquelyn would become one of the eminent historians of the South.

In late May, three months before we left Atlanta, Paul Anthony called me into his office to tell me of his intention to resign the executive directorship, a position he had held for six years. "As if our life were not already complicated enough," I wrote to my father, "Paul asked me directly if I would consider becoming the next executive director." As encouragement, he told me that Raymond Wheeler, the president of the Council whom I greatly admired, along with a couple of the executive committee members who knew me, thought I should become his successor. That was a stunner. Such a career change had many appeals. To direct the South's most effective and respected civil rights organization in this new era and to help shape both regional and national policies certainly spoke to my Fairhoper's sensibilities. In many ways it seemed a logical next step from the work that had engaged me for the previous fourteen years in Charlottesville. Over the summer, when Paul's intention to resign became public, several staff members came by my office to say they hoped I would become the next executive director.

I was flattered, of course, especially by the warmth and assurance of the men and women I had worked with over the previous year, but still we returned to Charlottesville without having made a decision. I told Paul and my staff colleagues that I would consider the offer if made, but that I was not courting it. I was tempted but doubts held me back. Did I really wish to leave academia? Did I really feel up to taking on the many strains that I knew would come with the job? My indecision stretched through the next several months.

Early in the fall, the executive committee appointed a search committee. I was invited to come to Atlanta for a formal interview. That much I felt I could do. Such a meeting would at least give me a firmer idea of what the job would be like should it be offered to me. The interview went well but, shortly after I returned, Raymond Wheeler called to say the committee was determined to appoint a black person. Offers were subsequently made to Harvey Gantt, Wylie Branton, and Andy Young. All expressed admiration of the Council but none was ready to become its executive director. When the last of these three declined the offer made to him Raymond telephoned to say a new round of interviews would soon begin. He remained my champion and assured me that several other members, black as well as white, favored me as well. To win the support of the full committee, however, I would have to come down for another meeting and "sell" myself.

When the date for my second interview came I developed what I'm sure was a case of psychosomatic flu. I telephoned Raymond to tell him I was unwell, that I could not come. He expressed his disappointment and, as a physician, wondered if there was another explanation of my hesitation. He had reason to wonder. Throughout my months of pondering the possibility I could never come to the point of truly feeling the job was right for me. Directing the Council was something I often thought I ought to do, but not something I wanted to do or felt I would do well at it. Fear that I might actually be offered the job and then feel obliged to accept it produced the physical reaction that sent me to bed. As it turned out, I might well not have been the committee's choice. That honor and burden went to my friend George Esser who had Ford Foundation connections and a strong record as a fundraiser. I had no such experience and was not of a mind to gain it.

My decision was the right one. And, as it turned out, I had my cake and ate it, too. At the 1972 annual meeting I was elected to membership in the Council and in 1974 to the executive committee, a position I held for the following twenty-four years, four of them (1984–88) as president.

IV

The university to which I returned in 1971 was different from and better than it had ever been. The barrier against women's entrance into the College of Arts & Sciences had been broken—by a lawsuit, faculty demands for coeducation, administrative leadership, and a national move toward casting away the institutions and mindsets that had excluded women from many universities and colleges. I had played a minor role in this process, simply signing the various petitions calling for change and lobbying a few members of the opposition. Perhaps the most useful thing I did, much later, was to urge Tami Curtis, one of my graduate students, to write a thesis on the coming of coeducation to the University. I believe her work, *Imperfect Progress* (1987), stands as the best study of the subject. The first class of 450 women entered the College in 1970; 550 more came the next year. They brought a new vibrancy to the classrooms, classrooms we teachers could now enter without the ugly feeling that women and blacks were barred from them. The enrollment of women (nearly all of them white) increased steadily every year, reaching 43 percent of the entering class by the fifth year of coeducation. Student opposition had been both vocal and sometimes vulgar but as coeducation became a reality, hassling and the old reverence for a male-only institution faded away. The women helped the process along by taking positions of leadership. Ann Brown, one of my favorite students, lost her campaign to become editor of the *Cavalier Daily*, so she founded *The Declaration*, an influential weekly with a leftward bent. Ann's friend Mary Bland Love, also a student of mine, did become managing editor of the *CD*.

Life and progress on the racial front was a different story. I was reminded of some of the difficulties not long ago by my friend Sydney Trent, one of my best students in the 1980s. She was a goddaughter of Barbara Johns—the famous teenager who ignited the student protests in Prince Edward County and the school integration struggle flowing from them. In a 2004 essay in the *Washington Post Magazine*, of which she is deputy editor, Sydney wrote of reading an article in 1983 reporting that the University of Virginia "was being threatened with a cutoff of federal funding for failure to increase its minority enrollment." With black students pressuring it, Sydney wrote, "the university announced it would accept any qualified minority student up to the first day of fall classes." She applied and was accepted.

"Enticed also by the school's academic reputation," she wrote, "I headed off to Charlottesville." At the end of the first semester, however, she wondered if she had done the right thing. "The liberal arts dean's voice dripped with condescension as she congratulated me on my straight B's." To Sydney those were low, not high grades; she simply had not worked as hard as she might have. Her reaction was instantaneous and memorable: "I felt like I'd taken my coat off in a cold wind. Was this, I asked myself, what we'd all yearned for—opportunities presented as though they were charity, with the smug assumption that we couldn't live up to them?" Such smug assumptions put her in mind of something her father had said to her, "that the worst kind of racism is the covert kind . . . because it carries with it the presumption that you're too stupid to know what's really going on." Painful though that encounter with her dean was, Sydney knew that "the more subtle racism my generation has faced is not as bad as the overt racism Barbara confronted so boldly in 1951." Her life was never threatened as was Barbara's and other black activists of the 1950s and '60s; and, because of their courage and tenacity, Sydney and other African Americans of her time could say and do things that were impossible a generation earlier.

By the 1970s, the antiracist white students, building on the work of their predecessors of the 1960s, had grown in both numbers and influence. Now dominant in the *CD* and the Student Council, they had a much wider following in the student body than the radicals of the '60s had commanded. The principal object of attack in the mid-'70s was University President Frank Hereford, the physics professor and former provost who had succeeded Edgar

Shannon in September 1974. The issue was his membership in the all-white Farmington Country Club, the social gathering place of the city's elite and a powerful symbol of their racist heritage. Edgar had resigned while he was president; Frank maintained his membership.

Even before Frank took office, Student Council president Larry Sabato launched a move to require all members of the university community—students, faculty, and administrators—to resign from Farmington. That act sparked a vigorous debate over the privacy rights of individuals versus the damage done to the University by membership in a whites-only club. In the spring of 1974, at President Shannon's request, Larry met with the Equal Opportunity Counselors, of which he was a student member, to ask them to make a joint statement. Larry recalls that he was "flabbergasted" by their response. The half-dozen or so white faculty and administrative members drew back, citing their club membership and the pleasures it provided. Linwood Jacobs, the only black member, stood alone, favoring the kind of statement Edgar asked Larry to propose. Edgar's response to the news Larry brought him was to dismiss the entire group, an act Larry rightly recalls as courageous and principled. Some months later, after he had assumed the presidency, Frank restored the dismissed persons to their former positions.

The joint move of the president of the University and the president of the Student Council did not succeed but Farmington remained out of bounds for university-sponsored events. Visiting job candidates, for example, could not be entertained there at university expense, a practice that was routine when I joined the faculty. Once Frank took over the presidency he became the focus of both student and faculty protest. With the *CD* leading the way, he was bombarded with demands that he break his ties with Farmington. Thirty years later Eston "Dusty" Melton, the paper's 1975–76 editor, brought a few of his warrior colleagues from those days to the University to recall the events of the tumult. I sat in the auditorium, brought into a reverie of that era by their undiminished enthusiasm and idealism. I carried home a packet of 150 or so items Dusty and his friends had collected and reproduced as archival evidence of their crusade. The next day I walked into my study to pull out my own (half that size) "Farmington Events" file, with copies of the few letters Dusty and I had exchanged at the height of battle.

My file also includes a copy of my letter to Frank and the original of his reply. Like others who wrote to him I stressed the impact his Farmington membership would have on our commitment (a commitment which he had publicly joined) to recruit black faculty and attract more black students. "What must I tell prospective black colleagues," I asked, "when they ask about the President's record as a leader in whom they, as black people, might have confidence?" Frank replied that he viewed "the elimination of racial discrimination at Farmington when it comes about—and I am confident that it will—as of greater importance than any immediate favorable reaction and results which my resignation might bring about."

Other faculty members wrote, some with more sting, some more gently. On November 20, 1975, the Arts & Sciences faculty, describing the Farmington membership as "detrimental to the University of Virginia's policy of affirmative action in the recruitment of black students, faculty and administrators," adopted a resolution calling upon the president to resign. The 144–54 vote was the sharpest evidence of a split between faculty and president I experienced in my forty years of teaching. The resolution had no immediate effect. Frank stood his ground, apparently still hoping he might rally enough members to bring about an end of the club's whites-only policies. Dusty took him to task in a *CD* editorial, writing: "For the president to claim that his membership is justified by his work to change club policies is to say that the future of Farmington is more important than the University's present, an assumption which we have repeatedly found unwarranted."

Early in the next year, however, Frank's belief that he might bring change could no longer be sustained. Farmington commissioned a poll of its members' views. By a vote of 1,918–1,066 they favored the status quo of racial exclusion. The club's board of directors then ruled that the ban on black guests and members would continue. On February 10, 1976, Frank announced his resignation, stating that the refusal to change was "damaging to our entire community" and "wholly unacceptable." A score or so others, including former president Colgate Darden and current Rector Joseph McConnell, also resigned.

In his editorial response Dusty did not describe Frank's resignation as a "victory." Tough as ever, he decried what he called the president's earlier "hypocrisy" so that his eventual resignation "brought a sense of relief rather than joy." I don't recall my own feelings when I heard the news but I probably had a different view. Once again, as in the '60s, students (now in alliance with an aroused faculty) had brought about a needed change. Two months before Frank's resignation, in an interview with *New York Times* reporter Drummond Ayres, I described the Farmington controversy as symptomatic of the "changing nature of the Old Dominion." The problem, I was quoted as saying, "is how the university can remain loyal to the traditions of an older Virginia and, at the same time, protect and further its reputation as a national and international university that appeals to people with the most disparate backgrounds." Frank's resignation from the country club was an important step toward resolving that problem.

The Farmington controversy faded after the resignations. Memories of it, however, and what the club stood for, had a long afterlife—at least for me. It remained on the banned list for another quarter-century, long after other private clubs had integrated and successfully appealed for the ban to be lifted. In 1997, the year I retired, the prestigious Raven Society asked to bestow its "Raven Award" on me, as a mark of my "many contributions to the University." I had been a critic of the society in the 1960s and '70s for its traditionalist stance and refusal to induct or honor any of our radical students, several of whom I had recommended. Much had changed since then and I might have accepted the award if the banquet at which I was to receive it was not to be held at Farmington. That was too much. Shortly after I retired, University President John Casteen telephoned to tell me that Farmington had requested that the ban be lifted. Its rules had changed; it had a few black members and blacks were admitted as guests. What did I think his response should be? I suggested that he wait until a request came from a faculty member. He did; the request came soon; the ban was lifted.

Not long after the lifting of the ban, during the academic year 2001–02, Glynn Key called to ask if I would be her dinner escort. The occasion was a banquet of the Alumni Association Board of Managers, of which Glynn was the new president. The venue was the Farmington Country Club. Glynn had been one of my favorite students in the mid-1980s. The first black woman to be president of the Honor Committee, she had also served as a student representative on the Board of Visitors. (She serves on the board now, a 2004 appointee of Governor Mark Warner and a 2008 appointee of Governor Tim Kaine.) The charm of my friend's invitation overcame my Farmington aversions. I put on my Sunday-best suit and walked into the club with Glynn on my arm. It was a good evening, amusingly punctuated by some of the older faculty members commenting, "How good to see *you* here, Paul." Old times there were not forgotten.

V

The Farmington controversy was the last of our great disputes over racial issues to garner national attention. There would, of course, be more disputes, many disappointments, and not a few bitter episodes in the years that followed. Given the enormity of the racist heritage of the nation, the state, and the University, it could hardly have been otherwise. But the black presence in the University slowly increased, sometimes accompanied by regrets (occasionally protests) because it was not substantial enough. Ironically (but perhaps not surprisingly), our progress in time became significant enough to arouse the blood lust of the far right, masquerading as disciples of Martin King. For example, Linda Chavez came to the University in 1999 to condemn our affirmative action policy because it "smacks of the kind of racism that has long plagued this nation." All over the country—from Rush Limbaugh to George Will—cries of "reverse discrimination" and abandonment of the King legacy rang out. Ms. Chavez thought we practiced a policy of "racial preference," a common charge of affirmative action critics. We had, indeed, practiced such a policy at one time —with perfection—when 100 percent of our preferred race made up the student body. Now when we were accused of an admissions policy based on racial preference, only 10 percent of the student body was black. We didn't seem to be very efficient in achieving our putative "preference." Shortly after she appeared here, Ms. Chavez accepted my invitation to lunch. I drove up to Leesburg hoping I might find a way to understand—and perhaps alter—her viewpoint. I didn't. I returned home to write a twenty-page pamphlet, ending with President Casteen's statement that our affirmative action admissions policy "is at base moral." We had come a long way. I argued that we could be held up as a model for the nation.

The last two decades or so of my active duty as a faculty member were strikingly different from the first two. During the earlier period my work was heavily focused on helping to break down the institutional and ideological barriers that kept us from becoming a university seeking and welcoming black students and faculty. By 1969 we had taken the first substantial steps toward removing those barriers. During the later period my race relations activities in the University took two main directions. One involved building and perfecting the black studies program I had brought into being in 1970 and, as part of that effort, helping to recruit black faculty. The other was teaching, both a much-enlarged twentieth-century Southern history class and a graduate seminar in which many of my students began the work on what would become their books on the civil rights struggles and related subjects. I used to joke that I decided to retire when one of my graduate students (Gregg Michel) wrote a dissertation on SSOC and the civil rights work of my students of the '60s.

Joe Washington, who took charge of the Black Studies program in 1970, stayed but a few years. He was succeeded by Vivian Gordon. A sociology student, Vivian had been my student in 1970; she took over the African American Studies program in 1974, the year she received her doctorate. Throughout the 1970s I was a member, sometimes chairman, of the committee on African American Studies. Ed Floyd, the Dean of the College then, began holding occasional meetings with the black faculty to discuss issues and plans for the future. Designating me an "honorary black," Ed included me in these meetings. We were two Alabama white boys bringing what we knew about racial matters to the table. Out of our discussions, especially in an October 1975 letter to Ed, I wrote that our conventional way of recruiting faculty—by departments according to perceived specialty needs—was a poor way of enlarging the black faculty. "Our appointments procedure," I wrote, "gives blacks equal treatment in the competition for jobs the definitions of which are reached without reference to our need for black scholars." The president, the provost, and the dean had all stressed our need to seek and recruit black scholars, but we had never given the priority to that need necessary to make it a reality.

All through these years, and especially after Vivian left in 1979, I hoped for a more-expansive program that would both put the black studies program closer to the center of the University's academic enterprises and find a way to adjust our recruitment procedures so that we might significantly enlarge the black faculty. To that end I was given the go-ahead to recruit Armstead Robinson, then at UCLA, to join the history department and to review and revise both our program and our recruitment procedures.

Armstead arrived in 1980 and immediately went to work. As nominal chair of the review committee, I met for lunch throughout the fall semester with Armstead, Ted Mason of the English department, and African history specialist Joe Miller. We called ourselves the Gang of Four. Before the semester's end we had crafted a proposal that was readily approved. Joe, Ted, and I made contributions, but the real creativity came from Armstead. We would keep in place the interdisciplinary major in African American Studies, expand the number of courses, and search for additional faculty. Most importantly, we would add a crucial research dimension. Armstead argued vigorously, and persuasively, that the academy's acknowledgement of intellectual and professional legitimacy came only with research and writing, not with teaching alone. To that end, our proposal looked to have annual research fellowships for both pre- and post-doctoral scholars, most of them from other universities.

Appointed by Dean Floyd to direct our program, Armstead named it the Woodson Institute for Afro-American and African Studies, after Carter G. Woodson, the "father of Negro history." He took charge in a whirlwind of activity. Our new director was no neophyte. As a Yale undergraduate he not only led the successful student demands for a black studies program but also co-edited *Black Studies in the University* (1969), the first major book on the subject. Under his leadership the Woodson Institute gained in fame and influence and Armstead became looked to by many as the father of black studies in the United States. With support both from the University and the Ford Foundation he quickly put into effect our plan to bring to the Institute both pre- and post-doctoral scholars. Eighty-three such fellows took

up residence during his fourteen-year tenure as director, a career brought
to an end in 1995 by his early death at age forty-eight.

The dozens of books that emerged from Institute fellows enriched
the study of Afro-American and African studies in many ways, giving
the Institute an international reputation as the place to come for research
and writing and, beyond that, firmly establishing black studies as a major
intellectual discipline. Not much time passed before Armstead created a
publication program with the university press to issue other books in the
field. Then, in 1982, I chaired a committee to create a center for the study
of civil rights within the Institute. Patricia Sullivan, an Emory Ph.D. and
a former Woodson Fellow, took over the directorship of the new program.
With all these achievements, and the wide approval of them within the
University (Edgar Shannon once served as chairman of the Institute's advisory board, a position I also held for six years) I often thought of how the
Black Students for Freedom leaders of 1968–69 would have been cheered
to see their dreams realized.

Armstead's effectiveness was enhanced by the close friendship he forged
with Ed Floyd, son of a white sharecropper from Eufaula, Alabama. He
and Armstead, the African American who grew up in Memphis, quickly
bonded. Their love of the same music brought Armstead to Ed's Lawn
Pavilion where they listened to old 78s in Ed's collection. On some of
those occasions they spoke of how to increase the number of black faculty
members. Ed was the kind of Southerner who combined a gentle personality and easy smile with a firm commitment to doing what he thought to
be right. I was pleased, but not surprised, when he agreed to Armstead's
proposal that the dean allocate to the Woodson director five positions for
the coming academic year. Armstead would identify desirable scholars and
offer them as free additions to the relevant departments. As I recall, those
appointments just about doubled the number of African Americans in
the Arts & Sciences faculty. The Floyd-Robinson initiative worked well
that year, demonstrating that outstanding black faculty could be recruited
in more than token numbers if the will and the imagination were there.
Those two ingredients would not always be present in the following years,
but what Armstead and Ed accomplished suggested a pattern that would

recur in the future. We were a better university when that happened.

VI

All through these years, even as the University acomplished progressive changes in which I took pride, my Fairhoper's idealism continued to be my standard of measurement. The Nancy Lewis story stood at the center of my thinking. I knew when I first wrote up her story that it could serve as a launch for a lecture on white supremacy's cancerous power over idealism. I had already seen in the archives the records of blacks being warned away from the beaches, kept out of the public school, told to be out of the town limits by nightfall and, eventually, coming up against that sign on the wharf. By the 1960s, when I was in the relative safety of the Virginia civil rights movement (split lips here; cracked heads in the Deep South), my activist mother was copying license-plate numbers at Klan rallies, wanting to march from Selma to Montgomery, and writing to me that Fairhope was becoming Wallace country—not a dime's worth of difference between it and Birmingham she was almost—but not quite—moved to say. An essay starting with the Nancy Lewis story might show how once that original decision for segregation had been made—once principle had been compromised—there was no turning back. And not only that: it could show the twin tragedy that, by the time the sign on the wharf was nailed in place, most Fairhope people had no idea it was an affront to the town's founding philosophy, its reason for being. Like the rest of the South, even Fairhope could not save itself.

I might have done this, but I didn't. Nancy Lewis wouldn't let me. The more I thought about her, the more she danced in my imagination as a real person. Who was she? Why had she come to this particular piece of land, to dispute its occupancy with my grandfather? All of the answers were not possible to find (of course, they never are), but many were, locked up in the federal manuscript census, wills, land deeds, tax records, the colony archives, a few reminiscences, and, finally, an interview with one of her descendants. Miss Rosetta Lewis, the eleventh and youngest child of William Alfred Lewis, Nancy's first born, had strong memories of her grandmother as well as of her parents, aunts, uncles, brothers, sisters, and cousins—memories which she generously shared with me. There was also a family Bible in which we could check some of my carefully gathered genealogical data. As the eleventh and youngest grandchild of E. B. Gaston, I felt a special kinship to Rosetta Lewis and treasured the bond that grew between us. Together, we two grandchildren worked to close a broken circle.

Nancy Lewis was born a slave in Lauderdale County, Mississippi, in 1841. Her father was born in the District of Columbia and her mother in Tennessee. We have no way of knowing when Nancy met her future husband, John. Three years older than she, he was born near Richmond, Virginia, a son of Virginia-born parents. John may have done something to stir his master's wrath—irascible planters sometimes turned their ungrateful slaves over to the slave traders as a means of punishment—or he may have been sold South with his mother as part of his owner's strategy to improve his material circumstances. John and Nancy somehow met and were married, in whatever ritual sanctioned by their owner, when Nancy was still a teenager and John hardly much more. The family Bible in Rosetta Lewis's living room tells us that their first child, William Alfred, was born in Meridian, Mississippi, on December 18, 1858. The second child, a daughter named Betty—the last Lewis born into slavery, came three years later, after the beginning of the war that would emancipate her.

Rosetta Lewis was a wonderful source of information and insight, but I longed for a time machine to allow me to interview her grandmother and grandfather. What were their hopes and beliefs? I could only infer them from the often-expressed views of their fellow slaves. One from South Carolina put it this way: "The land ought to belong to the man who . . . could work it, not to those who "sit in the house," profiting from the labor of others. "Freedom," another said, "is taking us from under the yoke of bondage and placing us where we can reap the fruits or our own labor." One of Nancy and John Lewis's fellow Mississippi slaves put it this way: "Gib us our own land and we take care ourselves; but widout land, de old massas can hire us or starve us, as dey please."

A powerful statement of my grandfather's belief that the "two great questions of chattel slavery and land monopoly . . . are nearer than Siamese twins," these declarations struck me as unvarnished Fairhope philosophy, echoes of which I found running through the pages of Henry George's *Progress and Poverty*. "As a man belongs to himself," George wrote, "so his labor when put in concrete form belongs to him."

By 1870, when the census taker made his rounds in Baldwin County, Alabama, he called at the Lewis household. John was employed as a turpentine hand, Nancy was listed as "keeping house" for her husband, their two Mississippi-born children, and the three-month-old baby, Mary, their first "freedom child," born on the site that one day would become Fairhope. "Gib us our own land and we take care ourselves," the Mississippi slave had said. John and Nancy Lewis now set out to prove how right he was.

Precisely how they got their land we shall never know, but a good guess would be that, perhaps on the advice of some of the local blacks they met when they arrived, they simply settled down on land belonging to an absentee owner. The site they chose was part of more than six thousand acres owned by Oscela and Sallie Wilson of Mobile. In 1881 the Wilsons sold these Baldwin County holdings to John Bowen, also of Mobile. Like the Wilsons, Bowen left the land undeveloped. He apparently had no interest in it, except for sport and speculation.

I guessed, from what I had learned, that John Lewis and John Bowen (or Bowen's agent) worked out an informal and probably unwritten agreement that gave the Lewises use of the land in exchange for payment of the taxes on it. I did find, in the incomplete tax records at the county courthouse, that John—and then Nancy, after John's death—paid the taxes on eighty acres of land belonging to John Bowen. For annual levies ranging from $1.35 to $2.33, John and Nancy got their land—eighty acres of it—and set out to look after themselves as free people.

It was a good place for free people. They cleared fifteen of the acres, built a home on the site, and looked after their animals—a horse, several cows, hogs, and goats (and, no doubt, dogs and cats and chickens, not mentioned in the tax records)—planted vegetables, fruit trees, and vineyards, and reared their family. Three sons—Joseph, John, and James—were born in the seventies. When Betty died in 1883, giving birth to her firstborn, a daughter named Rosa Lee Denton, the granddaughter joined the family, to be reared by Nancy.

There was seldom much extra cash in the household, but work was steady—William Alfred had joined his father as a turpentine hand by 1880—and the farm yielded an abundance of good food. Charles Hall, the tax collector in the 1880s, recalled many years later the loneliness of riding through Baldwin County. It was a welcome relief to reach the Lewis household. There, day or night, he recalled, John Lewis would "set me down to the best his farm could yield," which appears to have been both good and memorable. Special family occasions were marked by feasts of freshly roasted hog, according to Rosetta Lewis, who also remembers that her grandmother was a hardworking woman who could plow as well as John Lewis.

In this apparently free and secure world Nancy and John Lewis reared a closely knit and happy family. In my imagination I could see the Lewis boys and girls playing in the ravines and endless woods, just as I would a half-century later, or wandering the beach—fishing, perhaps crabbing, for the evening supper, or frolicking in the Bay, less than a half mile from home. Imagining their home place was a source of special poignancy for me because it would later become the campus for my "organic" school, the nurturing ground for my democratic ideals and home of many of my happiest childhood experiences.

The colonists from the north, coming to start their demonstration of the benefits of free land, arrived to intrude in the Lewis world in January of 1895. By that time John Bowen was dead and his heirs were apparently ready to reap the unearned increment from the sale of the Baldwin County lands. The colonists were invited to come to Mobile to talk over terms. No one ever mentioned an agreement with Nancy Lewis, now a widow for the past three years. The estate agent, of course, knew that she had no legal leg to stand on. Nancy, legal leg or not, felt differently. Too much of her life was invested in that land to give it up without a protest. She had also just paid the 1894 taxes on the place. It was appraised at $105 and the records show that she owned a horse, ten hogs, five cows, six goats, and personal property valued at $18. William Alfred was married and living nearby. Mary, also married, was living on the place with her husband. Rosa Lee and the boys were still at home.

Nancy denied the legal claims put to her by the colonists, but soon she had no choice but to make plans to move, to start over somewhere else. The law required that she be paid for her improvements—three years of peaceable and undisputed possession of a piece of land were grounds for compensation when dispossession resulted from proof of a title to the land—and the $100 the colonists paid generously exceeded the letter of the law.

I published this story in 1984, first as an article in the Virginia Quarterly Review and later in the year as the first chapter in a book of three essays I called *Women of Fair Hope*.

I wrote an epilogue, telling of a denouement that put the saga in a more complex light, leaving its meaning open to different interpretations. This is what happened and what I wrote:

Three months after Nancy was displaced, she and my grandfather met again, this time at the county courthouse. Once again it was the desire for land that made their paths cross and again there was potential for conflict between them. The occasion was the annual sale at the courthouse of land for nonpayment of taxes. Grandfather was there because he wanted a particular available forty-acre tract, very close to the colony site. With little spare cash, the colonists needed to take advantage of every bargain that might come their way. This promised to be a big one.

But Nancy Lewis was also there with her own compelling reason to buy that land: it was the site of her new home, the place she had removed to when she lost her land to the colony the previous February. Now she had come to pay the back taxes that would give her the clear title she lacked before. Learning of her presence and need, my grandfather made his decision. His colony had caused Nancy Lewis enough grief. There would be no more. As a white man, he could have pushed her aside and acquired the land for his colony; instead, he stepped aside himself, clearing the way for her to pay the back taxes of $4.58 and take legal possession. He later told his fellow colonists that, considering what had happened before between the colony and Nancy Lewis, he did not "deem it advisable" to thwart her will in this instance.

Nancy Lewis's new home was less than a mile from her old one. She lived there until she died fifteen years later, at the age of sixty-nine. The value of the land increased steadily. She later subdivided it, seeing that her heirs received a legal title to their shares. For her, the land was like a passport to freedom and security, a guarantee that she was fiercely determined to pass on to her children and to Rosa Lee.

During the last years of her life Nancy Lewis supported herself with odd jobs, occasionally as a gardener in Fairhope, continued to eat from her own garden, and accepted the care and support of her children as she grew older. By this time they were managing well on their own, but their mother took pride and satisfaction from knowing that she had given them land that could guarantee their independence in whatever uncertain years might lie ahead.

When she died, in July 1910, my grandfather wrote in his newspaper:

> Nancy Lewis, one of our old and respected colored citizens, died suddenly Monday morning. At the time Fairhope was founded, she lived in a cabin on what is now the Creswell property but being bought out by the Colony moved a little farther away where she has since lived. She left a large family of children and grandchildren.

The published version of the story ended with this obituary. Two longer chapters followed to complete the book—upbeat biographies of white women who had played major roles in the colony's history. Some months after publication the local bookstore owner put on an elegant shrimp and chardonnay autographing party. Many of my old friends were there, many more were people I didn't know. Rosetta Lewis was a special guest, reassuring me with her presence.

After our interview I had telephoned her a couple of times with questions. And when I finished the first draft I sent it to her for comment. "I truly enjoyed reading it," she replied, easing my anxiety. "All the family that read it was very appreciative of what you said because you told it just as it was. I am having several copies made for other members of the family." She modestly added, "Glad to know I was a small bit of help."

Now, with copies of the book piled up for purchase, she and I sat beside each other. As the people came up to the table for an autograph, I introduced her to them: "I'd like you to meet Miss Rosetta Lewis, Nancy

Lewis's granddaughter." To our left, as we gazed out the plate-glass window, we had a clear view of the site of Nancy Lewis's first homestead, at the end of a short street bordering a bank and a grocery store. There, ninety years earlier, our grandparents' hopes and passion for the land had made them uncomfortable rivals for its possession.

I returned to Charlottesville shortly after the book-signing party only to receive a telephone call a little later telling me of Miss Lewis's passing. I looked for a quiet place to mourn her loss and also to be grateful that, together, we had closed a circle.

Soon I began to wonder who would care about this story of our grandparents. Would it really matter that one more historian had written one more book? How would the discovery of a long-forgotten past enter into the present? Perhaps for Rosetta Lewis and me, sitting there side-by-side that afternoon in the bookstore, the past was not dead, nor even past. What chance was there, though, that anyone else would feel something of what we did?

Fairhope readers who spoke to me about the book seemed alternately puzzled and annoyed. Why, in a book about Fairhope's women, had I started off with an obscure African American, an ex-slave, who had nothing at all to do with the founding or building of our community? "Paul, honey," one of the town's older women asked of me, "what in the world were you thinking of?" Some expressed their disapproval more bluntly. But others, more puzzled than affronted, set off on their own searches for meaning, asking new questions of themselves and the history of which they now saw themselves a part. Then there were a few who understood straightaway. One of the remaining community radicals took me aside to tell me how he had read the story as a commentary on the roots of the racism which, in time, had helped to vitiate Fairhope's idealism. I told this friend about the sign on the wharf.

Whatever the immediate reactions, it was satisfying to know that I had brought into existence a woman who otherwise would never have had a known history. In my manic moments I told myself that this was surely history writing as a creative act. Nancy Lewis existed now, in the present; she had not before. Her story was part of recorded history, the real thing, with clear lessons to teach.

But as Professor Woodward once reminded us, "the lessons taught are not always the lessons learned," so I watched curiously to see how my discovery would make its way into Fairhope consciousness.

For a while there was little to observe. Then, when the community began preparations for its elaborate 1994 centennial celebration, a burst of activity began. Fairhope had long since turned away from its radical heritage and I wondered about how Chamber of Commerce boosters would twist history to suit their world views, so far removed from those of my father and grandfather. History for them was important because it made them historic, never mind for what reason. It made them special. Anxieties of this sort had already led me to write a second book about the community, telling of the founding idealists and their ideals.

I was called to consult on several planned dramatizations of the founding, some to be done by honest actors and playwrights. In the end, though, no parts were created for Nancy Lewis. One member of the play writing committee told me they discussed her, because they had read my book. There ought to be a plaque somewhere near the beach with her name on it maybe, but she didn't belong in the play because it was to be about Fairhope's founding and Nancy Lewis was not relevant to that story. I knew what Woodward meant about lessons taught and lessons learned.

She fared better in print. A local author, commissioned by the Chamber of Commerce to write a handsome coffee-table history, recapitulated the story as I told it and judged it to be another powerful, humbling example of the contradictions with which history is forever laced. With our perspective of a hundred years' passing, we can perceive that some version of the "Nancy Lewis story" is perhaps always present within the pattern of a people's founding. It reflects, in fact, the larger American experience, and is worthy of our continual remembrance, at the very least.

Finally, she found a permanent home on the pavement edging Fairhope Avenue, the main street. I bought one of the sixteen-inch square bricks centennial boosters were promoting to be inscribed with the names of ancestors, friends, and pioneer settlers. I bought one for Nancy Lewis and had it placed next to the ones I purchased for my parents. The inscription reads:

NANCY LEWIS

1841–1910

SHE LOVED THE LAND

Passersby may now be drawn to wonder about this woman who "loved the land." Perhaps some will try to discover how that love brought her, out of slavery, to the site of the future free-land colony, and ponder themselves the irony with which her meeting with my grandfather clothes the Fairhope story. They may also ponder the courage of her struggle to endure and to prevail—and the heavy price an unjust society placed on his mission to create a just society.

VII

Teaching, which had given me great pleasure from the start, took on a new dimension during the second half of my tenure. A much larger undergraduate course in twentieth-century Southern history was populated by whites and blacks, women and men. We read Faulkner, Woodward, Ellison, Anne Moody, James Agee and others whose works had rarely been on the shelves of Southern white families. The course was an eye-opener for many of the students, like the one who wrote she was surprised to learn that Harry Byrd, a man she had been reared to admire, had been the architect of massive resistance. In the last half of the 1980s we watched and discussed *Eyes on the Prize*, Henry Hampton's brilliant six-part documentary history of the civil rights movement. As one of the academic advisors on Henry's team I knew I could safely recommend it to my students as the most accurate accounting of the movement they could see. The responses were revealing. Many of the white students, from families that had rarely discussed racial events of the 1960s, were both horrified by the grotesque racist acts they saw on the screen and relieved that it was behind them. Their fellow black students, familiar from family lore with what horrified their white classmates, made a point of letting them know that, yes, things had changed for the better but the remnants of the white supremacy culture were still all around. That, of course, was one of Henry's objectives in making the film, to remind people that the past his film portrayed was not entirely past. Our discussions, in a racially integrated class, helped the students grasp that point. Many began to look more critically and realistically at the world in which they lived. They were awakened, changed people.

My graduate seminar, always a learning experience for me, brought me into the company of memorable young women and men, most of whom have become lifelong friends and, in their different ways, my mentors. My bonding with them was similar in some respects to the partnerships I formed with my undergraduate comrades during our civil rights struggles of the 1960s. The graduate students chose topics for their seminar papers and dissertations—and the books that emerged from them—that had been at the center of my earlier activist work, including emancipation in Virginia; black civil rights leaders; Southern white racial liberals; the Tuskegee civil rights movement; school desegregation in Charlottesville, Richmond, and New Orleans; the history of SSOC; racial integration in the military; and the rise of suburban politics and the white retreat from the cause of racial justice. In 1998, the year after my retirement, the University of Virginia Press published a book edited by Andy Lewis and Matt Lassiter that consisted of essays begun in my seminar. They called it *The Moderates' Dilemma: Massive Resistance to School Integration in Virginia*. I was doubly honored: it was dedicated to me and I was asked to write the foreword. Tears welled when I read, in the acknowledgments section, that "Professor Gaston's commitment to social activism and rigorous scholarship, spanning his forty-year career, demonstrates that there need be no separation between the two."

VIII

My twenty-four years on the Southern Regional Council executive committee brought me into the larger world of social activism. They broadened my understanding of struggles for racial justice and the extraordinary women and men who led those struggles, but also, alas, the complex series of events that eventually led to the disintegration of the SRC reach and influence.

The end of Jim Crow's formal reign, with the passage of the Civil Rights Act of 1964 and the Voting Rights Act of 1965, left in its wake knotty questions for advocates of racial justice. The combination of the SRC's Voter Education Project and the federal government's Voting Rights

Act enfranchised huge numbers of blacks throughout the South. What, though, could be done to connect voting with representation? Left to their own devices, white Southern political leaders would continue to defeat the efforts of African Americans to become members of Congress. Under the leadership of Steve Suitts, SRC's executive director from 1977 to 1995, we began a Voting Project that developed sophisticated computer technology to draw congressional district lines that would maximize the chances of African American successes. With influential black state legislators as our clients the lines were drawn as Steve and his staff had planned.

As I watched this successful program unfold I witnessed once again what had long seemed a truism to me. The white opposition to sharing schools, universities, work places, restaurants, motels, swimming pools, and the halls of Congress with black people was not overcome by instant changes of heart coming from religious faith, American ideals, or rational argument. It was undermined, instead, by experience, experience that did not come voluntarily, of actually having to share those and other places with their fellow black citizens. In the political realm, the SRC played a significant role in bringing these changes about. And many of its members became role models. Among present and former members of Congress from the Council I count John Lewis (Georgia); Benny Thompson (Mississippi); Carrie Meek (Florida), who was succeeded by her son, Kendrick Meek; and Jim Clyburn (South Carolina), now majority whip.

SRC members who were recruited to serve in Jimmy Carter's administration were Ray Marshall (secretary of labor), Patt Derian (assistant secretary of state for human rights), and Hodding Carter (state department press secretary). Ray brought with him thirty-year-old SRC staff member Alexis Herman as his assistant. She would later become the first African American woman to serve as Secretary of Labor in Bill Clinton's second term (1997–2001). A native of Mobile, across the Bay from Fairhope, Alexis was born the year after I graduated from high school but we shared stories about our youth in those two parts of south Alabama, so near but so different.

Steve Suitts, who served as executive director for eighteen of my twenty-four years on the executive committee, guided the Council wisely and with admirable moral force. In addition to his voting project, he wrote extensively and persuasively on issues of poverty; guided (with Ray Marshall's help) an annual report on working conditions in the South; introduced a new magazine, *Southern Changes* (all of its articles now on the web); recruited some of the most interesting and formidable people I have ever met for membership in both the larger Council and the smaller executive committee; fostered a creative school project under Marcia Klenbort's direction; oversaw *Will the Circle Be Unbroken?*, an award-winning radio history of the civil rights movement; expanded the Lillian Smith award program, bringing many of the South's best writers into the SRC orbit; and convened frequent conferences on the critical issues of political democracy and economic justice. All of these ventures helped to maintain the Council's historic role as the region's most vital interracial authority on matters of race and poverty.

For me, the quarterly meetings with the executive committee and the annual meetings of the whole Council were riveting learning experiences giving me greater knowledge of and deeper insight into the realities of the

With Laughlin McDonald of the ACLU, left, and Steve Suitts, SRC executive director.

Southern experience and Southern struggles for justice than I could possibly obtain from the books on my shelves or the archives in our libraries. United by a single mission, these comrades brought to our common task an extraordinary range of backgrounds, experiences, talents, and prescriptions. They made me a better historian than I would otherwise have been; or, perhaps better put, a better historian of the kind I wanted to be. With many of them I forged lasting friendships that enriched my personal life as they influenced the course of my professional life.

The friendships and the influence endure; the Council sadly faded into insignificance. In the years following Steve's 1995 resignation (he had already served eight years longer than any previous executive director) successive directors and interim directors tried new directions but failed to garner adequate foundation support or regional enthusiasm. I resigned from the executive committee in 1998, uncomfortable about the direction Steve's successor wanted to take us. Her successor, Luz Borrero, who had taken over an almost bankrupt organization, asked for help so I convened what I called a "conference of the elders" in Washington in 2003. The group consisted of Les Dunbar, Vernon Jordan, Hodding Carter, Lottie Shackelford, Julian Bond, and Charles Johnson. Luz was also present. We agreed that the Council should recapture its role as an authoritative research and information agency and suggested ways of funding it. I particularly favored (and had several times previously recommended) such an approach to offset the influence of the numerous right-wing foundations that dominated public discussion, especially on television. The Southern liberal voice was virtually absent from national discussion. Luz took our suggestions seriously but was unable to implement them. Discouraged, she resigned to take a position with the city of Atlanta offered by Mayor Shirley Franklin, a former SRC executive committee member. Luz's successors presided over an organization with ever-diminishing funds and influence. Many of us thought the time had come for a wake, but the remaining board members struggled on. As I write now, in the summer of 2008, the Council staff consists of but one person—an executive director—who hopes for revival but has found no means to that end.

IX

In 1986, at the mid-point of my SRC presidency, I received an invitation to teach a course on the American civil rights movement at the University of Cape Town (UCT). South Africa at that time was home to some of the world's most brutal repression of dark-skinned people. Shortly before leaving, I received a letter from Lindy Wilson who, with her husband Francis, had successfully lobbied for my invitation. They had been friends since 1963 when Francis came to study in the Virginia economics department and Lindy happened to take my course in Southern history. She was from "the other South," she told me.

"This has been a heavy week for me," she wrote in the early summer of 1986. "The morning of the emergency meant the arrest of one of our staff members, the Tuesday morning the detention of another plus the husband of another, plus the necessity of another to become unavailable. People have been picked up left, right and centre. One has the sense of ruthless determination." She finished off her letter with the arresting statement that "Our history is poised on the brink; you can almost smell it. And what will it be?"

Yes, I thought, what might it be? With a rising tide of resistance and repression, especially with the declaration of a state of emergency on June 12, I felt strongly drawn to have a look for myself. We did have some doubts about safety as we watched on television the awesome Casspirs (armored personnel carriers) roaming the city streets and the townships killing and arresting protesters. But we went, I to teach at UCT and Mary to work with a group helping to set up daycare centers in the townships. I stayed for ten weeks, she for seven. There were scary moments, including especially the time Lindy and Francis were arrested. They (and we) were fortunate that their detention was short-lived.

On my return I published an article entitled "A Southerner in South Africa." Even an "unreconstructed Southerner," I wrote, "would blink at the legislation that assigns living and working space exclusively on the basis of racial classification and confines blacks in urban townships, rural reserves, and single-sex workers' hostels—all hidden away from the white world." I recorded these and many other horrors (including the arrest of UCT student

On a picnic with South African friends (including Lindy and Francis Wilson and Mamphela Ramphele), 1986.

leaders and notices on the bulletin boards of those who were "in hiding") in my diary and again in the essay I later published. I was duly shaken by the realities of apartheid. I never underestimated the cruelty and barbarism of American racism at its worst, but what I witnessed in South Africa, however much it echoed themes in American history, seemed a world apart.

My class included a few persons designated "colored" as well as one "black" student who became one of my favorites. Henry Hampton had let me have rough cuts of *Eyes on the Prize* to show to my Cape Town class. On the day I screened the segment on Birmingham, with the jailing of the children, the shy black youngster walked up to speak to me and to ask how the Birmingham parents felt about their children going to jail. I could see the deep concern in his eyes. I had read of South African youngsters, like my student, being picked up, detained, and held for many months, if released at all. It was different in Birmingham, I told him; the parents worried but they knew their children would not be held long. More comparisons of the freedom struggles in the two Souths took place in our discussion sections. They were unanimous in their belief that the differences were greater than the similarities. But the similarities engaged them all as I was to write later: "the mixture of material and psychological forces undergirding white supremacy; the common experience of suffering and exploitation; the heroic will to overcome oppression; and the search for appropriate liberation strategies, leaders, and ideologies."

One bright winter day, at the invitation of my friend Ingrid, a doctor, I drove with her to her clinic, deep in the Crossroads township. Casspirs were reported to be roaming nearby, travel was forbidden, the area sealed off. When we received word that Ingrid's clinic would be free of surveillance at a certain time we set off. The clinic was clean and cheerful, packed with women and children. My tour of Crossroads with one of its residents was one of my most moving experiences. As we sat in one of the houses I noticed that the walls were lined with newspapers. I thought of Agee's *Let Us Now Praise Famous Men* with its detailed and loving descriptions of the homes of the three Alabama tenant families of the 1930s. I wished for his power to evoke the scene before me. Soon, though, word came that the Casspirs were coming our way. We hastened to Ingrid's car. Should we be stopped by the police on the way, she instructed, she would say I was an American come to make a contribution to the clinic. "Ingrid," I replied, "if the police do stop us and you tell them that and they let us go, I will most certainly make a contribution to your clinic—a big one!" They didn't spot us.

Crossroads, with its lovingly tended small gardens and patches of green in the sand, helped turn me into an optimist. To harbor optimism, one of my American friends told me, must owe to my new-found belief in South African "utopianism." Perhaps so. But, largely because of Francis and Lindy (who appeared to know everyone involved in the struggle), I met many of what in our civil rights era we would have called "movement people." Their "comradeship, character, courage, and vision," I wrote, "inspired hope for the future." Rather than urging South Africans to look on the United States as a model, I came back urging Americans to listen to the voices of the new South Africa struggling to be born.

One of the most powerful of those voices belonged to Neville Alexander. With a doctorate from a German university and further "education" as a political prisoner on the infamous Robben Island, where he was a "classmate" of Nelson Mandela, Neville told me over lunch one day that "America needs to be educated about the truly revolutionary changes that are in South Africa's future." Beyond the essential material and political changes he saw in his country's future, he said, "we are planning for new educational institutions and philosophies appropriate to a free society, rethinking the roles of the sexes, and questioning all forms of elitism." I went to bed one evening imagining a conversation among Neville, Marietta Johnson, and E. B. Gaston.

The friends Mary and I made—writers, academicians, filmmakers, clerics, lawyers, and physicians (of all racial designations)—unknowingly bolstered my own sense of self. They contrasted sharply with their counterparts back home, blurring almost completely the distinction Americans make between activist and detached observer. They had all the professional integrity we prize, but they seemed to value it primarily for its power to facilitate social change. I felt kinship.

That first trip to Cape Town would be followed by others over the next decade. I spent several months in 1989 studying the black consciousness movement and its leaders, especially Steve Biko and Mamphela Ramphele. In June 1990, largely owing to Mamphela's influence, I was invited to a week-long symposium on the legacy of Steve Biko. We met in Harare, Zimbabwe, so that the many black consciousness veterans in exile might attend. None could yet return to South Africa. As a white boy from Alabama (and the only American) present I was at first reluctant to be a discussion leader, but I got over that and made friends with black revolutionaries of a kind I had not known before.

I was back in Cape Town in 1994 in time to witness Nelson Mandela's historic election to the presidency. Standing shoulder-to-shoulder with thousands of ecstatic South Africans in the town hall square I felt the electricity of the crowd. We heard few of the words Mandela spoke, but it didn't matter; everyone knew he was talking about South Africans as free people. In 1996 I took my academic robes with me to march in the procession on the occasion of Mamphela's installation as vice chancellor (equivalent of our president) of the University of Cape Town, the first black woman ever to hold such a position. Her friends Nelson Mandela and Desmond Tutu, and her vibrant mother, were all part of the stunning program.

It was also during that 1996 visit that I met with members of the Truth and Reconciliation Commission in Johannesburg. I told them that such a commission had never appeared on the American landscape, how much truth had yet to be spoken, and how much reconciliation had yet to be forged. That had been a theme of one of my papers before the Southern Historical Association and in courses I taught for undergraduates at UVA on "the two Souths."

The riches I brought back from South Africa widened and deepened my understanding of movements for social justice. They also expanded my friendships with the actors on that stage. Those friends, like my SRC family, the progressive journalists I met through them, my '60s rebel comrades, my Southern history students, and my like-minded colleagues in other universities, formed the community where I felt at home, the men and women who nurtured my fair hopes for the future.

Epilogue

WITH FAIR HOPES

Among the great Southern writers I admire, James Agee stands high. I frequently asked my students to read *Let Us Now Praise Famous Men*, partly so I would have to read it again myself. Yet his books were few. He once wrote: "I'm a hard and in general fairly effective worker, but I'm horrified every time I reflect on the amount of life and gifts I have wasted or not used well enough, simply through some fundamental failures and lack in habits of self-discipline." I see myself in those words. I have started and then abandoned as many books as I have published. A dozen years ago I signed a contract with one of New York's great publishing houses to write what I thought would be a bold new interpretation of the civil rights movement. I never wrote the book. A half-completed manuscript on another subject lies buried somewhere in my study. The big social history of Fairhope I promised myself thirty years ago that I would write was never begun, its place later taken by two slender volumes about the community's origins, ideology, and early years.

A good Fairhoper should lament "fundamental failures" and "lack in habits of self-discipline." I have known both and the lamentations have been familiar companions. I was never a great fan of the New England writer Thoreau, but one of his aphorisms has long been posted on my list of "words to live and write by": "If a man does not keep pace with his companions perhaps it is because he hears a different drummer. Let him step to the music which he hears, however measured or far away." The music to which I have tried to march was neither measured nor far away: the Fairhope dream my grandfather brought with him to Alabama; the community and school he and Mrs. Johnson nurtured, trying to make good theories work; my father's keeping of the faith against impossible odds; my mother's counsel to look elsewhere to follow the Fairhope dream of a just world; and the decision Mary and I made together that our engagement with the world, our Fairhope mission, would be the nexus between race and justice.

The Nancy Lewis story in the first of my Fairhope books was aimed at that nexus. By 1994, ten years after *Women of Fair Hope* was published, Nancy Lewis had been acknowledged in both public and private ways and had entered the town's authorized history. Is this a happy story? Was this enough? Do we adequately capture her memory—make her past live authentically in our present—by seeing in her story the contradictions and complexities "with which history is forever laced," as the official historian put it? I think not. Far better for us not to allow "complexity and ambiguity" to stand as the most important things we should tell about her experience. Such a way of remembering the past, besides its banality, anaesthetizes fury, trivializes passion, and smothers struggles for justice. It helps us, in fact, to forget, to let the past live, but live benignly, approvingly, in the present, stripped of burden, rebuke, and challenge.

James Agee had something like this in mind when he said that "the deadliest blow the enemy of the human soul can strike is to do fury honor." Official acceptance, he believed, "is the one unmistakable symptom that salvation is beaten again, and is the one surest sign of fatal misunderstanding, and is the kiss of Judas." Strong language. Vintage Agee. I think both Rosetta Lewis's grandmother and my grandfather would have understood what he meant.

Both would understand that wherever the remembered past threatens privilege, power, and comfort it is likely to be muted, distorted, or suppressed. The process had long since begun in Fairhope, a tiny part of a great pattern all of us as historians have learned—or must now learn and combat. I think it is our understanding of the fierceness and high stakes of this struggle that makes us look with such a churning mixture of hope and doubt on the South African truth and reconciliation commission, anchored in the belief that wounds can be healed and a just society achieved only when the past is fully and honestly acknowledged.

Here at home we have more than enough honest telling about the South to keep the next generation of historians challenged. The writing and teaching and thinking about our past is full of the lack of awareness, the denials, erasures, fears, and manipulations I discovered in the Nancy Lewis story. I gained from the small experience I have described a deeper appreciation of our unique opportunities to tell truths about the South and a richer understanding of Miss Welty's belief that "one place comprehended can make us understand other places better," that "sense of places gives equilibrium" and that, "extended, it is direction too." I can imagine few more satisfying experiences for the historian.

But I also learned how small and fragile my accomplishment was. To change history by telling history is rarely within one person's grasp. To succeed we must work collectively, and with tenacity. My visits to South Africa put me in mind of this. There I listened to scholars whose teaching and writing were seamlessly bound to their anti-apartheid activism. That was a strong affirmation. I heard Fairhope music. Still, as I neared the decision to retire, surrounded as I was by colleagues (many of whom I liked and admired) who marched to drum beats altogether different from those that guided me, I felt occasional pangs of doubt and inadequacy. Then something quite extraordinary happened.

In March 1997, two months before my retirement, our Southern history graduate students convened their annual conference of students from other universities. The subject of this three-day meeting was "Struggles for Southern Justice." With only the foreknowledge that I was to give a talk on the opening night, I was stunned by what unfolded. First, my daughter, collaborating with my graduate students, invited dozens of former students and civil rights comrades to come. Those from out of town who could make it—they numbered in the forties—came to our home for a party Chinta orchestrated. Afterwards, when we arrived at the lecture hall for my talk, I learned that the conference was being dedicated to me. My speech dealt with the subjects closest to my heart: Fairhope, race, and the possibilities open to Southern historians. The 180-seat auditorium was close to full.

The next afternoon, in another large auditorium, we met for over two hours to listen to a dozen speakers recite my virtues. The length and flattery should have been embarrassing, and in some ways they were. But something else took place as a single principal theme wove its way through every speaker's remarks. My lingering self-doubts began to melt away.

Tom Gardner, whose name has appeared several times in this memoir, said my life of "scholarship and action" proved the point that, as he put it, "there is no grand canyon" between the two. There was a unique bond between the radical students of Tom's generation and me, he said: "We needed his history and he needed us, to bring that history to life." Jeff Norrell, recalling both his undergraduate and graduate study, spoke movingly of how our work together had helped him reconcile differences with his father. It had also shaped his sense of identity. From his student days onward he thought of himself as one committed to struggle for a better South who would link that struggle to both his professional and personal life.

Ray Gavins, the first black student to receive a Virginia Ph.D., wrote, in a letter read by Julian Bond, that our relationship proved that white and black could bond as though there were no color difference, two persons, two scholars, pursuing the same ends. Bob Pratt spoke the same message, recalling meals at our home and evening poker games with Gareth. Imogene Bunn, widow of Pastor Benjamin Bunn (in whose church many a civil rights gathering had taken place), wrote from her retirement home to remind me that she was my first "boss" in the Council on Human Relations, as chair of the employment opportunities committee. Eugene Williams, president of the local branch of the NAACP when I became a member in the late '50s, said that the invitation to speak on this occasion was the highest honor he had ever received. He recalled our work together on the executive committee and the friendship we forged, "at a time when we were not meant to be allowed to be friends." I began to tear up when he recited one progressive change after another that had taken place in our community, giving me far more credit than I deserved as their instigator. "I am sure you are at peace with yourself," he concluded, or almost concluded, before quickly admonishing me: "keep speaking out."

Every speaker came back to the "speaking out" theme, the nexus between scholarship and activism. They included my old friend and fellow

*With SRC president Lottie Shackleford and Julian Bond, at my 1997
retirement party.*

Alabamian Sheldon Hackney, then chairman of the National Endowment
for the Humanities; former graduate student John Kneebone of the Library
of Virginia; former undergraduate Woody Holton, historian and political
activist; my son Blaise (whose talk was shortest, applause garnered greatest,
laughter produced longest); and my Southern history colleague Ed Ayers,
generous and affectionate as ever. Vann Woodward, unable to attend, sent a
letter which read, in part, "Paul Gaston and I . . . share the conviction that
love of our native region could never be used to excuse silence as historians
about its faults, biases, and injustices. That would be a betrayal of our calling as well as of our people."

As a symbol of the theme that had dominated the afternoon, Julian (who
had been an SRC board member with me) read a letter signed by both the
Council's president and executive director announcing the creation of an

internship in my name, jointly sponsored by SRC and the University's Institute for Public History. I have always been grateful to Phyllis Leffler, the Institute's director, for her role in producing such a gift. Each summer a UVA student would be selected to work in the Council's Atlanta office. I could think of no happier or more thoughtful choice for a retirement present. I was also moved by the letter's description of me as "the keeper of our history and our conscience, insuring that our eyes are always on the prize."

One last recollection. Steve Suitts spoke movingly of our work together. It was by example, he said, that I taught him and the SRC board members about "the life of struggle." He closed by venturing an explanation. I was "rooted"—rooted in the "historical soul of Fairhope"; the heritage of white Southerners of good will committed to the struggle for social justice; and the University of Virginia, not as it had too often been, but as Mr. Jefferson envisioned its possibilities.

As I write these self-serving words I feel the embarrassment they bring; and, as Mary would certainly add, the poor taste. I suppose I can call up the presumed truism attributed to baseball pitcher/country philosopher Dizzy Dean—"It ain't braggin' if you done it"—but the real reason I record them is that they both transformed my life and led me to a deeper understanding of the institutions to which I had attached my values and mission: the Fairhope Single Tax Corporation; the Organic School; the Southern Regional Council; and the University of Virginia.

They did not wash away awareness of "gifts I have wasted" or my "lack in habits of self-discipline." Those were real and would be enduring. What they did was to make me comfortable with the gifts I had not wasted and the discipline I had been able to harness in using them. Or, to put it another way, they allowed me to accept my limitations and failures, not as defining characteristics but as realities that neither crippled nor inhibited what I wished to be. They liberated me in ways I had never anticipated, insuring that the "retirement years" would include plenty of "speaking out," just as Eugene commanded and Mary and I had hoped for when we chose the path we would follow more than a half-century ago.

What, though, of the institutions to which I had previously attached my values and aspirations? My university (like nearly all American institutions of higher learning) has become more diverse, more open to new ideas, more sensitive to different ways of life. But it never became the beacon for Southern progressives I had been encouraged to hope for, and, in the 1960s, had remained to work for. The Southern Regional Council, in the years after Steve's directorship, faded away. No Southern interracial research and advocacy agency has followed in its wake.

And Fairhope? Thirty years ago—as I wrote in the prologue—both the Organic School and the Single Tax Corporation had already lost touch with their founding principles. In a 2003 visit, I roamed the streets, talked to newcomers and old residents, and noted the arrival of what old timers were calling McMansion culture, as the simple but tasteful homes of the past, symbols of the community's egalitarian origins, were swept away. Land speculation was no longer controllable; the gap between rich and poor was widening. The woman I called on to cut my hair told me how wrong she found it for people "to be spending all that money on expensive houses when there are people homeless, people in the streets; people in poverty." I wanted to tell her that Fairhope was created to prevent precisely that. She seemed instinctively to understand. Reflecting on what she thought Fairhope's past to have been, she said "people got along, enjoyed what they had, lived a good life without all this showing off, this pretension, this looking down on you. People like me had a chance back then."

My new acquaintance's critique was perhaps too harsh, but I was not less negative than she in an essay I published the next year, describing Fairhope as "a fortified jewel of contented conservatism." And so it remains today, jewel-like and rightward tilting. But that one-dimensional judgment glides too easily over other realities. The creativity of Fairhope artists—especially its writers and painters—sets it apart from other Southern communities and forms a conscious link to the past when creativity and idealism were organically joined. Idealism and intellectual fervor can be found, not as common features of community life as they once were, but they are there, a stimulating presence. There are no more nudist colonies or women living in tree houses or barefoot seniors walking to town, but idiosyncrasies—in persons, lifestyles, and occupations—can still be found, and are tolerated. Beauty remains as well, the legendary sunsets drawing strollers to the pier every favorable evening. The Organic School, reconstituted and relocated, is making a valiant effort to restore Mrs. Johnson's pedagogy and principles; but with a miniscule enrollment its role in shaping the community's values is negligible. The reinvigorated Single Tax Colony, unable to be a demonstration of single-tax virtues, works with the town government to create a museum, a library, and an addition to the hospital, among other public structures and services.

All this said, the Fairhope demonstration has failed. The nexus between progress and poverty has not been broken; free land is no longer available; land speculation has become the rule, not the exception; and the "model" that the experiment hoped to provide has never been adopted by any unit of government, not the governments of the Town of Fairhope, Baldwin County, or the state of Alabama. There was a time when those who kept the faith put the blame for the colony's failure on miscreant members. I understand the temptation. But the underlying truth is that, even with the most faithful and talented leadership, success was not possible. The colony-owned land was too little, too scattered, too divided; the creation of a town government in 1908 and the subsequent transfer to it of colony services and properties removed the possibility of a model community based on the single-tax principle.

Despite these structural obstacles, my grandfather's charismatic leadership kept the idea of success alive for almost four decades, but in his last years he would tell my father of his fear that all would be lost. Dad stressed the colony's virtues and, in his writings, faithfully promoted Georgist doctrine, but he lived with the knowledge that the fair hopes he had been reared to cherish and for whose achievement he struggled were not to be realized.

My fair hopes, as Steve Suitts lyrically put it, were rooted in the "historical soul of Fairhope." Even before my mother counseled me to move away to pursue them, I knew, even if imperfectly, that my roots lay not in the physical community itself or in the challenge of reviving a demonstration that could not be revived. They lay, instead, in the blend of passion, idealism, and ambition that drove my grandfather to become a trenchant critic of the injustices of his age and a seeker of solutions. That was the essence of the utopia in which I came of age, my father and mother, in their different

30th wedding anniversary, England, 1982.

ways, transmitting to me my grandfather's hopes and values. That was a home I would never have to leave.

With Mary I found the way. Multiple injustices faced the America of our youth, but as Southerners we understood the greatest of these to be our region's cruel, inhumane—and, we thought, un-American—treatment of its dark-skinned population. Like my father and grandfather, I attached myself to institutions that would either disappear (the Southern Regional Council) or leave much more to be done (the University of Virginia). But unlike my forebears, those institutions would not define my mission, its success, or me.

The ideas, the things Mary and I cared about, had to be something ongoing, well past us. There is a phrase in the Talmud that says this much better: "It is not given to us to complete the task. Nor may we remove our hands from the plow." Charles Gomillion, the hero of the Tuskegee freedom movement, put it this way: "Keep everlastingly at it." And Ned Cobb, the Alabama sharecropper who could make the language sing, said simply, "It takes many a trip to the river to get clean."

~

ACKNOWLEDGMENTS

Midway through the writing of this autobiography, I began reading *Chance: In the House of Fate* by my friend the science writer Jennifer Ackerman. Adult memory, Jenny writes, "filters, sorts, judges, overlooks." The memory we claim to have "doesn't mirror events or return them like film; it recreates from choppy, fragmented impression and quick perceptual slices. . . . Some details slip away, unrecorded, or are misplaced in the mind's nebulous depths." In one of our exchanges, Jenny wrote of how "memory is not a storehouse or quiescent library from which we may pull a volume, but a fluid, organic process of storage and restorage."

For those of us who write autobiographies, especially those like me who call up memories stretching over three quarters of a century, the tricks our mind may play on us become a constant concern. More than once—indeed, many times—I had to confront the errant nature of what I thought I remembered. As one trained as a historian, who taught and wrote for forty years, it was part of my nature to be wary of other people's memories, recorded in interviews or structured in memoirs. As a historian I turned for authenticity to the archives, those primary sources contemporaneous to the events about which I wished to write. I was fortunate to have an abundance of them to check and amplify my memories. These included scores of letters, once stored in the attic of my grandparents, eventually to join nearly a thousand others in my parents' attic. My mother, and then my father after her early death, kept letters from me spanning three decades. The archives of the Fairhope Single Tax Corporation and the School of Organic

Education, the two principal institutions shaping my early life, were both of enormous help. The nearly complete files of our family newspaper, The Fairhope Courier, were likewise indispensable.

For the Virginia years my own extensive archives were supplemented by myriad institutional collections and, especially, the files of the student newspaper, The Cavalier Daily. During the latter part of my research I got in touch with George Taylor at the University of Michigan. He turned over to me copies of the substantial archives of the Black Students for Freedom. They had lain undisturbed for decades in his mother's garage in Hampton, Virginia. George and his fellow BSF leaders, especially John Charles Thomas, were later generous with their recollections of their struggles. My former student Bill Leary, a leader of the student chapter of the Virginia Council on Human Relations, turned over to me extensive records of that organization. Archives of the Southern Regional Council, with which I was associated for more than a quarter century, helped to fill out and keep a watchful eye on my recollections. I rarely kept diaries, but those from my early teenage years and again during my South African trips were indispensable.

Many individuals, in various but always constructive ways, generously offered their help to me. John T. Casteen, president of my university, set up a travel account that allowed me to interview several of my students from the 1960s; he also provided funds for a research assistant. I am grateful both for the material support and the confidence it bespoke. Three research assistants—Sarah Maxwell, Anne Foster, and Julia Trechsel—made my work far easier and more effective than it would have been had I been on my own. Anne also read some of the chapters, offering insightful responses and consistent enthusiasm. As I neared the end of the work, Jeanne Manis helped me deal with doubts about the outcome and to persevere until the last sentence was written.

I owe a very special word of thanks to my friends Bill Chafe and Larry Goodwyn of Duke University. I was a fellow in their Civil Rights Center more than thirty years ago when they told me I must drop everything to write about Fairhope. "Fairhope is about freedom, too," they retorted when I protested that I had come to them to write a book about the civil rights movement. I subsequently wrote two small books about Fairhope's origins and early history, but never the large social history I then thought I would write. This is not that history, but the confidence Bill and Larry gave me all those years ago emboldened me to write this story of what the Fairhope idea did to shape my life. I also owe much to the South African filmmaker Lindy Wilson, my friend who began urging me, many years ago, to write a book much like this one

Several friends and family members read the manuscript. My colleague Phyllis Leffler, whose course on the history of the University of Virginia I have had the privilege of visiting many times, read the chapters on the University with the expertise I very much needed. Larry Sabato furnished an account of a revealing event in the ongoing struggle at the University that I knew nothing about. I am grateful to him for that and for the enthusiasm he expressed about the book. George Gilmore, who has served as both President and Secretary of the Fairhope Single Tax Corporation, read the entire manuscript. He pounced fruitfully on numerous stylistic glitches and, much to my relief, wrote approvingly of my interpretations, many of which he knows will not be accepted by the people of Fairhope today. My colleague and neighbor, Bill Abbot, has read my previous books, always teaching me how to be a better, more thoughtful writer. He read this one, encouraging me to believe in it even as he found points of interpretation he did not share. One could not have a better friend, neighbor, and colleague.

Charlotte Crystal and Jayne Riew, two masters of constructive criticism, favored me with their editorial skills. Few pages escaped their calls for improvement as they showed me how to say, with greater clarity and simplicity, exactly what I was trying to say, but hadn't. I was buoyed by their unfailing confidence in the work and was enriched by the friendship I formed with each of them.

My three children—Blaise, Chinta, and Gareth—read the manuscript as it moved along, were unfailingly enthusiastic, offered editing suggestions, and called for the inclusion of some of their special memories. I am also grateful to my sister-in-law, Clare Shoemyen, and her husband, Janos, for their thoughtful reading and their suggestions. My wife, Mary, either lived through or had heard about virtually everything I have written in the book. She was always there to check my memory against hers, to offer interpre-

Guest helmsman on the schooner Shearwater, *New York Harbor, 2005*

tations that had escaped me, and, in her quiet way, to assure me that the book should be written.

Randall Williams and Suzanne La Rosa hold a special place in both my personal and professional life. As editor and publisher, respectively, of NewSouth Books, they have, under one label or another, published three of my books as well as a collection of essays to which I was a contributor. The combination of personal concern and expert guidance is the best I have ever experienced. An author could not be more fortunate.

～

Index

Gordon, Howard, 276
Gordon, Vivian, 311–312
Graham, Frank, 163, 177, 226
Graham, Harold, 79
Graham, Temple, 79
Gray, Claire, 70–71
Grayson, William J., 129
Great Depression, The, 32, 70, 79, 130
Greek societies, 113, 120, 126
Greenbacks, 39
Green, Fletcher, 165–166, 167, 203–204, 231, 256
Greeno, Dr. H. S., 55–56
Green, Paul, 163
Greenwich, Connecticut, 61–62
Gregg, Dell, 88
Griffin, L. Francis, 198
Griffith, D. W., 252
Gronlund, Laurence, 34, 35
Gulf of Mexico, 72, 79–80, 133, 200
Gulf Shores, Alabama, 139
Gwathmey, Richard, 269, 270, 278–279

H

Hackney, Sheldon, 302, 303, 336
Hale, Pat, 168, 203, 206
Hall, Charles, 317
Hall, Gus, 210
Hall, Jacquelyn, 303
Hamlett, Ed, 250
Hammond, Tom, 192, 193, 194–195, 208–209, 211, 220
Hampton, Henry, 329
Hampton Institute, 135
Hancock, Gordon Blaine, 294
Hannah Moore School, 138
Harris, Clarice, 269
Harris, Edna Rockwell, 71–73, 79, 84
Harrison, William Henry, 183
Harris, Robert, 240–241, 269
Harris, Wes, 212, 239–241, 244, 272, 275, 276, 278, 281, 286
Hawkinds, Marian Russell (cousin), 78
Hay, James, Jr., 174, 190
Henley, Thomas, 217, 221–223
Henry George School of Social Science, 103
Hereford, Frank, 306–308
Herman, Alexis, 324
Herndon, Angelo, 257
Herring, Alice, 57
Hickey, Roger, 241, 242–243, 248, 249
Hickman, Ron, 277
Hill, Lister, 109

Hilson, Chester, 99–100
Hilton, James, 96
Holt, Mike, 231
Holton, Linwood, 142, 290
Holton, Woody, 336
Homer, Frank, 261, 266
Hoover, Herbert, 183
House Un-American Activities Committee, 145–146
Howie family, 98, 116
Howland, Edward, 57
Howland, Marie, 57, 76–77
Huffman, John, 79
Huffman, Lorena (aunt), 79
Humphrey, Hubert, 111–112, 114
Hunnell, Jimmy, 47
Hunter, Charlayne, 209–210
Hynes, Liz, 117, 127
Hynes, Sam, 117, 127

I

individualism, 44
industrial education, 135
Ingrid, 329–330
Institute for Research in Social Science, 163
integration, 23, 103–104, 119, 184–199, 260–284, 306
  in sports, 193–194
  resistance to, 175–179, 179–180, 184, 255
interposition, 177
Iowa, 40, 47, 53
  populism in, 41–42
  Populist Party, 13

J

Jackson, Alice, 177
Jackson, Andrew, 183
Jackson, Brenda, 213
Jackson, Ed, 213, 227
Jackson, Edwana, 213
Jackson, Jimmie Lee, 232, 235
Jackson State College, 287
Jacobs, Linwood, 307
Jacobsson, Knud, 147, 159
Jamestown, Virginia, 103
Jefferson Society (UVA), 195–196
Jefferson, Thomas, 131, 170, 173, 175, 176, 179, 190, 191, 194, 200–202, 236, 279
Jensen, Eric, 161
Jim Crow, 49–54, 98–100, 175–179, 179–180, 184–187, 246, 259, 260, 293, 295, 297, 323–324
John Randolph Society, 195